EVALUATION PRACTICE
for PROJECTS with
YOUNG PEOPLE

SAGE was founded in 1965 by Sara Miller McCune to support the dissemination of usable knowledge by publishing innovative and high-quality research and teaching content. Today, we publish more than 750 journals, including those of more than 300 learned societies, more than 800 new books per year, and a growing range of library products including archives, data, case studies, reports, conference highlights, and video. SAGE remains majority-owned by our founder, and after Sara's lifetime will become owned by a charitable trust that secures our continued independence.

Los Angeles | London | Washington DC | New Delhi | Singapore

Kaz Stuart, Lucy Maynard and Caroline Rouncefield

EVALUATION PRACTICE
for PROJECTS with
YOUNG PEOPLE

A Guide to Creative Research

$SAGE

Los Angeles | London | New Delhi
Singapore | Washington DC

Los Angeles | London | New Delhi
Singapore | Washington DC

SAGE Publications Ltd
1 Oliver's Yard
55 City Road
London EC1Y 1SP

SAGE Publications Inc.
2455 Teller Road
Thousand Oaks, California 91320

SAGE Publications India Pvt Ltd
B 1/I 1 Mohan Cooperative Industrial Area
Mathura Road
New Delhi 110 044

SAGE Publications Asia-Pacific Pte Ltd
3 Church Street
#10-04 Samsung Hub
Singapore 049483

Library of Congress Control Number: 2014949126

British Library Cataloguing in Publication data

A catalogue record for this book is available from
the British Library

Editor: Jai Seaman
Assistant editor: Lily Mehrbod
Production editor: Victoria Nicholas
Copyeditor: Rose Campbell
Proofreader: Rosemary Morlin
Indexer: Silvia Benvenuto
Marketing manager: Sally Ransom
Cover design: Shaun Mercier
Typeset by: C&M Digitals (P) Ltd, Chennai, India
Printed and bound by CPI Group (UK) Ltd,
Croydon, CR0 4YY

MIX
Paper from
responsible sources
FSC® C013604

ISBN 978–1–4462–7599–3
ISBN 978–1–4462–7600–6 (pbk)

CONTENTS

LIST OF FIGURES
AND TABLES

Figures

Tables

ABOUT THE AUTHORS

So why have we written this book and what do we know about evaluation? We thought that you might want to know a little about our stake in this book, so that you can see what our drivers are and how they might have influenced what we have suggested!

Kaz – I have worked in education, social care, outdoor education and youth work as a front line worker, manager and, at times, leader. I have encountered the challenge of measurement of progress in all of these settings. The emphasis on impact evidence varied across contexts, but one constant was the need to develop a form of evaluation that: benefited the young people I worked with; allowed me to stay true to my values as a practitioner; and met the needs of the organisation that I was employed by. I taught research methods on a Masters programme in Leading Integrated Children's Services at the University of Cumbria, I was the Head of Research at Brathay Trust, a youth work organisation, and am now a director at Indigo Children's Services supporting children's centres, schools and children's services to provide outstanding services for children and families. Evidencing the efficacy of services and impact for young people remains a constant challenge in all of these roles and is the impetus for this book.

Lucy – I've worked both nationally and internationally as a practitioner, educator, evaluator and researcher in the area of youth development. My interests in the area are rooted firmly in practice, the foundations of which were laid whilst working in the USA as an experiential educator. My interest in understanding practice increasingly led me to study at undergraduate, Masters and doctoral levels. In 2011 I completed my PhD in empowerment and critical pedagogy, working with young people and practitioners to understand the process of empowerment in youth development. Now, as the Head of Research at Brathay Trust, I work alongside practitioners and students to understand, evaluate and develop our practice.

Caroline – I originally came to the University of Cumbria with a background in mainstream psychology. However, I have always been interested in young people and the challenges they face, and in thinking about how psychology can be used in practical, useful ways to help practitioners understand and support young people. My MSc in Applied Psychology and PhD in Community Psychology allowed me to focus on these interests. For many years I worked with Youth Workers both in training and in the field. I also worked directly with young people on a range of projects, including diversion projects and youth homelessness. I currently teach psychology and research methods to wide range of students (including youth work, criminology, policing and social science students) at the University of Cumbria.

ACKNOWLEDGEMENTS

This book is dedicated to all the inspiring young people that have worked with us over the years; to all the dedicated practitioners with whom we have developed our evaluation practice; and all the academics with whom we have shaped key ideas. We would also like to acknowledge our organisations, Brathay Trust and the University of Cumbria who have supported us to write this book, and of course, our families who have supported us every step of the way.

COMPANION WEBSITE

This book is supported by a brand new companion website (https://study.sagepub.com/evaluationpractice). The website offers a wide range of free teaching and learning resources, including:

- **Author Videos** introducing the book and looking at a range of issues associated with evaluation and young people.
- **Tools & Templates for Evaluation with Young People** including a range of activity materials.
- **SAGE Journal Articles**: free access to selected further readings listed by topic.
- **Links** to relevant and useful websites.
- **Glossary** of key terms.

INTRODUCTION

Welcome to this book! Given that you have picked it up and started to read it, we really hope that it helps answer some of the questions and dilemmas that you may have about evaluation and help you in the work that you do. That is certainly what we intended.

Setting the Scene

Our approach in writing this book was to provide anyone called upon to carry out evaluations with young people, an accessible, 'hands-on' guide to planning, implementing and interpreting evaluations. That is not to say that we have made things overly simple but we have made sure that every chapter is applied, practical and full of tips, pauses for thought and practice examples to help you make sense of what we say in terms of your day-to-day work.

As you can tell from the title of the book, we focus on **evaluation**. We have done this because the current climate of work with young people demands it. There is a growing trend in many of the applied, 'people', professions towards **evidence based practice** and in demonstrating the efficacy of the work that they do. In evidence based practice, evaluations are commonly used to investigate what works, and why. Usually this is done with a view to informing future policy, practice developments or to secure funding. Work with young people is one of the many sectors being called upon to provide evidence of the impact of their work.

This book has three purposes:

- To provide an overview of the current evaluation context, the rise of evidence based practice and the growing demands on workers to evaluate their work.
- To give a practical guide to understanding what evaluation is and how to plan, implement and assess different forms of evaluations.
- As practitioners we know that 'doing evaluations' is not a simple process, particularly for those who work with children and young people. Evaluation is a process that is

tied up with a range of practical, ethical and philosophical challenges. Although tricky, we believe that many of the challenges met by practitioners are surmountable. We therefore aim to discuss some of the challenges we have faced in carrying out evaluations and share with you our ideas about how we tackle these issues in practice.

Key Terms in the Book

So what do we mean by evaluation? Evaluation is sometimes seen as a form of research, and in fact uses the exact same methods of design, data collection and analysis techniques as research. However, evaluation is a very specific form of research with a definite goal, stakeholders, an agenda, and criteria for success. This is then known as 'pure' research. Research is much broader than this, and refers to the types of work where people pose questions and try to find things out. Pure research does not have to have any stakeholders; instead it asks questions for the sake of finding something out, quite a different endeavour from evaluation. Let's say we were investigating young people who are not in education, employment or training. A pure researcher might be interested in why the young people have been given this status, by whom, and what it means to them, whereas an evaluator would be evaluating how effective a programme was at changing this status, getting young people into education, employment or training. Therefore, evaluation is a very specific form of research. When we use the word evaluation throughout this book we mean: ascertaining the amount, number, value, quality or importance of programme/s, assessing it/them on the basis of evidence. This definition of evaluation is common to a range of academic and practitioner organisations (HM Treasury, 2011; Charities Evaluation Services, 2014; Community Sustainability Engagement, 2014). When we talk about evaluation we refer to the good practice of youth workers reflecting on their work and evaluating what went well and what could have gone better. We do not subscribe to the drive for evaluation 'for the sake of it' or the continual drive for the measurement of results that is prevalent in the UK. We propose evaluation as a useful reflective approach already in use by youth workers, an approach that develops the quality of practice, and an approach that can demonstrate the impact of work when useful.

Pause for Thought

- Have you ever carried out research or evaluation? What did you do?
- What were the key characteristics of the evaluation?
- What were the key characteristics of the research?
- What was it that made the two endeavours look different?
- What was it that made them similar?
- What could a pure research question and an evaluation question look like for a project that you run with young people?

We also use the term 'youth work' throughout the book. When we use this term we are referring to all work with young people, rather than 'Youth Work', which is a well-defined and specific way of working with young people in the UK and guided by the National Youth Agency. When we talk about working with young people we are referring to the wide spectrum of work that goes on with young people, from formal classroom projects, through to informal detached youth work. We have simply adopted the phrase 'youth work' as a shorthand for all types of work with young people. However, when we talk about youth work we are also referring to a type of work which is underpinned by a set of values and principles and we believe these should be fundamental to all youth work practice.

There are some characteristics that define what we mean by 'work with young people', and these are value based. The work that we refer to throughout this book is:

- Respectful
- Promotes young people's rights, choice and decisions
- Promotes the safety and welfare of young people
- Is anti-oppressive and promotes **social justice**
- Is developmental – aiming to enable the young people to develop from the strengths that they already possess.

A final key characteristic of this book is that the type of evaluation that we most recommend for work with young people is creative. We have found through personal experience that creative methods enable young people to engage in evaluation in a meaningful way and to benefit themselves from the experience. By 'creative methods' we mean approaches that are artistic, physical and experiential, rather than paper based forms. That is not to dismiss the role of traditional forms of evaluation, but to offer an alternative and more engaging approach. As such we will refer to creative methods throughout the book chapters.

Who Is This Book For?

This book is useful for anyone who works with young people. You could be a student, a front-line worker, a manager or a leader; this book is still for you, no matter what level you work at. You may be delivering youth work, outdoor learning, community development, social work or family work based projects. The book is aimed mainly at evaluating projects that are non-formal, or not delivered in formal settings such as schools and colleges. That does not mean that it is not relevant to teachers and tutors, just that we focus on types of work that are planned and that can be unpredictable!

The book is written by three authors from the UK. It is therefore predominantly written from a UK perspective, with many UK examples of practice. Despite this UK focus, the practices, methods and tensions that it covers speak to an international audience, and we have made explicit links to projects overseas to encourage the reader to think globally about evaluation.

How Have We Written this Book?

In order to help you develop practical evaluation skills for projects with young people, we will provide you with a combination of theory and practice. We believe that theory is helpful in bringing understanding to the practice of evaluation, and wish to avoid overly academic language and terminology that can often put people off reading about it. Hence, we aim to use accessible theory to illuminate the subject and only the most necessary jargon with clear explanations. We also bring practice examples into the book to provide insight into how the theory relates to real life. These should help you to contextualise what you are learning, and will give you a touchstone with your own projects. Most of the examples we use are drawn from our own practice, warts and all! However, we have also included examples from youth work around the world. We are not simply reflecting when we talk about these practices, our descriptions of them intend to develop your understanding of evaluation, and we use case studies because knowledge is always contextual. These qualities mean that we are using what academics call **praxis** in this book (Kemmis, 2009). Praxis is a term that came from Aristotle and refers to the way in which we make meaning from experience and theory that informs our actions. It is not simply a reflective task, praxis also has at its heart a commitment to human well-being and respect for others. We hope that you will then engage in praxis yourselves, thinking about your evaluation practices and how they respect others and promote human well-being in the light of the theory and practice described in this book. We hope that we integrate theory and practice into a useful practice guide for practitioners working with young people. This means that we are able to span the gap between an ideological perspective and a pragmatic perspective. Ideologically, youth workers might believe that they should not set outcomes as youth work is led by young people, and that it is impossible to 'measure' attainment of soft outcomes such as self-confidence. Pragmatically, youth workers may think that they have to set outcomes to be able to plan effectively and to promote growth for young people and that they need to measure progress in order to secure funding and future contracts. In this book we integrate theory and practice, for example, by bringing the theory of participatory youth work alive in a practical form of evaluation. With this integration we reconcile many of the tensions between ideology and pragmatic approaches to working with young people. We do not attempt to hide the tensions, but acknowledge them and provide some ideas for working through them yourself.

When you think about your practice in the light of new theoretical knowledge, or when you think about the theories that you have read about from theoretical perspectives, you are engaging in praxis. This is an excellent form of **reflective practice**, another core aspect of this book that is explored more in Chapter 2.

Chapter Overviews

Chapter 1 sets the scene for the rest of the book as it describes a range of projects with young people, the contextual drivers for evaluation, and the tensions that exist between practice and context. The chapter concludes by offering an approach to evaluation that will enhance the projects that practitioners are delivering.

Having understood the challenges that evaluation has to resolve, Chapter 2 looks at various approaches to evaluation. This chapter discusses two very different ways of thinking about evaluation and outlines how they dramatically shape what you do in practice. The key arguments for creative methods are presented here as suitable for all types of evaluation with young people. The chapter really gives you the big picture thinking that is often not visible in evaluation reports, and that is fundamental to their design.

The next step in evaluation design is to consider the ethical issues that may arise in your study. Chapter 3 describes what some of these may be, and offers you a range of guides. In this chapter we consider both the rights of the child and child protection issues using contemporary dilemmas – such as the use of social media to conduct research with young people.

Chapter 4 will provide an overview of different types of evaluations, with step-by-step questions that lead you from the purpose of your evaluation to the selection of an evaluation through to the overall design of the evaluation process.

The discussion of power introduced in Chapters 2 and 3 is further developed in Chapter 5. Here the theme is explored in more depth, identifying the power of commissioners, the organisation, practitioners, evaluators (if they are not the same as the practitioners) and young people. Participatory evaluation work is explored as an evaluation approach that explicitly addresses power issues and that has benefits in enhancing the learning for the participants.

Chapter 6 will guide you through stages of planning, ensuring that you have the right paradigm, methods and tools using a theory of change framework. Reflective practice is central to this chapter, and engagement with the materials will encourage you to reflect on and develop your own evaluation practice.

Chapter 7 picks up on the data collection tools mentioned in the last chapter. The advantages and disadvantages of a wide range of data collection tools will be introduced allowing you to choose the ones most appropriate for the young people you are working with. These tools can all be downloaded from the SAGE website.

Chapter 8 builds on the debates introduced in Chapter 2 and presents mixed methods as combining different forms of evaluation and as a paradigm in its own right. The strengths and weaknesses of mixed method approaches will be discussed and illuminated by case studies, along with clear guidance on how to conduct a study in this way.

Having collected your data, the next step is data analysis. Chapter 9 presents a simple six-step process that involves collating, sorting, analysing, interpreting, checking and drawing conclusions from data. Key approaches to data analysis, linked to each of the methods, are presented with a step-by-step approach to turning data into meaningful findings.

Chapter 10 follows on from this, discussing the different ways that you might write up your evaluation findings depending on the audience you are writing for. Choices about the content, language and presentation format will be given for verbal and written presentations.

The conclusion pulls together key strands from each chapter of the book and discusses some of the challenges of applying the learning from your study into future projects. The conclusion makes the case for carrying out evaluation in projects with young people in order to raise the quality of practice, to promote learning and development for practitioners and young people, to demonstrate the value of the project and to promote non-formal approaches to work with young people.

Our Big Ideas About Evaluation

Before launching into the first chapter we wanted to leave you with some fundamental pointers on evaluation. These are our BIG IDEAS!

1. Evaluation involves measuring the effectiveness of programmes or projects for young people against the outcomes they intend to achieve. Programme evaluation has mainly been used by stakeholders to evaluate the effectiveness of programmes and assess value for money. However, evaluations can, and do have other purposes.
2. Evaluations are key to the reflective practitioner, helping them assess what is or is not effective in their practice.
3. Evaluation can be used with young people to help give them an idea about how they are getting on. If shared with the young person, evaluation can become a really useful coaching, teaching, or youth work tool.
4. Evaluation is already a natural part of youth work practice in review sessions. What we need to find are ways of capturing the discussions of learning that already occur.
5. We believe that evaluation really helps practitioners to reflect on their practice and leads to practice development. We also believe that evaluation is vitally important for organisations to ensure quality of provision, knowledge management, practice development, data for fundraising and marketing and so on. Overall, we think evaluation is REALLY important!
6. We think that the evaluation process is quite simple, as long as it is thought about at the start of the project rather than at the end! It involves four simple steps:

   (a) Think of the questions and criteria for success
   (b) Gather data in an appropriate way
   (c) Analyse the data to see what it says
   (d) Apply the learning to the next project.

We believe that the evaluation process follows a cycle very much like an experiential learning cycle (Kolb, 1984), or an action research cycle (Lewin, 1946). This has been discussed more recently in the context of social action by Mullender, Ward and Fleming (2013). Hence when we talk about evaluation in this book we will often refer to the reflective evaluation cycle throughout this book. This process is shown diagrammatically in Figure I.1. Each step is simple and difficult, as tensions may emerge within each one.

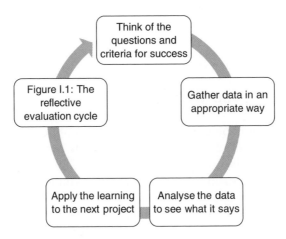

Figure I.1   The reflective evaluation cycle

We think that creative methods are absolutely central to engaging young people in a meaningful way with the evaluation process, and so this book focusses not only on planning evaluations generically but takes a specific focus on creative and participatory methods.

Finally, we think that when evaluation is used in the ways described above it can lead to emancipation for all the stakeholders, providing a voice for all, with the findings contributing to social justice.

How to Use this Book

You may want to read this book from start to finish, or you may prefer to dip in and out of it. To make both of these possible, and to help busy people learn effectively, we have built in a range of learning features.

- *Chapter Overview*: Each chapter starts with a bullet-pointed list of the key areas covered so that you can quickly see if it is the one for you to read.
- *Case Study*: There is one case study that is used as an example throughout the book. The example is the 'Step Up' Project. We have used one case study consistently throughout to help you relate the different topics in each of the chapters to the same piece of work. There are more details about the case study on the following page.
- *Vignettes*: We have filled the book with vignettes of international research practice to provide you with clear examples of important points.
- *Pause for Thought*: We interrupt the text after key points to allow you to reflect on and apply the key points made in the chapter to your own practice or context.
- *Summary and Key Points*: These recap on the key points that were made in the chapter to help you reflect on what to take away.
- *Further Reading*: This signposts you to other more in-depth reading about how to do evaluation and to examples of best evaluation practice. We explain why we have suggested each one to help you make the links.

Additionally, this text is only part of the book – there is also accompanying material on the SAGE website – this includes a set of downloadable evaluation tools.

 The Step Up Case Study

The Step Up project will be used as a case study throughout the book so that you can relate all the different sections of the book to one project.

Step Up was a two-year project involving 26 community based and 27 residential sessions of experiential learning for 'looked after' young people. The 16 young people who attended the project had been referred by a variety of agencies but volunteered to participate. The young people had been referred because they were in care and at risk of not attaining their target grades at schools. They were all 14–16 years old.

The project was commissioned by the local authority with the overall aim of increasing attainment and decreasing unauthorised absence.

We all hope that you enjoy reading it!

1

THE EVALUATION
CONTEXT

Chapter Overview

- The challenges in evaluating work with young people

- The difference between formal, non-formal and informal learning

- The challenges and dilemmas workers face when they are asked to design, implement and analyse evaluations

- The difference between proximal and distal outcomes

- The approach to evaluation presented in the rest of this book.

Work with Young People

Youth work is founded in a set of core values and principles which, besides guiding youth work practice, informs the practice of evaluation with young people. However, although these values are key to practice, they make evaluation with young people a difficult, complex endeavour and can present the youth worker with a range of practical and ethical challenges when called upon to carry out evaluations. Historically, the values underlying youth work do not sit easily with traditional approaches to evaluation, particularly those forms which adopt a 'scientific methodology' or which fail to put the young person at the heart of the evaluation process. This chapter describes some of the current pressures placed on youth workers, the dilemmas evaluation poses and our responses to them. The discussion, methods, approaches and case studies we present are based on our experience of working with young people over a number of years and within various contexts. We believe the distinct purpose, values and approaches of youth work, and its basis in the principles and practices of informal and non-formal education, presents 'evaluators' with a range of challenges. However, we also believe that these challenges enable us to use a fresh perspective from which to address evaluation.

Challenge Number 1: The Distinctiveness of Young People's Non-formal Learning

For readers who are not youth workers, the meaning of 'youth work' can be difficult to pin down. 'Youth work' has been used to refer to a wide variety of activities, from working with a group of scouts, running a youth club or making contact with groups of young people on an estate to addressing anti-social behaviour.

The definition of youth work used in this book is from the National Youth Agency in the UK:

> Youth work helps young people learn about themselves, others and society, through informal educational activities which combine enjoyment, challenge and learning.
>
> Youth workers work typically with young people aged between 11 and 25. Their work seeks to promote young people's personal and social development and enable them to have a voice, influence and place in their communities and society as a whole.
>
> Youth work offers young people safe spaces to explore their identity, experience decision-making, increase their confidence, develop inter-personal skills and think through the consequences of their actions. This leads to better informed choices, changes in activity and improved outcomes for young people. (NYA, 2014b)

As a learning experience youth work is influenced by key educationalists' ideas, such as the importance of emancipatory education (Friere, 1972), the role of race, capitalism and gender in the perpetuation of oppression and the need to celebrate invisible histories and cultures (hooks, 1994), and the role of critical pedagogy and **empowerment** (Giroux, 2001; McLaren et al., 2010); it is important to revisit the principles of these key figures when planning an evaluation of youth work.

As the NYA quote above shows, youth workers are often defined as **informal educators** (Rosseter, 1987), and youth work is often described as an informal process (Merton et al., 2004; NYA, 2014b). We, and others, believe that the word 'informal' can be problematic, and it has been increasingly suggested that the appropriate term for planned interventions with clear purposes being applied throughout Europe is 'non-formal education' (Festeu and Humberstone, 2006).

When we talk about projects with young people in this book we refer to non-formal learning. Non-formal learning involves learning through planned activities that take place outside school or college, but which involve some form of facilitation.

The evaluation practice described in this book can also be applied to formal and informal learning settings, but principally we refer to non-formal projects throughout this text. So what is the difference?

Non-formal learning is learning outside the formal school, vocational training or university system. Non-formal learning takes place through planned activities, in other words, activities that have goals and timelines. Non-formal learning involves facilitation. This does not equate to 'teaching' as the role of the student as an active participant is stressed. It tends to be short-term, voluntary, and have few if any pre-requisites, although it can have a curriculum and can overlap with formal learning (Batsleer, 2008). Youth work is often non-formal in that there may be a session plan and intended outcomes. A session watching a DVD might, for example, have intended outcomes that include listening skills, discussion and increased awareness of the subject on the DVD. The session plan might also detail what the youth workers will do with the young people to enable them to gain the outcomes from watching the DVD.

Informal learning is learning that is not organised or structured in terms of goals, time or instruction. There is no teaching or facilitation and as such it refers to skills acquired through life and work experience in the private and social lives of learners. It also includes the informal learning that occurs around educational activities, rather than as an intended aspect of a planned educational intervention. Young people hanging out in the park together may learn social skills for example. This spontaneous informal learning may also occur in a formal setting, with young people, for example, learning about social norms in a classroom setting whilst formally being taught, say, geography.

Formal learning is planned learning that takes place in schools, colleges and universities. It involves a teacher planning a series of lessons that cover a curriculum and can be highly bureaucratic and institutionalised. The teacher may use interactive teaching styles, or may predominantly 'transmit' or tell the young people what they need to know. A lesson on citizenship for example may require the young people or 'students' to listen to the teacher, read a section of text, and then complete some comprehension questions.

The key difference between these forms of learning is the degree of power that young people have. In formal learning the young person has very little power over what is planned, delivered or assessed. In informal learning the young person has all the power. In contrast, non-formal learning shares power with young people and takes the development of the young people themselves and of their life-world as the point of engagement (Batsleer, 2008).

The differences between these types of learning are set out in Table 1.1. The difference between these three forms of learning is significant in evaluation as two of them are predisposed to having a predetermined set of outcomes to work towards, and one intentionally has no outcomes. Because formal learning is pre-planned, it is predictable and relatively straightforward to monitor and 'measure' through the attainment of targets at key stages, and eventually through qualifications (often called **'hard' outcomes**). Non-formal learning is less predictable, although there are goals and timelines, these are flexible and outcomes are often more concerned with the social or personal development of the young person (**'developmental outcomes' or 'soft outcomes'**). As a consequence, planning, implementing, monitoring and 'measuring' outcomes is a complex process. Informal learning is completely unpredictable and so even more difficult to monitor and 'measure'. Perhaps because of this, formal learning has often been privileged as the 'best' way to learn, as it is simpler to evidence attainment.

Table 1.1   The key differences between formal, non-formal and informal learning

	Formal Learning	Non-formal Learning	Informal Learning
Role of the teacher/educator/facilitator	Teachers	Facilitators	No adult role
Role of the learner	Students	Young people	Self-directed learner
Type of planning	Set curriculum and lesson plans	Flexible session plans	No plans
Who has responsibility for planning	Teachers have responsibility for learning	Joint responsibility for learning	Learner directed
Type of learning	Passive, transmission	Active	Active
Setting	In school or formal setting	Outside of school or formal setting	No setting – can happen anywhere
Evidence of achievement	Attainment targets Qualifications	Outcome based	None

Youth workers have championed the non-formal/informal approach to working with young people, as has the United Nations Education, Scientific and Cultural Organisation (UNESCO, 2012) who have recently called for the validation of non-formal and informal learning in the EU by 2015 to ensure that the outcomes of formal, non-formal and informal learning are equally valued. This drive is also championed by the Organisation for Economic Growth and Development (Werquin, 2010).

Unfortunately, this move comes with a cost. Given the nature, aims and practices of informal and non-formal education 'demonstrating success' has proved notoriously difficult. However, it is exactly these forms of learning that youth work practitioners are being asked to evaluate and demonstrate the 'success' of. It is clear that one of the challenges for people working with young people in informal or non-formal settings is to develop effective and appropriate ways of evaluating and demonstrating the success of their practice, of this distinct form of learning.

Pause for Thought

Think about a project that you have been involved in:

- How would you classify the type of learning? Identify critical elements within this using Table 1.1.

- Why does it not fit into other types of learning?

- What are some of the 'hard' and 'soft' outcomes of the project?

Challenge Number 2: The Professional Context

The discussion of formal, non-formal and informal learning showed that previously formal learning has been privileged as it was possible to evidence outcomes and attainment in this style of learning. Education, and the well-being of young people more generally is often subject to changes in the political leadership of countries. This can lead to differences between countries at different points in history. Currently in the UK it is the age of evidence. Here, evidence currently counts above all else in the realms of policy making, health, social care, education and youth work. In the next section we identify some of the other recent pressures coming to bear on youth work at local, national and global scales, including drives for the free market economy, managerialism and individuation.

The free market economy

The drive for **free market economy** is based on assumptions that competition and user choice will raise quality as organisations compete to offer the best service to consumers. As youth work projects are pitched against one another in price wars for funding, the result may actually be a decrease in quality as the temptation is to reduce services to reduce costs (Baldwin, 2011: 188). Supermarkets, one could argue, need a free market economy to keep them competitive to ensure that their profits are balanced with low prices for customers. They deal with food commodities and profit margins. Youth services, on the other hand, do not have consumers who pay them money. They are largely funded by local authorities or trust funds. Forcing such organisations into competition does not therefore benefit the end consumer – the young person – nor are services necessarily improved by fierce competition. The free market economy drives evaluation to demonstrate the **cost benefits** of youth work.

The free market economy is now also a global phenomenon, with the United Nations and OECD developing many European and global databases of indicators showing how well countries manage to look after their young people (among other things). The first youth work indicators have just been developed by the Commonwealth, called the Youth Development Index (The Commonwealth, 2013). This index has measured educational, health, employment, and civic and political participation of young people aged 15–29 across all the Commonwealth countries. Some of the indicators, for example, are: D1.3 Youth Literacy, D2.3 Teenage Pregnancy Rates, D3.1 15–24 Unemployed, D4.1 Youth Policies and Representation, D5.1 Youth Volunteering. This index could be seen as a global free youth market economy. Such data sets may increase global free markets, and exert further pressure on youth work.

Managerialism

Managerialism has held sway in the last decade, underpinned by the assumption that employees need 'managing' to provide high quality services. In the UK the

Government introduced and increasingly tightened a school inspection service (DCSF, 2007: 85), enabling the government to manage schools with key performance indicators. Managerialism imposes conformity on youth work in order to allow comparisons to be made (Spence, 2004: 263). The impact of this discourse is not limited to youth work, and Jefferies (2011) identified the effect of the managerialism on social work as; 'fail[ing] to honour and recognise the variety, richness and diversity of human experience ... and to measure both what individuals view as a high priority in their lives and the resources that they themselves can bring to bear in addressing their circumstances' (2011: 30). This resonates with work with young people.

In the youth work context in the UK, this process started in 2001, with *Transforming Youth Work: Developing Excellent Youth Services for Young People* (DfEE, 2001). This created the need for outcomes to be measured in youth work in the UK and hailed an era of increased accountability devolved from central government (Spence, 2004: 261). Despite such changes, the 2011 UK Select Committee on Youth Work (2011) still condemned the lack of evidence of outcomes across the youth work sector in the UK. This has led to a drive for evidence based practice.

Evidence based practice is based on the belief that the efficacy of 'programmes' can be shown in a scientific way. The terminology and methodology are borrowed from the medical world where there are observable and measurable changes from any intervention. Some believe that these assumptions do not hold true for social sciences. There are now a number of websites that publish lists of youth work programmes that are evidence based (for example, see Puttick and Mulgan, 2010; Blueprints for Youth Development, 2013). Funding may increasingly be made available for programmes that can demonstrate evidence based practice, excluding many others. Establishing clear **causal links** between an intervention and an outcome is not as simple in youth work as in medicine. If a patient takes a pill and then gets better, the likelihood that the pill caused the improvement is obvious. If a teenager comes to a youth work session and then gets a job, there are many factors that could have led to that outcome – attribution of causality is not simple or measurable. You may find that you want to bid for contracts for projects that demand evidence based practice, and this can be problematic, especially when linked to the discourse of value for money.

The effect of managerialism on youth workers can be profound. Continual monitoring and management can erode professional trust:

> If people feel that they are not trusted to provide a quality service and, moreover, are forced to undertake elaborate activities to prove that they are in fact doing a good job ... they often become either; demoralised and demotivated or else motivated to behave in a more self-protective manner. (Le Grand, 2003: 57)

Evidence based practice seems to be replacing 'professional judgement'. In this context, you may need to consider how you can evaluate projects without adding to the bureaucratic burden felt by staff, how you can monitor without eroding trust, how you can evaluate without being perceived to manage performance, and whether your evaluation is justified, or simply conforming to a culture of measurement madness.

Individuation

When attempts are made to standardise services for young people and measure set outcomes, individual young people are at risk of being labelled as having **deficits** as they 'do not' achieve outcomes. A focus on what young people do not have, such as the 'not in education, employment or training' (or 'NEET') label in the UK creates 'patronising approaches to social inclusion that characterise specific groups as victims' (Davis, 2011: 135). This deficit approach stands in contrast to an asset based approach that starts with the strengths and capabilities that young people have. The implicit assumption is that if they have not achieved the indicators then it is the fault of the individuals, and this can be seen to potentially displace the state's responsibilities (Jeffs and Smith, 2002). Services aimed at supporting such individuals have become more 'targeted' and 'needs-led'. These are logical approaches to meeting the needs of groups, and yet also support an individual deficit focus, detracting from consideration of the causality of the communities and societal environments that they are located in. This agenda might drive an evaluation to identify the extent to which a programme has 'met the needs' of these young people and enabled them to 'achieve outcomes'. The danger is that this evaluation may miss the socioeconomic factors that conspire against the success of the young people and the project.

Individuation is compounded by the media. Franklin and Franklin (1990) argue that the image of young people in the media typically reflects two conflicting, yet powerful stereotypes of groups of young people.

On the one hand there is the 'model' adolescent who has 'knuckled down' and achieved something worthwhile, often against considerable odds. More often than not, these young people are referred to as 'young people' and described in glowing terms. On the other hand there are the 'anti-social hooligans' or the 'sexually precocious'. Such young people are presented as passive victims that need protection. The example (Figure 1.1), is taken from the UK paper *The Daily Mail*. The lead headline for this story is: 'An adult at 18? Not any more: Adolescence now ends at 25 to prevent young people getting an inferiority complex'. The picture shows a young man, seated in what looks like a doctor's surgery. The photograph that the *Daily Mail* has chosen to illustrate this story shows an anxious looking young man. He has a worried expression, downcast eyes, he is hiding his face behind his hands. This conveys a sense of the young man's vulnerability and need for help from the professional, in this case a male doctor or psychologist. The reader is encouraged to link this young man's apparent ill ease or anxiety to the 'inferiority complex' mentioned in the headline. This conveys a negative stereotype of young people.

These individuals are described as 'youth' or adolescents and the language associated with them is negative, often highly emotive. These young people are described as a threat to society, something to be controlled. Another stereotype presents young people as vulnerable, at risk from every direction.

Figure 1.1   An illustration of the vulnerability of young people as portrayed by the press (Woollaston, 2013)

These debates allow us to individualise young people, to locate the 'problem' within them, rather than out in society. This is called 'individuation' and 'problematising' young people. They also allow us to socially exclude and subjugate young people by defining them as different from us, this is called '**othering**' (Butler, 1990).

These debates are called '**discourses**' by academics. Certainly, these discourses, and the stereotypes that they perpetuate, are at odds with the values and principles underlying youth work that we outlined above. However, unfortunately, there is a growing pressure on youth workers in the UK to treat young people as the problem and a view that successful youth work involves 'removing the problem', 'reducing its extent' or 'increasing positive behaviour'.

It is crucial that youth workers are aware of such discourses and of the potential impact that such views can have on their practice, how they evidence the success of their practice or what is seen as successful youth work. Although youth work acknowledges that it will be called upon to work with society's 'problem youths', youth workers need to be aware that they can control the discourses that surround young people and stamp their perspective on, for example, who is the problem (or if there is a 'problem' at all), what is to be done and how and what counts as success. Being aware of, and challenging, the discourses and stereotypes that surround young people, and adopting evaluation tools which are able to reflect the principles and values of youth work are two steps towards controlling this. Certainly a major challenge for youth workers over the next decade is to find a balance that enables them to stay true to these principles and values, and provide the kind of work that they have always done, whilst providing programme and evaluation data that satisfies stakeholders and funders, and that can influence policy change. One of the intentions of this book is to provide practitioners with the tools to do just this.

Some of these messages are global trends, such as the sexually precocious young woman who 'deserves what she gets', and the role of alcohol as an acceptable form of relaxation and fun. Others are firmly rooted in some countries' national policy, such as, in the UK, the 'hoodie'-wearing anti-social youth and 'chavs', who are young people of the lower class who display brash and loutish behaviour and wear real or imitation designer clothes (Oxford Dictionary, 2013). Whatever the source, such messages affect what happens in localities, in organisations and in your day-to-day practice. Accordingly, what you do in practice affects organisa-tional activity, local practice, and to some extent national and international trends. Lipsky (1980) describes front-line staff as power holders, as it is only through you that any of these messages become embedded in practice. This means that it is important for you to think through what these messages mean to you, and the extent to which you will allow them to shape what you do. It may sometimes feel like you are powerless in the face of some of the policy drives, but this is not the case – only you decide how you act; you have agency. Figure 1.2 shows the nested levels of influence, with your practice firmly situated in the centre, and arrows showing the mutual influence of context on your practice, and of your practice on context.

Figure 1.2   Levels of influence on practice

This diagram prompts some questions which you can tackle in the pause for thought.

```
┌─────────────────────────────────────────────────────────────────┐
│                        Pause for Thought                          │
│                                                                   │
│   •  What is your organisation doing with all of these drivers? What are you driven to do?   │
│                                                                   │
│   •  What is the local context? What goes on in your part of the country?   │
│                                                                   │
│   •  What is your national context? How is it driving evaluation practice?   │
│                                                                   │
│   •  What is the global context? How is that affecting your practice?   │
└─────────────────────────────────────────────────────────────────┘
```

Challenge Number 3: The Value Base of Youth Work

At the heart of youth work is a set of values and principles. Although these have been modified over the years, these core features define youth work today. Youth work is about supporting young people's personal development, their sense of identity and how that governs how they act in the world. It is also about supporting their development in becoming social beings in the world (Young, 1999: 3). Identity work is central to personal development along with critical moral enquiries into why the world operates the way it does to govern identity.

Alongside personal and social development, an overall aim of youth work is to give young people insight into the society that they live in, and the ability to make positive choices on the basis of that increased awareness. In other words, it is **emancipatory**. Perhaps as a result of the central position of identity and emancipation in youth work, Chouhan (2009: 60) says that the key characteristic of youth work is anti-oppressive practice. **Anti-oppressive practice** is tackling oppression and discrimination, working to alleviate oppression and to bring about equality and social justice (NYA, 2004).

Buchroth and Parkin (2010: 65) state that 'youth work is inherently always an educational activity, based on dialogue and conversation, working with the issues that people bring from their everyday lives'. This means that personal experiences are valued, and participatory practice is important. Because of this, conversation is a central means of achieving outcomes. The positioning of something as everyday as conversation in youth work has led to criticism of the profession, but is not to be underestimated. 'The recognition that conversation lies at the heart of youth work practice should not obscure the complexity of the role: conversation is necessary but not sufficient in most forms of work with young people' (Payne, 2009: 225). Unfortunately, this has, on more than one occasion led to youth work getting a 'bad press', and being described as 'vague' or 'insubstantial' or as 'just having a chat'. Dispelling the stereotypes around youth work, such as the 'image of the cosy' chat or 'youth workers just hanging out with young people' is one of the challenges that professionals face in defending what they do.

Davies (2005: 22), helpfully, in summary describes seven defining features of youth work:

- Young people's voluntary participation
- Seeking to tip balances of power in their favour
- Responsive
- Offers new experiences and challenging activities
- Free from prejudice or discrimination
- Based on the young people's interests, current activities, styles and emotional concerns
- Respecting and working through their peer networks.

More recently Sapin (2013), proposed a framework for professional youth work practice. At the heart of this framework are a set of values (including having a positive, participatory, anti-oppressive approach and respect for human rights and equality) and principles (voluntary participation, proactive anti-oppression, establishing dialogue, confidentiality and accountability) which must inform practice. Like Sapin, we agree these are core to youth work practice. However, we also believe that these should also be core to evaluation practice. These core values are summarised in Table 1.2.

Table 1.2   The core values of youth work

• Supporting personal development
• Supporting social development
• Supporting identity formation
• Raising critical consciousness
• Supporting empowerment
• Anti-oppressive practice
• Valuing personal experiences
• Participatory practice
• Responsive to needs, interests and preferences

Whilst this table shows the values of youth work, these are generalisable to non-formal work with young people. This list of values raises the issue of how evaluations that are increasingly pressured and driven by free marketisation, managerialism and individuation can uphold the values of youth work.

Challenge Number 4: The Difficulties of Measuring Youth Work

These core values and principles present youth work with a variety of challenges in the current 'performance culture' discussed above. Not only is informal and non-formal learning difficult to explain, plan and implement, but its outcomes and impact are notoriously difficult to pin down and measure, whether in the short, medium or long term. This has been compounded by personal development outcomes being labelled as 'soft outcomes', which devalues them. This approach has been criticised by feminist and emancipatory researchers, and we prefer and use the term 'developmental outcomes'.

Second is the issue of measuring distance travelled. If an ideological position is adopted in youth work, and an informal learning process is used, then the end point of work will not be known or predetermined by outcomes. This poses a challenge for measuring change as it cannot be anticipated, and so measured, before it has occurred. Thirdly, we needed to consider how we could measure the acquisition of set characteristics when young people are considered unique, for example:

- How can we compare young people when they are unique?
- How can we measure personal development when there is no nationally or internationally agreed scale for doing so, as there is with height?
- How can we evaluate if there is no set curriculum, yet how can we have a curriculum when youth work is young person led?
- How can we claim that youth work changed the young people when there are so many other factors at play in their lives?

Youth work has stood by its principles and values and has resisted the curriculum's outcomes and measurement. If it continues to do so, however, some believe that non-formal projects may end in 'oblivion', as evidence based practice is increasingly the only practice that is funded.

Explaining and evidencing the youth work process so that it is tangible, visible and valued is clearly key to its future, but how to do this whilst maintaining the value basis of youth work is clearly critical. Many youth workers do use creative methods and activities to evaluate their work, but this practice is threatened by the current focus on scientific 'proof' of success. These tensions have inspired us to write this book, to provide the sector with ways of evaluating youth work that is young person centred, participatory, empowering, respectful and anti-oppressive. We hope you also embrace this challenge and come with us through the next chapters.

Vignette 1.1   Brathay Trust's Values

Brathay Trust is a youth development centre with both urban and rural sites of practice. Brathay has used **experiential learning** to promote youth development since 1946. On average, 5000 young people a year attend programmes. These programmes are asset based and build on the strengths that young people have, helping them to overcome a range of disadvantages that are having a negative impact on their lives.

When Brathay established an evaluation department it considered its practice value system and contrasted it to the external value system of measurement imposed upon it. This comparison showed the challenge that they faced in developing an evaluation system that was true to internal values, and that met the needs of the external context. The lists are shown in Table 1.3.

Table 1.3 Brathay Trust's internal and external contextual values

Internal Values	External Contextual Values
• Respect for the individual	• Evidence based
• Learning and experience	• Outcome focused
• Primacy of the youth work process	• Quality
• Human centred – fulfilling potential	• Indicators of success
• Anti-oppressive and anti-discriminatory	• Quantitative data
• Social justice	• Value for money

Reflecting on this comparison allowed the organisation to understand the difficulties and challenges that they faced, and to decide where to give ground, and where to stand firm on their values, justifying their position to funders and commissioners.

Pause for Thought

Think about a project that you have been involved in:

- Create a map of its internal and external values, like the one in Table 1.3.

- How contradictory are these values? What might you do to reconcile them?

- Write a list of the outcomes that your project works towards (if any). Is it clear to you how to evaluate each one?

A Unique Evaluation Challenge

We believe that the current context puts youth work at the heart of a perfect storm, pitted against a barrage of criticisms and pressures to justify the sector (Ellis and Gregory, 2008: v).

Whilst the issue of evidence has challenged the third sector, it has been specifically targeted at youth work in the UK. As the Select Committee on Youth (2011: 23) concluded:

We accept that the outcomes of individual youth work relationships can be hard to quantify and the impact of encounters with young people may take time to become clear and be complex. In that context, it is hard to reject the basic tenet expounded by a range of youth service representatives and young people themselves, that 'you know good youth work when you see it'.

Such a critique of UK youth work led to a number of attempts to defend youth work (see, for example, In Defence of Youth Work, 2013) and in 2013, the Catalyst Consortium were commissioned by the Department for Education in the UK to generate an outcomes framework for youth work. Although going some way to helping youth workers communicate the success of their projects, it has been taken by some as further evidence of the standardisation and so managerialism of youth work and an erosion of informal education's standing (Ord, quoted in Goddard, 2012). Despite this critique, we have found no evidence of it being used in this manner.

Vignette 1.2   The Catalyst outcomes framework

The Catalyst Consortium includes four UK-based youth organisations (NCVYS, NYA, Social Enterprise UK and the Young Foundation). They created an outcomes framework for youth work that was: 'Designed to support understanding and measurement of the connection between intrinsic personal development outcomes and longer extrinsic outcomes' (Young Foundation, 2013: 2). The outcomes framework includes seven outcomes as shown in Figure 1.3. These are designed to be a holistic planning tool that prompts practitioners to think about the range of outcomes that their programmes might address in as broad a context as possible. To convey this, the framework shows seven key sets of capabilities (shaded). Practitioners may focus on one or more of these sets, but would not focus on all of them in a single programme. The framework also shows a suggested list of smaller capabilities that are attached to each of the main capabilities. These are examples of capabilities, rather than an exhaustive list, as suggested by the 'thought bubble' shape of the boxes.

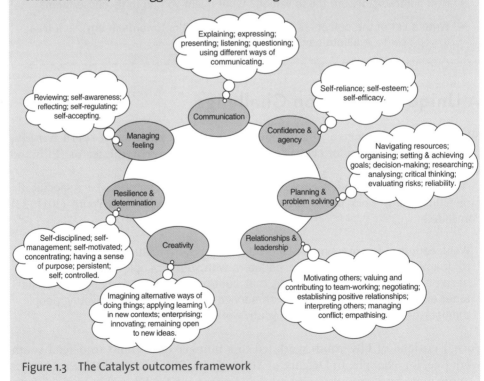

Figure 1.3   The Catalyst outcomes framework

The diagram suggests that these are food for thought, rather than a deterministic list. Despite this, the framework has been taken by some (Ord quoted in Goddard 2012: 26) as a predetermined check list which has then been used to determine the goals of work with young people.

Reflecting on this, Brathay's use of the outcome framework has created a consistent form of reporting against one set of outcomes, whilst still providing practitioners with flexibility in planning programmes. Before the outcome framework Brathay's work seemed diverse and eclectic, now, using this framework for annual reporting, Brathay's practice can be seen as a coherent approach to youth work.

This example is evidence of how a contradiction between drivers and professional values can have a dramatic impact on practice. Some youth workers feel that the very philosophy of youth work is challenged by the notion of intended outcomes:

> For youth workers, the ideal is to affirm the positive aspects of young people's collective as well as individual identities, to enable them to better understand their present. From this perspective, they encourage constructive and reflective understanding in the here and now ('starting where the young people are at') in order to create futures which by definition cannot be pre-planned. Hence the dominant ethos in youth work is one of 'process' rather than 'outcome'. (Spence, 2004: 262)

Others find outcomes supportive, believing that they allow practitioners to effectively plan and evaluate the impact of their work. The notion of intended outcomes is, however, less contentious in non-formal youth work settings. As described earlier, non-formal learning has intended outcomes. These remain flexible and responsive to the needs of the young person, and are planned from knowledge of the young person, but remain a guide to the youth worker delivering the session, in what they hope to achieve. When set with the young person this is a highly participative and supportive process. From this perspective, measurement of outcomes (set with the young people) is unproblematic.

An issue arises in informal and non-formal youth work when the outcomes that are set by commissioners or funders of projects are long-term, or distal. In our experience we are often set outcomes that relate to desistance from offending. These are not outcomes that young people would write, they are not short term, and they are not meaningful. After years of difficulties with such drivers, we now explain to commissioners that we can only achieve these outcomes through short-term or proximal personal development outcomes. We are confident that we can evidence personal development and that this contributes to distal outcomes, but we can rarely show long-term outcomes ourselves as we do not always work with young people on long-term projects. Figure 1.4 shows the relationship between proximal and distal outcomes used at the Brathay Trust. Whilst the diagram is useful, it does raise questions about whether it positions some outcomes as more valid than others as they are in a pyramid. The idea was to show distance, rather than value. What the figure does convey is the potential for tension when commissioners want to deliver distal outcomes in the short term.

Figure 1.4   Proximal and distal outcomes (simplified from Stuart and Maynard, 2012)

The practice of youth work happens between a young person and a youth worker (including evaluation practice). The drivers and challenges that have been identified act on that youth work practice, creating a range of tensions and pressures. See if you recognise any of the pressures in Figure 1.5, and the extent to which you have control over them.

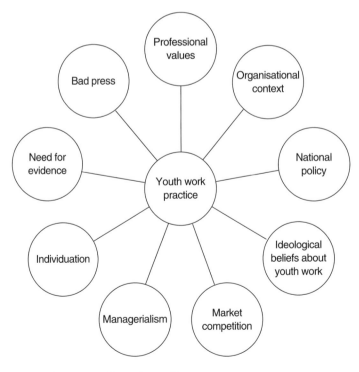

Figure 1.5   Forces acting on youth work practice

At this point we would like to return to the Step Up case study that is referred to throughout this book.

 Step Up Case Study

The Step Up project was commissioned with the overall aim of increasing attainment and decreasing unauthorised absence, but it was immediately seen that the young people needed to have greater self-confidence and self-esteem in order to make any progress. What was meaningful for the young people was the extent to which they felt good about themselves, rather than school attendance data. This is a clear example of proximal outcomes (personal development), contributing to distal outcomes (attainment and attendance), a realisation that the project team made after they mapped the outcomes at the end of year one in a 'theory of change map'. The practitioners were interested in whether their practice was promoting self-esteem and confidence. The organisation was interested in whether the programme was benefiting the young people on their terms, and the commissioner wanted to know if the grades of the young people were improving.

This highlights how one seemingly simple project can mean vastly different things to the different stakeholders. These are all aspects of the same programme, as shown in Figure 1.6, but they all have very different forms of evaluation at their hearts.

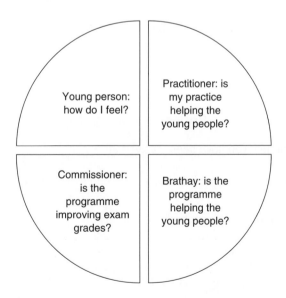

Figure 1.6   The different stakeholder questions in the Step Up Project evaluation

(Continued)

(Continued)

Rather than seeing these differences as an irreconcilable barrier, the project was evaluated in a way that was meaningful for each of the stakeholders, and the different forms of data combined to create a rich, multifaceted evaluation of the project. However, it took a lot of time and effort to avert the potential disaster that such varied demands could have created. We achieved this by investing time in the relationships between all four stakeholders, ensuring that their expectations could all be met.

We have described four key challenges and the unique context of evaluating youth work. Some organisations, understandably, use these challenges as barriers that prevent them from evaluating work with young people. Many organisations also do not evaluate because of a range of internal organisational barriers. You may need to overcome these as well as the contextual challenges before you can get going. Some of the most common reasons for avoiding evaluation are that:

- It is perceived as 'too difficult' or 'too time consuming' (Airthrey Ltd, 2013).
- There is a lack of understanding, miscommunication and confusion about which evaluation approach to adopt.
- The main evaluation 'method' is often seen as end of programme 'reactionnaire' (Kirkpatrick and Kirkpatrick, 2006).
- The feedback mechanisms to inform programme design and review are often missing or are ad hoc/anecdotal, leading to the belief that evaluation does not change anything and so is meaningless.
- The evaluation processes are believed to get in the way of good youth work, rather than supporting it.

Pause for Thought

Think about a project you have been involved in:

- What are the organisational barriers that could prevent an evaluation from happening?
- How would you overcome each of the barriers?

Our Evaluation Approach

We believe that non-formal projects with young people do have intended outcomes. These are not deterministic, or at odds with the values of youth work. Rather, these intended outcomes are often negotiated, participatory and open to change. Projects that have outcomes allow young people and practitioners to conceptualise what they are aiming to learn, achieve or attain, and so enhance the learning experience by clarifying the shared goal of the endeavour. Reflecting on progress against the outcomes becomes the basis of good non-formal learning, as participants and facilitators jointly think through the gains made, the progress along the road. If this reflection is underpinned by facilitative tools that promote learning, then the young people, the staff, and the service make gains.

When we talk about evaluation practice for projects with young people we mean practice that supports learning and emancipation. Supportive evaluation tools can enhance learning from the perspective of all the stakeholders (see Figure 1.6), and can take account of intended and unintended outcomes. This mediates a middle way between the contextual demands and values of youth work. From this perspective we advocate creative methods throughout the book.

Summary

In this chapter we have identified the differences between different types of work with young people and the difference that these can fundamentally make to evaluation design. We have identified the contextual challenges that face evaluators and summarise how these create a unique context for evaluation at the moment. We also identify some of the organisational barriers that might hinder evaluation. Despite these challenges, we have found through our own practice, that youth workers' skills are ideally suited to the evaluation. The rest of this book focuses on the practical ways that practitioners can evidence the outcomes of their work whilst still holding true to the participatory, anti-oppressive, voluntaristic and emancipatory nature of non-formal projects with young people. We suggest that creative methods are ideal to support this.

Key Points

1. The techniques in this book refer to non-formal projects with young people, although they may also be of use in formal and informal settings.
2. The international context of evaluation drives practitioners to evidence outcomes, and tends to focus on long-term outcomes, rather than those that are closer to and more meaningful to young people.
3. Non-formal work with young people uses outcomes and as such offers possibilities for outcome measurement.
4. Informal learning, which many youth workers argue they use, makes it difficult to measure outcomes, and as such evaluation and monitoring is ideologically rejected by many youth workers.
5. This book presents a range of ways to evaluate non-formal projects that supports learning for young people and practitioners, and meets the needs of the provider organisation and of the commissioner.

Further Reading

Axford, N. and Morpeth, L. (2013) *Evidence-based Programs in Children's Services: A Critical Appraisal* presents the case for and against evidence based practice in children's services, which is now impacting on youth work.

NYA (2014) *Commissioning Toolkit* shows how commissioners of youth work services are advised to think about outcomes in youth work in the UK.

In Defence of Youth Work is a UK-based campaign group supporting informal, creative, voluntary and collective youth work. Their homepage presents their argument against the use of outcomes in youth work.

Spence, J. (2004) *Targeting, Accountability and Youth Work Practice in Youth Work Practice* demonstrates how regulation and managerialism has developed in youth work.

Harris, V. (2009) *Community Work Skills Manual* has a very practical section on evaluation and action research.

2

EVALUATION METHODOLOGY

Chapter Overview

- The key beliefs and assumptions that underpin evaluation, and the key differences between them
- The reflective evaluation cycle
- The value of creative evaluation methods.

Introduction

As we have discussed in the introduction to this book, evaluation is a form of research. Evaluation, therefore, can use many of the same methods as pure research in order to assess the effectiveness of projects with young people. Because of this overlap, there is some technical language used in this chapter, don't be put off. We explain these terms all as we go along, and there is a glossary to help too.

The approach a practitioner takes to evaluation is based upon certain beliefs and assumptions he or she holds about the world and about the nature and acquisition of knowledge. These beliefs and assumptions have an important impact on the range of methods available. Briefly, these beliefs and assumptions are concerned with what our view of reality is (or our **ontology**), how we believe knowledge comes about (our **epistemology**) and our approach to knowledge generation (our **methodology**). These key beliefs are intrinsically linked. Before we plan an evaluation, it is important to understand what these three terms mean. This understanding will enable us to articulate our beliefs and assumptions about our evaluation and explain and justify why we are adopting a particular approach. The discussions around methodology, epistemology and ontology play a critical role in how the 'evaluator' plans, implements and analyses the evaluation. Hence, it is vital for anyone who is interested in carrying out evaluations to have an understanding of these ideas and their implications for the evaluation process. This chapter introduces these concepts and how they have come to inform evaluation design.

First Assumptions: Ontology

Our evaluation is guided by our worldview, our view of the nature of reality. This is our ontological perspective, or our ontology. There are two main ontological positions in the social sciences, these are '**realism**' and '**relativism**'. Realism argues that there is a reality 'out there' which exists independently of us. Relativist argues that there is no reality outside our perception. These two ontological views determine the **paradigm**, or way of thinking, in which our evaluation sits. Just as there are two main ontological views, there are two broad paradigms: Positivism and Post-positivism.

Positivism is the paradigm of traditional science and is the oldest, most dominant, view of social science. Positivism adopts a 'realist' ontology that assumes there is an objective reality 'out there' which is independent of our perception. This paradigm aims to seek knowledge about the world and it seeks proof for theories. It is based on the assumption that there is one reality, that is black or white; right or wrong and verifiable by empirical evidence. This paradigm values evaluation that is empirical, objective, independent, neutral, hygienic and value-free. When applying this to the social world, or youth work, only directly observable and measurable behaviours are considered as worthwhile of study. Unobservable phenomena, such as meanings and intentions, cannot be objectively evaluated and thus are not valid (Haralambos, 1985).

Vignette 2.1 introduces a positivistic approach to evaluation. The vignette illustrates some of the key features of a positivist approach and shows how value is placed on observation, control and the objective measurement of the impact of an intervention on the target population.

Vignette 2.1   Tapping Youth as Agents for Change: Evaluation of a Peer Leadership HIV/AIDS Intervention (Pearlman et al., 2002)

The purpose of this evaluation was to assess the impact of a community-based HIV/AIDS peer leadership prevention programme on newly enrolled peer leaders and youth enrolled as peer educators. The evaluation was quasi-experimental, seeking to estimate the causal impact of the intervention on young people. The population sample included 235 young people, 164 peer leaders and 71 young people (in a comparison group). They were drawn from nine communities in Massachusetts, USA. The intervention consisted of a short course and on-going group work with an adult advisor to plan and implement HIV/AIDS outreach activities for young people. A confidential questionnaire was administered at the beginning and after the intervention to measure (a) HIV/AIDS knowledge, (b) planning and presenting skills, (c) self-efficacy, (d) perception of one's self as a change agent in the community, and (e) sexual risk-taking behaviours.

Reflecting on this case study we can see a quantitative approach to evaluation. Two groups are given the same questionnaire that collected numeric data to allow the evaluators to rate the extent to which the programme had increased peer leadership in the group who came on the programme versus a group who did not. In this way it is seeking to test the theory that the programme led to change. There were no attempts to understand the young people's experiences in depth, or to understand the reasons for the answers that they provided in the questionnaires.

Post-positivism holds an alternative and **relativist** viewpoint that believes one reality is not possible in a social world. Post-positivistic perspectives are based on the assumption that there are multiple versions of reality, that reality is subjective, socially constructed and interpreted. This paradigm values meanings and intentions, and thus, variability and the personal. Value is placed on the meanings that young people might assign to the world around them (Denzin and Lincoln, 2003). As a result, there are multiple realities in existence which are interpreted by the evaluator, the participants of the investigation, and the reader (Creswell, 1997).

Post-positivist perspectives are also referred to in different ways, depending on the influence and the focus of the evaluation. Most commonly, you might have heard the terms **interpretivism** and **constructivism**. We use the term post-positivism in this book as an umbrella term. Another important term to introduce you to is **participative**, or emancipatory evaluation. This form of evaluation seeks to involve participants as much as possible in the design, collection and analysis of the data, so that they gain as much, if not more than the evaluators. This form of evaluation sits firmly in post-positivism as the positivistic approach would not allow for non-evaluators to be involved in any stage of the process wishing to keep it objective and neutral. Participative evaluation is covered in detail in Chapter 5.

Vignette 2.2 introduces a post-positivist approach to evaluation. The vignette shows how value is placed on understanding, rather than measurement, and thus the importance of the subjective and multiple realities of the participants.

Vignette 2.2   Qualitative Evaluation of the Project P.A.T.H.S. Based on the Perceptions of the Programme Participants (Shek et al., 2006)

This evaluation was carried out to understand the perceptions of the students participating in the Tier 1 Program of the P.A.T.H.S. Project (Positive Adolescent Training through Holistic Social Programmes). P.A.T.H.S. is a youth enhancement

(Continued)

(Continued)

programme that attempts to promote holistic youth development in Hong Kong. Five focus groups with 43 students recruited from four schools were conducted to generate qualitative data to evaluate the programme. There was a specific focus on how the students described the programme and they were encouraged to verbalise their views and perceptions of the programme. The focus group facilitators were conscious of the importance of adopting an open attitude to encourage the students to express different views, including both positive and negative views.

Reflecting on this vignette reveals a very different approach to Vignette 2.1. Here a small group is recruited rather than a large sample being used. There is no control group. It is assumed that the experiences of this group will account for any change without a control group to test against. They meet in focus groups to discuss the changes that have happened for them rather than completing an individual anonymous questionnaire. This means that they can build meaning together and learn from the focus group as much as the evaluators. The only data collected are experiences recorded as words. In-depth understanding rather than generalisations were sought.

Although this book will give an overview of the different methods, our position as practitioners is situated within a post-positivistic paradigm, which aligns with the values and assumptions of non-formal learning. We believe that the evaluation of projects working with young people will hold multiple realities and will be subjective and complex. This means they are not black and white or right or wrong. Therefore, we feel, evaluations of projects working with young people are best approached from a post-positivist perspective.

Second Assumptions: Epistemology

Our ontological views inform our assumptions about how knowledge is constructed, or our **epistemology**.

In the social sciences positivism has been dominant for many years and considered to be the most reliable way of building our knowledge of the world. At the heart of positivism is '**empiricism**' or the '**empirical method**'. Empiricism requires that our study of the social world is based on empirical observations, or on things that we can directly experience (e.g. see, hear). Hence, in building our knowledge of the world we need to gather data, directly through experience and observation, and carry out our evaluation only on that which can be observed and measured. In order to test out theories or assumptions people hold about the world and establish 'the truth', it is essential to positivists that we are able to test these theories or assumptions. By using the methods based on the empirical method (such as experiments), positivism seeks to establish facts that prove or disprove our theories and assumptions. In positivism, knowledge builds through a continuous process of hypothesis testing. In this approach knowledge is constructed by the evaluator who is seen as detached and objective. As facts accumulate, so too does knowledge. The key goals of positivism are to produce knowledge which is **reliable** (refers to the consistency of the knowledge gained), **valid** (which refers to the extent to which the knowledge gained reflects reality) **replicable** (the ability of a method to repeat and produce the same findings) and **generalisable** (results from a small number of cases can be applied to the wider population).

Epistemology, the question of who can know and therefore construct knowledge, from a positivistic paradigm asserts that the observer/evaluator holds the power to investigate and thus construct knowledge objectively. Vignette 2.1, Tapping Youth as Agents for Change, shows how the evaluation valued measurement in areas pre-defined as important by the evaluator.

In stark contrast the post-positivistic paradigm assumes that knowledge is con-structed 'with' or 'by' all social actors (e.g. young people) and that each construc-tion might be very different. In terms of youth work, post-positivism assumes that young people have each constructed their own view of the world and these need to be recognised, described and understood. In this paradigm the evaluator is interested in finding out more about each social actor's view about the world and how that might, for example, impact on their behaviour. In this perspective the social actor and evaluator are on equal footing, all accounts hold equal weight, and young people are encouraged to actively participate within the evaluation, rather be a passive subject of the evaluation and evaluator as an external expert. Because this paradigm is based on the assumption that there are multiple perspec-tives to take into account when constructing knowledge, it aims to ensure that individual versions of the truth are acknowledged and represented. The assump-tion holds that all human action is meaningful and has to be interpreted and understood in the context of social practice. The aim of evaluation is to gain an understanding of the ways in which people make sense of their social worlds.

Knowledge gained through this paradigm is very descriptive and is not concerned with generalisations, prediction and control but with patterns and systems of meaning that young people use to make sense of their worlds, with interpretation, meaning and illumination taking a key role (Sarantakos, 1998). Unlike positivism, which assumes that everyone shares the same meaning system, post-positivism acknowledges that people experience social and physical reality differently. In this context, facts are regarded as fluid and embedded within a meaning system of people; they are not impartial, objective and neutral (Neuman, 1997). Vignette 2.2 shows how the evalu-ation was open to themes emerging from the young people themselves, rather than being predefined. In this sense, it valued the young people as experts of their experi-ence and had knowledge for the evaluator to learn from.

Third Assumptions: Methodology

The approach to the evaluation, or methodology, is based on both ontological and epistemological assumptions. In positivism, the evaluator's role is to gather data, through empirical observation and measurement, and establish 'facts', such as the 'laws' that govern behaviour. In a positivistic approach, the evaluator is considered as separate from the evaluation. They are objective, unbiased, value-neutral and capable of ensuring that personal views or feelings do not intrude on the evaluation process or on their interpretation of the data. The evaluator is a neutral scientist, who is expert and holds the power in the evaluation process.

Vignette 2.1 shows how the evaluation was objective with the evaluator separated from the project.

In a post-positivistic paradigm, the evaluator acquires an insider's perspective of young people's actions, interpretations and definitions of the situation (Schwandt, 2003). Schwandt adds that our active participation in the life-worlds of others is crucial in order to grasp the context in which action takes place. In order for the evaluator from this paradigm to acquire knowledge of the social world they first have to 'get to know' the context within which they are to work and try to get a feeling for how people in that context 'see the world' and construct meaning. This is a **'naturalistic'** methodology, which means that we try to understand what is happening in as natural a setting as possible, for example, joining in with the game of pool (Lincoln and Guba, 1985; Denzin and Lincoln, 2003). This approach would also enable the evaluator to get beyond some of the deficit discourses of 'youth' and some of the assumptions about young people's experiences of school, home life and relationships and it works from an open mind, with no preconceptions or hypotheses in mind.

Vignette 2.2 showed how the evaluators adopted an 'open attitude' working with the young people to encourage them to give honest opinions. The relationship the evaluator built with the young people was important to this process.

A Summary of Positivism and Post-positivism

As discussed, ontology, epistemology and methodology can all broadly be thought of as positivist or post-positivist. As such, we wanted to summarise both of these paradigms before moving on.

Positivism has been dominant for many years in the social sciences and was considered to be the most reliable way of establishing knowledge. With its dependence on objectivity, isolation of 'variables' and 'control', measurement and statistical analysis, positivism has been accused of reductionism and of dehumanising its participants. By removing young people, and their behaviour, from the very rich tapestries their lives are immersed in, by ignoring culture, history and diversity and by failing to account for subjective experience or the meanings young people attached to their world, positivism is accused of reducing complex social behaviour to simple, causal links and numerical counts that don't actually tell us anything meaningful about the behaviours they are supposed to represent. By seeing people as essentially the same and as 'governed' by the same laws, positivism ignores individuality or that people are conscious, possess free will and are reflexively engaged in their worlds and their behaviour. Positivism also claims that the evaluator is neutral in the evaluation process. This means that important questions about 'the evaluator' and their impact on the evaluation process (such as why did they chose to ask particular questions or interpret the data in a certain way) are not asked (Guba and Lincoln, 1994). Finally, the positivist approach fails to consider the power dynamics inherent in the evaluation relationship. In positivism the evaluator holds the power – they choose the evaluation question and method, and implement their evaluation on young people. The evaluator is traditionally only interested in the 'data', not the thoughts or feelings stakeholders have about the evaluation process. The evaluator and young people are not equal in this process and evaluation is 'done to' not 'done with' young people.

On the other hand, post-positivism values young people centrally within the evaluation process. It provides opposition to all the criticism of positivism above. It is therefore more in keeping with youth work values and principles, particularly in relation to voluntary participation, collaboration, empowerment and respect. In particular, a post-positivist approach which employs creative methods supports young people to have power in the evaluation process. This increases engagement and provides a greater depth to data and can even potentially enhance the project itself, as it asks young people to explicitly think about their experience.

Pause for Thought

Think about a project you have been involved in:

- What was it important to find out, for example, proof or understanding (your ontological assumptions)?
- Who had knowledge and how was it constructed (your epistemological assumptions)?
- What approach was taken to finding this out (your methodological assumptions)?

We can think of our ontological, epistemological and methodological assumptions as three simple questions:

1. What do we want to know?
2. Who has this knowledge?
3. How do we find this out?

These form the foundation of the first stage of the evaluation cycle introduced at the beginning of this book. When we 'think of questions and criteria for success' (the first stage of the cycle), we must explore our ontological (what do we want to know), epistemological (who has this knowledge) and methodological (how do we find this out) assumptions. These guide what the evaluation aims to find out and our evaluation questions.

Although we recognise that positivism and post-positivism inform a range of different evaluations methods, and at times as practitioners we will be called upon to design, implement and interpret 'positivistic' forms of evaluation, this book is situated within a post-positivist paradigm. This is because we believe that the core values and principles of youth work and non-formal learning closely align with this paradigm. For example, the value placed upon voluntary participation, collaboration, empowerment and respect is key to youth work, and post-positivism enables us as evaluators to respect these. Similarly, when the evaluator is subjectively involved within this process (as with post-positivist method) they are in a better position to understand and represent it. Relativist accounts also require the evaluator to acknowledge and state their bias. This is aligned with and achieved through reflective practice.

The Reflective Evaluation Cycle

Reflective practice is a common term used in youth work practice. It refers to a form of professional learning. Reflection, in this context, is 'in' and 'on' practice (Schön, 1983). Bolton (2010) states that 'Reflection is a state of mind, an on-going constituent part of practice, not a technique or curriculum element' (Bolton, 2010: 3). As evaluators and youth workers, reflective practice is an important part of our daily work. It is important in these contexts because it allows us to discuss complex issues of power and ethical practice. Evaluation and youth work are both full of such issues and as such reflective practice is important as it is applied to relatively complicated, ill-structured ideas for which there is not an obvious solution and is largely based on the further processing of knowledge and the understanding we already possess (Moon, 2004).

Reflective practice can enable us to think about ourselves, our assumptions, our approach, wider society and culture. It can enable enquiry into:

- What you know but do not know you know
- What you know but want to hide or forget
- How to resolve practical dilemmas
- How actions match beliefs
- How to change what you are doing
- The extent of your power and agency
- Relationships with given social, cultural and political structures
- What you think, feel and value and how that impacts on evaluation. (developed from Bolton, 2010: 4)

In post-positivism, the position of the evaluator is central to the collection and interpretation of data. The evaluation process and its outcomes are a product of their construction of understanding. It is therefore essential that reflective practice is central within this process in order to represent a thorough and fair evaluation of practice.

The reflective evaluation cycle presented in the introduction, is a tool to help structure reflective practice. In the introduction it was populated with words that helped you evaluate in a reflective way. Figure 2.1 adapts the model with words that help you reflect on your evaluation practice.

As you can see from the wording and suggested questions, the reflective evaluation cycle can help you to reveal ontological, epistemological and methodological positions adopted by yourself and stakeholders, revealing tensions in evaluation practice. Only through quality reflective practice can the evaluator be aware of and manage this dilemma.

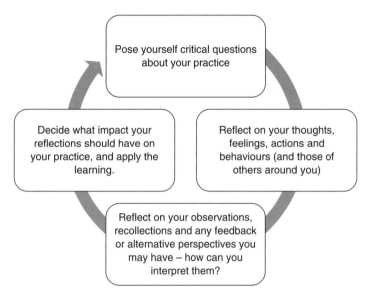

Figure 2.1   The reflective evaluation cycle as a tool for reflective practice

Methods

Within our methodological approach we decide our **methods**. This is the specific ways in which we will collect data. These are often referred to as **quantitative** and **qualitative** methods. It is commonly assumed that quantitative methods are aligned with a positivistic paradigm, whereas qualitative methods are aligned with a post-positivistic paradigm.

The basic aim of quantitative methods is to explore social phenomena via systematic, empirical investigation techniques, such as experiments or surveys that result in quantifiable data and can be analysed by the use of statistical, mathematical techniques. Ideally experiments are conducted within a laboratory or a field setting where a high degree of control and measurement is possible. Quantitative methods produce numerical data for statistical analysis (types of analysis are discussed further in Chapter 9). This is exemplified in Vignette 2.1.

The primary aim of qualitative methods is to acquire a detailed description of the social situation being studied and focus on the meaning that people attach to their lives and experiences. Qualitative methods produce narratives and rich descriptions which are analysed for key themes. Vignette 2.2 exemplifies this approach with focus groups that allowed the conversation to be directed by the young people and the data to be richly descriptive. Table 2.1, shows examples of common quantitative and qualitative methods.

Table 2.1   Examples of evaluation methods

Examples of Typical Quantitative Methods	Examples of Typical Qualitative Methods
Questionnaire	Interviews
Experiment	Focus groups
Observation	Participant observation
Secondary data (official statistics)	Case studies

Mixed Methods

Many people think that qualitative and quantitative methods are incompatible because they use methods from opposing paradigms. However, we frequently find ourselves using both qualitative and quantitative data. We believe it is important to utilise the advantages of both in order to meet the needs of an evaluation. We have come to the conclusion that our evaluations will be most useful when thought of as 'no stories without statistics and no statistics without stories'. Each method qualifies the other and provides a more rounded picture. This approach is in keeping with practice, as well as hearing the demands for quantitative proof alongside explanations of change within the current political climate. This is known as a **mixed methods** approach to evaluation. A mixed methods approach seeks to allow the two methods to complement each other whilst accepting that each fundamentally seeks the same goal – providing answers to evaluation questions. The mixed methods approach is discussed further in Chapter 8.

In youth work practice, people often start with a method, rather than the approach they want to take. This is because few youth workers are given the time to explore the assumptions behind evaluations. We may hear them say 'I'll survey the young people to see if their self-esteem has improved'. The risk of starting with the method (such as surveying in this example) is that we do not consider all of the assumptions that underpin the method. This is crucial in order to ascertain if it is the most appropriate method (Will the young people engage with a survey?), as well as to justify its use to achieve the aims of the evaluation (Is it just self-esteem you want to evaluate? What questions will you ask and why are these appropriate?).

Remember the three simple questions: What do we want to know? Who has this knowledge? How do we find this out?

Pause for Thought

Think of a young people's project you have been involved in.

- What methods were used to evaluate the project?
- Were these qualitative, quantitative or mixed methods?
- Were the assumptions which the methods were based upon clear, so as to justify their use?

Table 2.4 summarises the discussion so far in the context of a project for young people. In this example, the young people were referred by a youth offending team to the project which aimed to reduce offending and promote engagement in posi-tive activities. Table 2.2 shows how an evaluation of the project could come from two opposing paradigms.

Table 2.2 An overview of two opposing paradigms

| | | Paradigm | |
		Positivism	Post-positivism
What do we want to know?	Ontology (perception of reality)	The evaluation seeks to prove whether the project met its aims or not. Evaluation question: Did young people reduce their rate of offending and increase their engagement in positive activities? By how much?	The evaluation seeks to understand if and how the project met its aims for all participants. Evaluation question: What were the experiences of those involved in the project and how did the project contribute to young people reducing their offending and increasing their engagement in positive activities?
Who has this knowledge?	Epistemology (construction of knowledge)	Knowledge is constructed through the evaluator's objective, detached, independent, neutral and value free analysis.	Knowledge is co-created and all perspectives are valued. It is subjective, concerned with all interpretations, social constructions or meanings that are made. Practitioners and young people are considered experts in their own experience for the evaluator to learn from.
How do we find this out?	Methodology (approach)	The evaluator stays separate from the project in order to stay objective. They seek pre-existing data.	The evaluator works with (or is) the practitioner and/or young people. They want to get an inside and in-depth understanding of what happens within the project that contributes to young people reducing offending and engaging in positive activities.
	Methods	The evaluator analyses youth offending data for the duration of the project, as well as six months before and after. Comparison of data, pre-project, during project, and six months on, as well as comparing to a control group who did not attend the project or statistics from an offending population with the same demographics.	The evaluator takes part in the project as much as possible as a participant observer, taking field notes of what they see going on. They seek clarity of their observations by conducting informal interviews with participants and staff, during and after the project.
	Analysis	Statistical analysis of numerical data to show changes in rates of offending and engagement in positive activities. Data compared to control group.	All data is analysed for key themes and rich descriptions that show what the project meant to young people and how it contributed to any changes in offending and engagement in positive activities.

After considering the method that you will use, the next planning stage is to decide upon data collection tools, and the analytical approach. These are explained later in the book in Chapters 7 and 9 respectively.

Creative Methods

The ontological, epistemological and methodological assumptions of post-positivism described here open the door to subjective evaluation methods that best suit young people and the context of the project. These assumptions lead us to a consideration of **creative methods**.

As discussed in the opening chapters of this book, we are increasingly required to evidence our practice. However, this does not necessarily mean that young people cannot have a voice in evaluation design, or even lead evaluation. Robust data about the project, its impact and its shortcomings, is most easily gained when young people want to engage in the process. This is best achieved when the evaluation tools are in keeping and integrated within the project. Considering the ways in which to make evaluation fit the needs of the young people and the context that they are working in, ensures that, at the very least, the evaluation is engaging and, where possible, that young people have ownership and power in the process. Prosser (2009) advocates using creative methods because they make the evaluation process more playful, engaging and motivating.

We believe that creative methods make evaluation more accessible to young people. In our experience, written questionnaires (aka school test) and formal interviews (aka police interrogations) prohibit many of the young people we work with from participating. A key quality of creative tools is therefore their ability to level the power between young people and evaluator, increasing the value of young people's expression over the evaluator's mental, or written, framework of questions.

A further advantage of creative methods is that they are non-language based. They utilise more senses, opening creative channels and communicating through preferred means, allowing a more holistic understanding to develop (Jewitt and Van Leeuwen, 2004). The very process of engaging in a creative process forces young people to reflect on experiences, choose how to represent them, and then describe what they have represented and why. This is a more considered cognitive process than answering a question, and some argue that it leads to better quality data (Gauntlett, 2007; Bolton, 2010). The multisensory approach used in creative methods also means that they are accessible to young people who may have limited language skills for a range of reasons, so they can open participation. Gauntlett (2007) also advocates that creative tools provide a depth of data that may not be possible through other non-creative means.

It is important to highlight that creative methods can be either quantitative or qualitative. This might seem surprising after reading the last chapter, However, creative methods are more about the way in which we engage with young people, rather than the type of data that is produced. Thus, we can collect quantitative data using creative methods. One example of a creative method is called 'Line outs'.

This is a process where young people line up along a physical or metaphorical line to reflect how they rate themselves on the criteria selected, such as self-confidence. This is an energetic and engaging method to collect numerical data.

There are critiques of creative methods that need to be considered before using them. Creative methods can prompt anxiety for young people; they may worry 'I'm not creative enough!' This shows the importance of methods being in keeping with the project context. When they are carefully tailored into a programme, they then appear a natural part of the programme, overcoming criticisms that creative methods are artificial or non-naturalistic (Pink, 2007). There are difficulties posed by the open nature of creative methods. Exactly because there are no carefully crafted questions, the young people may say more than they wished to, or more than we wished them to. As a result of this risk, Prosser (2000b) warns of there being an absence of ethical frameworks for creative methods. This is particularly important as youth work evaluators potentially ask young people to open creative channels that may elicit deep reflections that are uncomfortable or upsetting. This is considered further in the discussion of ethics in Chapter 4. As might be expected, creative methods are valued by post-positivists, and undervalued by the positivistic paradigm (McIntosh and Sobiechowska, 2009).

Pause for Thought

- Make a list of data collection methods (e.g. interviews, surveys, etc.).
- How could each of these be creatively adapted to be more engaging for young people?
- How could you integrate these within a project you have experience of?

Stakeholders

The evaluation approach is also dependent on the beliefs of the project stakeholders. Stakeholders are individuals, groups or organisations who are involved with the operation or outcomes of the project and include policy makers, commissioners, managers, funders, staff and young people. All of these people could be affected directly or indirectly by the project's activities. They may be able to influence the project – by assisting with funding or benefiting from its results, or use the project data and/or evaluation outcomes. As a result, they may literally have different 'stakes' in the evaluation process. Different stakeholders may have different evaluation questions based on different worldviews and assumptions. For example, in a youth offending project, a youth worker may be interested in showing that a young person has increased in confidence and belief in themselves, that they can achieve more; whereas the youth work organisation commissioned to deliver the project, may be more interested in evidencing how the project has contributed to reduced offending. In turn, the project commissioner may be interested in changes in the rate of offending; and the young people themselves may simply be concerned with not wanting to fill out yet another questionnaire! Therefore, our evaluation approach must be designed in partnership with all stakeholders in order to consider and understand all perspectives, so that we can ask the right questions and gather appropriate data. Of key significance in this discussion is the notion of power. Ensuring equity and inclusion of all stakeholders is essential, particularly the participation of young people. Power is discussed further in Chapter 5. Table 2.3 may help you think through the beliefs and expectations of the stakeholders involved in your evaluation.

Table 2.3   Stakeholder views when planning an evaluation

	Why do they want it?	What will they gain?	What design do they want?	What data collection works for them?	How do they want it analysed?	What do they want to do with it?
Young person						
Evaluator						
Organisation						
Funder						
Public						

Mapping the different views of the stakeholders above may help you identify areas of tension and could also show that the process will be straightforward as everyone agrees, or had no opinion. We signpost further reading for stakeholder analysis tools at the end of this chapter. We can see this methodological process in the context of the Step Up case study below.

 Step Up Case Study

Table 2.4 shows the assumptions behind the evaluation of the project which aimed to improve school attendance and raise attainment of looked after young people in the 14–16 cohort.

Table 2.4   The post-positivistic assumptions underpinning the Step Up case study

What do we want to know?	A post-positivistic ontological approach	Assumption: We want to understand if the project contributes to young people improving their attendance and attainment and in what ways?
Who has this knowledge?	A post-positivistic epistemological approach	Assumption: Young people and practitioners have knowledge that can qualify numerical data. They are the experts of their experience and can inform our understanding of how to best support young people to increase their attendance and attainment.

How do we find this out?	A post-positivistic methodological approach	Assumption: The evaluator works with the practitioners and young people to get an inside and in-depth understanding of young people's experiences and what happens within the project that contributes to young people improving their attendance and attainment.
	Using mixed methods	The evaluator gathers qualitative and quantitative data. Quantitative attendance and attainment data is gathered from school databases. Comparison of data, pre-project, post-project, and six months on as well as comparing to year group data. Journey posters are used as a stimulus for individual interviews. Practitioners write pen-portraits for each young person. All project materials are gathered (e.g. Asdan folders, creative projects, photos and video footage).
	Analysis	Statistical analysis of quantitative data to show any changes in attendance and attainment. Qualitative data analysis for key themes in young people's experiences and to understand what contributes to young people increasing their attendance and attainment.

This shows that the ontology and epistemology were both post positivistic, and the methods were mixed. This allowed the evaluator to use a wide range of creative and statistical data together to present the facts around attainment with an in-depth understanding of how attainment had been increased or why it remained static. The commissioners had originally thought that they wanted a purely positivistic study, but after some discussion with them they also wanted to illuminate any statistical data with the experiences of the young people to provide a comprehensive understanding of what the programme achieved and how it achieved it.

Summary

This chapter has introduced some fundamental concepts. Ontology, epistemology and methodology and methods are often invisible in evaluations, but are the vital building blocks of a good evaluation design. Each of these elements can be positivistic or post–positivistic, and we have encouraged you to consider how your beliefs map onto these. Reflective practice was introduced as a key way in which you can keep your beliefs and the beliefs of others in sight during the evaluation process and ensure your design choices align. Stakeholder analysis was also introduced as a key tool to aid your management of different expectations in the evaluation process. Creative methods were also introduced as an engaging and empowering way to conduct evaluation, a theme that will continue throughout the text.

Key Points

1. Evaluators need to understand and articulate the values and assumptions that underpin their approach to the evaluation. This should incorporate all stakeholder needs and assumptions.
2. Creative methods can be qualitative or quantitative, but are underpinned by post-positivist values and assumptions. These values and assumptions align with youth work.
3. Adopting a creative approach is more engaging for young people. It can enhance the evaluation, as well as the project itself. For example, enabling a range of young people to engage, facilitating fun ways to participate, creating time and space for reflection, and enabling expression in a variety of non-verbal ways.
4. A good reflective youth worker who conducts reviews is also a good evaluator, as the skills of youth work are directly transferable into evaluation.

Further Reading

Community Sustainability Engagement (2014) *The Evaluation Toolbox* provides an accessible overview of what evaluation is and how to do it.

Denscombe, M. (2010) *The Good Research Guide* for small-scale social research projects provides an introduction to research that is accessible and practical.

Mindtools (2014) Stakeholder Analysis is one of a series of online business tools, providing step-by-step guides.

Gauntlett, D. (2007) *Creative Explorations* explains in Chapters 6–8 how Lego can be used to explore identity. This is a useful insight into how creative methods can elicit deep data.

Squirrell, G. (2012) *Evaluation in Action: Theory and Practice for Effective Evaluation* presents a clear and simple guide to evaluation as opposed to 'research'. It is generic, rather than geared to youth work, but remains an invaluable guide to planning and carrying out evaluations.

3

EVALUATION
ETHICS

Chapter Overview

- What is ethics?
- Key ethical considerations
- Challenging traditional notions of ethics.

Introduction

Because evaluations influence policy, practice and people's lives, it is important that they are carried out with care. Simply being involved in the evaluation process as well as reading the findings of the evaluation can have an impact on people's lives. Because of this, evaluators have to ensure they consider all possible ethical issues in their duty of care to safeguard participants.

Due to their importance, these ethical considerations are highly debated and this is magnified in the context of working with young people. The context of non-formal and informal learning with young people poses specific and complex ethical considerations. This is because of the hybrid position young people fall into – not yet considered an adult, but no longer considered a child.

This chapter will help to understand the ethical considerations that need to be included when carrying out evaluations on projects with young people. The chapter is split into two halves; the first will provide an overview of key ethical considerations, as well as discussing each in more depth in relation to evaluating projects with young people. The second half will take a critical perspective of this discussion, taking into account challenges to traditional notions of ethics that may not have considered the power dynamics at play, but which are central when working with young people. Here is a reminder of the core values or ethics of youth work from Chapter 1:

- Supporting personal, social and identity development
- Raising critical consciousness
- Supporting empowerment
- Anti-oppressive practice
- Valuing of personal experiences
- Voluntarism and participatory practice
- Being responsive to young people's needs, interests and preferences.

This is an excellent checklist to keep in mind when planning an evaluation. If an evaluation of youth work projects does not contribute to these, then we are perhaps already infringing the ethics of our youth work practice before we consider evaluation ethics. On the whole, good youth work ethics lead to good evaluation ethics. A more detailed critical discussion can be found in Batsleer (2010).

What is Ethics?

The term ethics is taken from the Greek 'ethos', from Plato and Aristotle. It literally translates to the 'customary or habitual way of behaving', and is often interpreted as the study of good and bad conduct. Later, Immanuel Kant called for moral actions that were based on a pure respect for duty. More recently, the *Oxford English Dictionary* (2013) gives three significant definitions: (1) 'the moral system of a particular writer or school of thought' (1651); (2) 'the rules of conduct recognised in certain limited departments of human life' (1789); and (3) 'the science of human duty in its widest extent' (1690).

These definitions have formed the foundations for professional groups to establish codes and standards of behaviour to regulate the actions of their members (Shephard, 2002). Most notable, was the establishment of the Belmont Report, which became the primary ethical framework for protecting human subjects in the United States (Zimmerman, 1997). The main catalyst for this and subsequent regulations is most commonly quoted to be the 'Bad Blood' case, detailed in Vignette 3.1.

Vignette 3.1   Bad Blood (Fourtner et al., 2007)

The Tuskegee syphilis experiment was an infamous study conducted between 1932 and 1972 by the U.S. Public Health Service to investigate the natural progression of untreated syphilis. Six hundred African American men working as sharecroppers were recruited on to the study. The men were told they were being treated for 'bad blood' – a term used for various illnesses, including syphilis, anaemia and fatigue. They were given free medical care, meals and free burial insurance for participating in the study. However, they were never told they had syphilis, nor were they ever treated for it and were prevented from accessing treatment elsewhere. The ethics of the study were criticised as the researchers knowingly failed to treat the men even after penicillin was found in the 1940s to be an effective cure for the disease.

The study now stands as a benchmark case in the importance of proper ethical procedures and, in particular, participants being fully informed before they consent (known as informed consent and discussed further later in this chapter). The study marked major changes in US laws and regulations internationally of studies involving human subjects, including the ethical review panels that most research and evaluation has to pass through today.

Reflecting on this we can see that despite the impact the study has had on the ethical debate, it highlights key critical questions we should be constantly asking ourselves:

- Are young people always aware that an evaluation is taking place?
- Do we always ensure that young people are fully informed of what a project or evaluation will entail, or do we assume certain things for them, for example, that they will want to be involved, or that they will be happy using a certain evaluation method?
- In what ways do adults assume they can withhold certain information from young people? For example we may consider the importance of informed consent when we are wanting to speak directly to young people in an interview, but do we consider the same level of importance when an evaluator is observing a course and has no specific or formal interaction with young people?

Key Ethical Considerations

We will now describe some of the key ethical considerations that are often quoted when evaluating projects with young people. It may be helpful to use these areas as an ethical checklist for your evaluation.

Purpose and gain

It is important that we consider from the outset, who will gain from the evaluation. We must ask ourselves this question and explicitly state this within the design and report process. We must consider all stakeholders within this: young people, project workers, organisations, funders, families, communities and policy holders. What is critical within these considerations, is when young people will not gain. This is commonly when the evaluation is not participatory and the focus is on gaining proof or understanding for the other stakeholders, for example to prove to a funder that the project was successful and a good use of their money. The project worker might want to evaluate in order to better understand the elements of the programme so as to develop it for the young people currently involved. In this case, it should be made clear how the young people will directly gain from providing feedback. However, this is different from if the project workers want to evaluate in order to better understand the programme so as to develop it for another cohort of young people. We must question if it is ethical to 'take' the knowledge and experience from the young people for the gain of other stakeholders. The evaluator cannot assume that the young person will gladly do this. Permission needs to be sought, which should acknowledge the young person as having an expert contribution to make (permission is discussed further below). However, as we have discussed in the previous chapters of this book, the evaluation of projects with young people should consider the same values as practice with young people. Of particular importance, in this instance, is valuing participation. Young people can gain from the type of evaluation that has an ultimate purpose of reporting to funders. But this needs to be seen with equal value and thus be given equal attention in the design of the evaluation. To not do this may see any value placed on young people's participation as tokenistic. If there is no gain to the young people at all, this should be made explicit within the design and made clear to the young people.

Risk of harm

Consideration needs to be paid to any potential risk of harm. This should be viewed from the perspective of all stakeholders, as well as the project's impact as a whole. This can be thought of in terms of risk of the project failing (for example, due to insufficient data), risk of damaging information about the service provider (Squirrell, 2012), or the risk of distress to participants or an adverse impact on stakeholders. Our discussion here focuses on the last of these three risks.

In considering all stakeholders, we should question all eventualities. This can be viewed in terms of psychological, emotional or physical risk. Firstly, the evaluation process should not be emotionally distressing or psychologically damaging. If the process becomes emotional for the participant we should offer support, offer to cease the evaluation process and offer to follow up with the project workers normally working with the young person for ongoing support. For example, in interviews with young women from a domestic violence project, a young woman became distressed within the interview after recalling elements of her domestic violence through the interview. This young woman chose to carry on with the interview, but we should make it very clear that the interview can stop.

Related to this, evaluators should be aware of diversity and multi-cultural understanding. This includes religious practices, LGBT culture, working classes' culture, etc. For example, some cultures may require female-only focus groups. We should be aware of our own culture and ethnicity in the evaluation process. This links to our reflective practice, which has been discussed elsewhere in this book.

Secondly, young people should not be put at any physical risk from others by taking part. This could be in terms of the location of the data collection being in a dangerous geographical area or perhaps the location being too public and exposing of young people's engagement. For example, young men involved in gang and knife crime may be cautious of being involved in evaluating projects, for fear of physical harm if being seen talking to evaluators.

When considering all stakeholders, we should also consider ourselves as the evaluators within this. Again this should be considered in terms of psychological, emotional and physical safety. Evaluators should have appropriate background checks and be trained to the appropriate standard. Evaluators should not work beyond their boundaries, but always working within our remit and training (Weiss, 1998). The lines can become particularly blurred with therapeutic practice, which is evident with some of the examples shared within this chapter. We should safeguard ourselves as evaluators, just as we do as youth workers, in the locations we choose to work. Data collection should be carried out in places suitably quiet enough to ensure privacy and yet suitably visible enough to safeguard all parties.

We should also ensure we have the appropriate supervisory support structures in place to manage our own emotional and psychological safety.

Informed consent

Before conducting any evaluation consent should be gained from young people, their parents/carers (although please see discussion below regarding Gillick competence, for a critical discussion of parent/carer consent) and other stakeholders (Christian, 2005; Liamputtong, 2007). This consent should be fully informed. To understand this in more detail we can draw from Emanuel et al. (2000) who state this should include 'the provision of information to participants, about purpose of the research [or evaluation], its procedures, potential risks, benefits and alternatives, so that the individual understands this information and can make a voluntary decision whether to enroll and continue to participate' (p. 2703).

Informed consent should typically include the following, as well as any other considerations specific to a particular project:

- Purpose – including evaluation questions and the intended use of the evaluation
- Confidentiality and anonymity – including the use of pseudonyms (or code names)
- Security of the data – including who will have access to the data, where the data will be stored and for how long, and how the data will be disposed of
- Young people's access to their own data any time
- Participant validation
- Their right to withdraw their information at any point
- How the evaluation will be written up and who will see it.

Informed consent needs to be accessible to young people and therefore needs to be explained in ways that they will find intelligible. Usually this is in both a written and verbal form, where questions can be answered. This should also be considerate of language issues, to ensure that young people are truly informed.

We need to ensure that informed consent is given and gained from young people themselves and not just their gatekeepers, for example, managers, youth workers, or parents/carers. It may be that these gatekeepers think it is fine for us to access young people for information, but we must not assume this. Equally, we should not assume that those gatekeepers that prevent access to young people are actually representing the young people's wishes. This is discussed further later in this chapter with regard to the issue of power.

We should be aware that some young people may feel coerced into consenting. This may be through peers, youth workers, parents/carers, or the evaluator. We need to ensure that young people understand that they are not obliged to consent and as evaluators we need to ensure that the young people will feel no repercussions of their choice by, for example, any of the aforementioned other stakeholders. Squirrell (2012) identifies how this may be a particular issue with 'captive' young people, for example those in a young offenders institution.

This links to the area of incentives. This is a highly contentious area for two key reasons. Firstly, linking to the previous point regarding coercion, young people may feel they have to participate because they are receiving something in return. Further, they may feel they have to say the 'right thing' in order to receive the incentive. This, obviously, may lead to inaccurate data. Secondly, there is debate about what type of incentive young people should receive. Some argue, from an equitable perspective, that this should be a monetary payment. Others argue that this is not always appropriate when working with vulnerable young people, as they may use their money for drugs or alcohol. They suggest incentives such as food vouchers or cinema tickets. This is obviously context specific and again should be negotiated with the organisation in the evaluation design phase.

Young people should be made aware that they have the right to withdraw their consent from the evaluation process at any point – beginning, middle and end (and up to a pre-agreed point, where the evaluation report is written up). It should be made clear that they don't have to participate in all activities or answer all questions. They have the right to choose what they answer. Squirrell (2012) states the importance of also ensuring that young people have no obligation to state why they are withdrawing.

Anonymity and confidentiality

Young people should be assured their anonymity and that their name or any information that could identify them will not be used in the dissemination of findings. This is also true for the process. For example, Weiss (1998) highlights the importance of not telling 'one respondent what another has said ... they will be able to piece together their identities' (p. 94).

Squirrell (2012) highlights how photos, tapes and videos add an extra level of complexity to the discussion of anonymity. There needs to be specific reference to this within the informed consent process.

Weiss goes on to state that anonymity should be ensured, unless an individual gives specific permission to be identified. We have come across young people several times, who wish to be identified. This has often been because they feel strongly about a matter and want to help other young people learn from their experience. However, this should be seriously considered, particularly when working with more vulnerable or disadvantaged young people. They may regret this choice in the future. They may also inadvertently identify other young people by association. This should also be considered if professionals or organisations choose to be identified, as this could also inadvertently identify young people wishing to stay anonymous. This discussion of choice is addressed later in this chapter and alternative options are discussed.

Young people should also be assured any information they share will be confidential. This however is another problematic matter. Confidentiality can be assured for some things, for example dislike of a particular activity or worker, but cannot be assured for others, for example in the case of disclosures of harm.

Dealing with disclosure is a discrete element associated with both confidentially and risk. Confidentiality can only be assured up until there is a safeguarding issue. This should be made clear to young people from the beginning and be reiterated if the evaluator senses a young person is starting to disclose something. This is a very blurred and disputed area. Some suggest that any disclosure relating to harm to self, harm to others, or criminality, should be reported. Some people debate the criminality element, suggesting that this would be impossible when working with young offenders for example. We suggest that you negotiate this with the project management team and align, as much as possible, to their safeguarding policy. This blurriness was also experienced within the Step Up case study, exemplified below.

 Step Up Case Study

A standard organisational ethical checklist was completed during the planning of the evaluation of the Step Up project. This ensured that young people were protected from harm, that they would gain from the evaluation, that they had their identities protected, that they consented, and they understood how the evaluation would be used. The checklist process also identified a risk of the young people disclosing personal information that may need to be passed on to other services for safeguarding reasons, and the protocols for doing so were discussed. During the Step Up project, we carried out part of the on-going evaluation at a residential at the end of the first year. We were scheduled to carry out a group journey mapping session leading to individual journey mapping and interviews. Journey mapping is a creative technique where the participants create a visual representation of their experiences in the form of a map. The group had a powerful experience at the residential and some of the participants came to a point where they felt comfortable enough during the journey mapping session to disclose information that caused safeguarding concerns, such as previous criminal offences and people that they associated with who might pose a risk to them. The questions we asked and the timing of the session in the residential and the overall project culminated in, what we felt was, opening a can of worms. We supported the young people in the moment, managing their needs and expectations. We discussed stopping the session with the youth workers and arranged the youth workers' support for the young people both during and after the residential. The youth workers were particularly challenged by this as they now had to follow up on multiple

(Continued)

(Continued)

disclosures and deal with these collectively as a group away on residential. We had the sense that they wished we had never asked any evaluation questions. We questioned if we should have asked these particular questions about the young people's experiences of learning and the factors that jeopardise it at this particular time. The disclosures were beyond the scope of the evaluation, but our questions had triggered their responses.

Reflecting on this, the case study highlights the need to be constantly vigilant for ethical issues. An initial checklist will not suffice. In this situation the ethical checklist showed that there was a risk of young people disclosing. That raised awareness, but still did not help with the in-the-moment responses that the evaluator needed to manage the young people's, staff's and organisation's needs regarding the disclosures. Ethics are always in the moment and of the moment, as well as pre-planned. This is discussed further later in this chapter.

Pause for Thought

Think about a project you have been involved in:

- Do you have any similar experiences of young people disclosing information during a simple discussion?

- How did you/would you deal with this situation?

As we identified in Chapter 2, creative methods can utilise more senses, open creative channels and thus evoke deeper consideration (Jewitt and Van Leeuwen, 2004; Gauntlett, 2007; Bolton, 2010). This obviously needs to be considered, understood and supported through the ethical process.

Participant validation

Wherever possible, written up information should be taken back to young people to check the evaluator's interpretation. Lincoln and Guba (1985) proposed that this is a crucial technique for establishing validity and credibility. This may also often allow the narrative to refine and develop.

Sharing and dissemination

Young people should be aware of, and consent to, how the evaluation report is disseminated. The report should be available to all stakeholders in an accessible format. As much as possible, the ethical considerations taken within a project should be made clear to all recipients or readers of the evaluation. This shows credibility to evaluators as professional and considerate, as well as adding validity to the evaluation report.

Ethics panels and committees

In some cases evaluators are required to have their evaluation ethics cleared by a panel of experts. This may be within a university or academic structure, or for larger research organisations or departments this maybe an internal feature. For some smaller youth organisations, such as the Brathay Trust, we have a partnership agreement with a university that allows us to apply for ethical clearance through their ethics panel. This may not always be possible for everyone carrying out evaluations of projects with young people. However, ethical procedures still need to be adhered to for the same reasons as we have discussed above. To not adhere to them not only might make the evaluation unethical in some way, but we are at risk of only considering ethics to get past the ethics panel, rather than for the actual safeguarding of the young people.

Challenging Traditional Notions of Ethics

Ethics are rooted in the traditional sciences discussed in Chapter 2. Just as the methods of this positivist paradigm do not meet the needs of evaluation of projects with young people, it can be expected that ethics from this paradigm will not be suitable either.

Negative ethical principles

Sometimes, ethics can feel like a list of negative things to be avoided. For example, ethical guidelines tend to be a list of what should be avoided, such as, harm, deception, coercion, etc. Essentially these are all negative. Stern (2011) suggested we should move away from negative ethics to more positive virtues that the ethical process can foster. He lists examples such as sincerity, trust, courage, kindness, modesty, humility, truthfulness, respect and being open to criticism.

Unrealistic ethical principles

Ethical guidelines have been criticised for being unrealistic and unworkable in practice. Pain (2008) described them as a narrow and inflexible set of rules. Participatory evaluation in particular may not fit into some sets of guidelines. Such set guidelines cannot be applied as a blanket approach to every situation and one size does not fit all (Heath et al., 2009). This approach also assumes that ethics are static and that evaluation methodology doesn't change. This is particularly troublesome when running participatory evaluation with young people, who may change the focus of the evaluation or their preferred data collection tool. This can lead to ethical guidelines feeling restricting to the potential of the evaluation and, more importantly, the young people's engagement. How do we compromise between staying with planned evaluation activity when a young person is choosing to engage in their own way?

Consent

Kellett (2010) argues that it is only relatively recently that young people have been asked for their consent. Previously parents and carers had been asked to consent to young people being involved. This dialogue excludes young people and does not consider their thoughts and opinions. Furthermore, we should question whether young people have consented to their parents or carers being contacted. This does not consider if young people want their parents or carers to know about the evaluation they might want to get involved in. They might prefer not to take part than have parents/carers become involved. This is obviously their choice and it should not be removed from them by the adults involved.

This also alludes to 'taking' information from young people as though they are an object to be studied, rather than a living, breathing and thinking human being. This seems particularly incongruent if the evaluation then goes on to interview young people and ask them about certain matters. If young people are able to articulate their opinion on such matters, then surely they are able and have rights in the consent process. This sits within the broader discussion of evaluation questions and agendas still largely being the province of adults (Roberts, 2008). Young people's lives are thus poorly served by some of social science's traditional methods. This is a problem when evaluation starts with adults, rather than collectively with young people. It assumes that the adults know everything beforehand and know what is best for young people.

This discussion is related to the one above, regarding ethics being static and restricting. Informed consent can also be restrictive if it is a static rather than dynamic process. This is problematic when the course of the evaluation changes and, for example, new methods have not been consented to by parents/carers.

Vignette 3.2   Gillick Competency and Fraser Guidelines (NSPCC, 2012)

In 1982 Mrs Victoria Gillick took her local health authority (West Norfolk and Wisbech Area Health Authority) and the Department of Health and Social Security to court in an attempt to stop doctors from giving contraceptive advice or treatment to young people under 16 without parental consent. The case went to the High Court where Mr Justice Woolf dismissed Mrs Gillick's claims. The Court of Appeal reversed this decision, but in 1985 it went to the House of Lords and the Law Lords (Lord Scarman, Lord Fraser and Lord Bridge) ruled in favour of the original judgement delivered by Mr Justice Woolf:

...whether or not a child is capable of giving the necessary consent will depend on the child's maturity and understanding and the nature of the consent required. The child must be capable of making a reasonable assessment of the advantages and disadvantages of the treatment proposed, so the consent, if given, can be properly and fairly described as true consent. (House of Lords, 1985)

The Fraser guidelines refer to the guidelines set out by Lord Fraser in his judgement of the Gillick case in the House of Lords (1985), which apply specifically to contraceptive advice.

Lord Scarman's comments in his judgement of the Gillick case in the House of Lords (1985) are often referred to as the test of 'Gillick competency':

... it is not enough that she should understand the nature of the advice which is being given: she must also have a sufficient maturity to understand what is involved.

He also commented more generally on parents/carers versus children's rights:

Parental right yields to the child's right to make his own decisions when he reaches a sufficient understanding and intelligence to be capable of making up his own mind on the matter requiring decision.

Since the Gillick case, legal, health and social work professionals continue to debate the issues of a child's rights to consent to or refuse treatment, and how to balance children's rights with the duty of child protection professionals to act in the best interests of the child. Further court rulings, new legislation and revised guidance continue to amend the legal position.

Reflecting on this, we can see how the implications extend into evaluation. As young people need to consent to being involved in an evaluation it begs the question of whether you consider someone under 16 able to give consent, or whether you will need to gain consent from parents and carers. Your organisation or local authority may have some guidance or rules on this which you will need to know.

Power

This discussion is related to the concept of power. Power is discussed in greater detail in Chapter 5, but it is an important part of the discussion here also. Pain (2008) referred to this as a top-down model, where adults (evaluators or parents/carers) have control over the process. This means that only adults define and distinguish risks and benefits. This, in turn, assumes that adults know all the risks and benefits, when in all eventuality, each situation is different and has its own set of risks and benefits, which are best known to the young people, not the adult. It therefore seems somewhat backward to have to gain ethical clearance beforehand to carry out evaluation in a situation you may know little about compared to young people.

Several authors have called for power and control to be shared in the ethical process. This can, in turn, be a valuable process for young people in understanding that they have a voice and rights. This is best achieved by ensuring a phased ethical review (Manzo and Brightbill, 2007) or 'process consent' (Munhall, 1991). Pain (2008) described this as developing ethics iteratively and something which is on-going. This step-by-step process makes room for young people's voices as well as for adaptations in response to changing priorities and procedures. This also ensures that when ethical clearance is needed before any work can commence with young people, it is explicit within the first phase of clearance that other phases will follow and that these will be inclusive of young people's participation. This is exemplified in the debate that exists as to why the evaluator should decide beforehand if the participant's identity will be anonymous. Critiques question whether this should not be for the participant to decide, through mutual discussion and understanding. As we discussed earlier in this chapter, several young people we have worked with have wanted their names to be included in evaluation reports. Some, after discussion, have decided this would not be best for them, some have decided only their first name, some have decided not to include other defining information, such as hometown, whereas others have chosen their own pseudonym. The significance here is that there was discussion leading to informed consent.

Vignette 3.3   Phased Ethical Review (Maynard, 2011)

This was exemplified in the evaluation of a project set up for young women at risk of sexual exploitation. The approved ethical considerations had stated that any disclosure would be taken through an official process and included all of the paperwork that this would involve. In reality, the evaluator developed such good rapport with the young people that disclosures started to happen at an overwhelming rate. It was impossible to follow the procedure stated in the ethical clearance. A more appropriate method was found namely taking all disclosures to the young person's key worker to ascertain if they were aware of the content of the disclosure. If they were, and had dealt with it, or were dealing with it, then the evaluator needed to do nothing more. If they were not aware of it, then the official procedures were followed.

Reflecting on this we can see that traditional, one-off, ethical procedures would have certainly been restrictive to this clearly engaging process for young people. Likewise, some evaluators might have been discouraged from continuing the evaluation, with the inconceivable amount of paperwork associated with reporting the safeguarding issues. A phased ethical review provided the opportunity to readjust and devise a more achievable, yet still ethical framework.

Manzo and Brightbill (2007) and Pain (2008) both describe this process of developing ethics relationally. This is 'with' young people and acknowledges differences in understandings of what is ethical and how people would like to be treated. It subscribes to the belief that ethics will vary between individuals and social groups. Their participatory values or principles are shown in Table 3.1. These participatory practices suggest the need for reflective practice.

Table 3.1   Manzo and Brightbill's participatory principles (2007)

Representation	All knowledge is situated, not neutral. [Evaluators] should not represent participants alone; participants can represent themselves throughout the research process.
Accountability	Not only accountable to institutions and peers, but also to participants, partners and communities. Ultimately these stakeholders decide if research is ethically sound and valid.
Social responsiveness	[Evaluators] take responsibility to the needs of the participants (not just their own agendas). This takes priority over institutional demands.
Agency	Requires ethical behaviour, reflection and scrutiny from participants.
Reflexivity	Ethical dilemmas not viewed as a 'snapshot', but as a process (on-going and changing). All are reflexive in this process.

Balancing protection with participation

This critique does not intend to completely reject the importance of ethical procedures and the safeguarding of all young people. But it denies young people the opportunity to safeguard themselves and have a voice in the debate. Protection and participation could be, and should be, mutually reinforcing (Lansdown, 2013). Landsdown draws from the Convention on the Rights of the Child in this argument, stating two key components:

> General comment No.13, The right of the child to freedom from all forms of violence (UNCHR, 1989).

A child rights-based approach requires a paradigm shift towards respecting and promoting the dignity and integrity of children as rights-holders not victims. Children's rights to be heard and to have their views given due weight must be respected in all decision-making processes, and central to protection strategies and programmes.

> General Comment No.12, The right of the child to be heard. (UNCHR, 1989)

This is both a substantive right and a general principle to inform the realisation of all other rights – a means and an end. It is the right to be heard and taken seriously. This is an entitlement and not a privilege. The concept of participation is embodied in a cluster of articles recognising the child as a social actor – Articles 5, 12–17.

Summary

This chapter has introduced the concept of ethics and outlined a range of common ethical considerations. Youth work ethics and evaluation ethics at times align and differ. Each has been highlighted as needing consideration when planning and conducting evaluations. Vignettes have shown that ethical considerations are not a one off, but rather, a continual process. Evaluations involving under-16-year-olds demand particular thought regarding the role of consent. Evaluations that adopt creative methods were highlighted as needing particular ethical attention. The second half of the chapter explored some of the difficulties with 'simple' sets of ethical checklists and explored the assumptions and power that lie behind them. These issues demand that evaluators carefully consider their own views on ethics, and find their own way to manage the tension between protection and participation.

Key Points

1. Youth work and evaluation have ethics that govern their practice. Good youth work is often representative of good evaluation as they share a similar ethical base.
2. Use an ethical checklist when you plan an evaluation ensuring that you cover all the main aspects: purpose and gain, risk of harm, informed consent, anonymity and confidentiality, participant validation and sharing and disseminating.
3. Ethics can be framed as positive lists of attributes to be aspired to as well as negative lists of things to be avoided.
4. Be alert to ethical issues that emerge as you conduct your evaluation, as they arise dynamically in the power relations of youth work and evaluation.
5. Reflection is key to ethical practice as it is only through considered reflection that you can become aware of the power that you, as an evaluator and youth worker, exert over the evaluation process.

Further Reading

Batsleer, J. (2010) 'Youth workers as researchers: Ethical issues in practitioner and participatory research' gives detailed critical discussion of key ethical issues in researching and evaluating youth work practice.

Economic Social Research Council (2013) *Research Ethics Guide Book for Social Scientists* is a comprehensive ethical framework and guidebook if you want a more academic approach.

International Program for Evaluation Development Training (2013) *Evaluation Ethics, Politics, Standards and Guiding Principles* provides an online resource which elaborates on the potential ethical and political challenges facing evaluators and gives examples of guiding principles and standards.

Liamputtong, P. (2006) *Researching the Vulnerable: A Guide to Sensitive Research Methods* provides an ethical, practical and methodological guide to working with people at the margins of society.

Mauthner, M. et al. (2002) *Ethics in Qualitative Research* examines ethics with sensitive populations and offers practical ways to manage dilemmas.

Simons, H. (2009) *Case Study Research in Practice* discusses in Chapter 6 the issue of data ownership.

4

TYPES OF EVALUATION

Chapter Overview

- Why evaluate?
- The difference between scientific, quasi-experimental, developmental and participative evaluation
- How to choose an evaluation
- How to distinguish and choose an impact or process evaluation
- How to decide whether your evaluation is formative or summative.

Introduction

It is important to think through what it is that the evaluation is seeking to discover and to select the type of evaluation design that suits the evaluation questions and context. There are a variety of reasons why organisations engage in evaluation. As we have seen in Chapter 1, there is an increasing pressure on organisations to be accountable and provide the best service for customers within the budgets they have. Evaluation plays a key role in developing effective interventions. However, we have also seen that there is an increasing requirement for workers from a number of sectors to use evaluation to reflect on and develop their practice. In Chapter 1, we also argued that evaluation is a powerful tool to inform your practice or, indeed, organisational, national and global practice. Here are some reminders of why organisations carry out evaluations:

- To link individual learning and its impact to both the programme's aims/outcomes and the business's needs
- To be a natural part of review for individuals and the organisation
- To clarify what (content) the programme is trying to achieve and how (process)
- To establish where the programme is working well or in need of further improvements
- To close the loop with feedback on progress against needs
- To help us find out whether an intervention is working or not
- To help us find out what works or doesn't work in an intervention
- To collect evidence about the success of an intervention – proof that it works
- To collect evidence to justify our practice
- To reflect on and improve our practice.

As we have seen in Chapter 2 there are a number of paradigms that inform the evaluation method we eventually choose to use. However, there are a number of other factors that will inform the final form of our evaluation – including what exactly we are aiming to evaluate and why – and it is these questions that we address in this chapter to start to guide your evaluation design.

The Purpose and Focus of Evaluation

Evaluations have a specific focus in that they seek to determine something's merit, worth, value or significance (Scriven, 1991; Clark, 1999; Patton, 2008). Typically evaluations are used to 'determine the degree to which a planned programme achieves its desired objective' (Suchman, 1967), its 'impact' (i.e. the change, effect or influence that the intervention or programme has had on the beneficiaries) or how and why an intervention is successful (or not). Often the longer-term aims of evaluations are not to 'prove' but to 'improve' (Shufflebean and Shinkfield, 1985).

Evaluation is something that most people engage in at one time or another. It is the critical, thoughtful engagement in the world around us. When we evaluate we collect and weigh up a variety of data and make judgements about how successful (or not) something is and why. We use evaluations to improve how we do things (or avoid making mistakes in the future), including everything from buying a new car to evaluating a project!

The most common distinctions made are between evaluation approaches that focus on evaluating the **outcomes** of an intervention (and so, for example, whether or not an intervention has met its targets in reducing youth nuisance or increasing community participation) and those that focus on evaluating what is going on in an intervention, or the **process** (such as why is an activity – such as a drama club – successful in reducing youth nuisance). Understanding the differences between these two types of evaluation is key to evaluation planning.

Outcome and impact evaluations

Probably the most common focus of evaluation is an **outcome evaluation**. These aim to establish how well a programme, project or intervention works overall and whether, for example, its targets have been achieved? In outcome evaluations, the evaluator may also take into account how parts of the programme or project influence the outcome, as well as implementation issues, but overall they are interested in the achievement of goals.

Outcome evaluations are typically concerned with whether the effects achieved are those which were intended. Hence, 'outcomes' are usually identified at the outset of the intervention and the success of the intervention is usually measured in terms of whether the outcomes have been achieved. In order to be able to evaluate the outcomes of an intervention, outcomes need to tangible, measurable and observable – for example, the number of young people with improved communication skills, numbers of certificates gained, the number of arrests, number of pregnancies. In Chapter 1 we introduced the notion of 'proximal' and 'distal' outcomes. You may have noticed then that some of the proximal outcomes are not naturally quantitative, and so are more difficult to measure. This has, historically, led some people to discount them, focusing on the more quantifiable distal outcomes alone. We challenge this, and have developed creative tools that can be combined with scales and measures to quantify all outcomes.

Outcomes need to be defined in terms of an agreed realistic timeframe in order to be measured and 'to count' and they need to be attributable to the project and so traced back into the project's outputs, inputs and decisions about making an impact. If outcomes are linked to too many and different variables this can make it hard to evaluate exactly what has happened.

In order to demonstrate the extent to which outcomes have been achieved, outcome evaluations often employ '**distance travelled**' tools. This means that the young people report, or are observed, or measured against all the project outcomes at the start and the end of the project to demonstrate how much distance they have travelled, the ground that they have gained in each. Sometimes this is also repeated sometime after the project has ended in order to show that the gains have endured.

Outcome evaluations help answer questions such as:

- Has the overall programme goal or aim been achieved?
- What factors outside the programme have contributed or hindered the desired change?
- What unintended outcomes have occurred as a result of the programme?

Outcome evaluations are often tied up with assessing impact. However, there is a subtle difference between **impact** and outcomes. Typically, **impact evaluations** consider what has happened as a result of a project and aim to establish exactly what is different or what has changed. Impacts are not always intended or identified as a target at the outset of a project. There might be, for example, a number of impacts on a community that arise out of a particular project, that were never envisaged at the outset of the project. For example, it might be that a drama project to engage young people in the community leads to the setting up of a drama club for young people.

Evaluating impact can be very complicated. To get a good measure of impact, an evaluation may need to incorporate extended periods of time after the project has finished, in order to establish a realistic evaluation of its impact. An evaluator also needs to consider that there are different types of impact and that some types might be much more difficult to gauge than others because they are not easy to measure or have been felt by communities who are hard to access. Further, impact evaluation may also need to show the cause and effect between the project and the impact, this is called **attribution**.

Impact evaluations help answer questions such as:

- How well has the project achieved its objectives?
- How well have the desired short–term changes been achieved?

The important factor to bear in mind here is that outcome or impact evaluations are focused on one question: whether the outcomes had been achieved, and what was the impact of those changes.

Vignette 4.1   The Copenhagen Youth Project (Copenhagen Youth Association, 2013)

The Copenhagen Youth Project: 'works in partnership with young people to create and sustain a positive youth culture that inspires young people to plan, initiate and lead their own projects' (CYA, 2013). They provide positive activities, mentors, education, training and support. Their outcomes are to increase aspirations, increase motivation and challenge behaviour.

Their last outcome evaluation showed that:

- 40% of the 12–14-year-old young people had increased aspirations and a newfound desire to learn, and the same was true of 70% of the 15–21-year-old young people.
- 60% of the young people had increased motivation and chose positive routes.
- 50% of the young people developed awareness of the consequences of their behaviour and learnt to control their behaviour in a positive way.

Do you think that this is an outcome or an impact evaluation?

Reflecting on this, we can see that the evidence shows positive outcomes for some of the young people, which is excellent. It does, however, beg the question of why so many young people did not gain outcomes. Nor do these statements inform us whether the same or different young people gained the different outcomes. Nor do we know how this outcome data was gained – who decided that the young people had progressed, and what criteria were used in the decision. This perhaps highlights the need for transparency in reporting, to avoid raising more questions than you answer when you present your findings. There was not any evidence provided to connect the outcomes to the programme, nor do we know how the programme achieved these outcomes, precisely because the evaluation is limited to outcomes. This provides a good insight into the advantages (simple powerful statements of outcomes) versus the disadvantages (no indication of how outcomes were achieved) of outcome evaluations.

Process evaluations

Process evaluations focus on how well a programme is operating and can be used as freestanding evaluations or in conjunction with impact assessment as part of a more comprehensive evaluation. As freestanding evaluations, process evaluations yield quality assurance information, assessing the extent to which a programme is implemented as intended and whether it is operating up to the standards established for it. When a programme is new, a process evaluation can provide valuable feedback to stakeholders about the progress that is being made in implementing the intervention.

The success of a project is obviously one measure of the effectiveness of a process. When targets are not met, process evaluations help us to diagnose what went wrong. Looking at what is going on in a project or programme and working out why it is not achieving its targets as it infolds is a key use of process evaluations. Process evaluations enable us to look at a range of variables which might be impacting on the effectiveness of an intervention including the practitioner, the participants or the actual intervention (e.g. activity). Process evaluations aim to detect strengths and weaknesses in a project or intervention, often with the intention of improving future practice. This process of on-going evaluation and adapting practice is a key part of developmental evaluations and reflective practice. Process evaluations involve the systematic observation and study of what actually occurs in the intervention, often as a way of assessing how the intended outcomes have been worked towards and how effective this method was.

Where process evaluation is an on-going function involving repeated measurements over time, it is referred to as programme **monitoring**. Process monitoring is the systematic and continual documentation of key aspects of programme performance to assess whether the programme is operating as intended or according to some benchmark or standard.

Monitoring refers to setting targets and milestones to measure progress and achievement and whether the inputs are producing the planned outputs. In other words, monitoring sees whether the project is consistent with the design (CIVICUS, 2001). The key difference between monitoring and evaluation is that evaluation is about placing a value judgement on the information gathered during a project, including the monitoring data. The assessment of a project's success (its evaluation) can be different based on whose value judgement is used. For example, a project manager's evaluation may be different from that of the project's participants, or other stakeholders (CIVICUS, 2001).

Process evaluations will help to answer questions such as:

- Has the project reached the target group?
- Are all project activities reaching all parts of the target group?
- Are the participants and stakeholders satisfied with all aspects of the programme?
- Are all activities being implemented as intended – if not, why not?
- What, if any, changes have been made to intended activities?
- Are all materials, information and presentations suitable for the target audience?

The advantage of process evaluations is that they clearly show what the programme has done, what was delivered, how it went. The clear disadvantage is that they do not necessarily provide any evidence of what was achieved, which the outcome evaluations do.

A second common distinction made in the timing of the evaluation is that it can be either on-going or at the end of the project, **formative** or **summative**.

Formative evaluations

Formative evaluations are done to provide feedback for those trying to improve something. They may be outcome or process orientated. They are intended to help in the development of the programme. Formative evaluations are different to process evaluation in that process evaluations may simply assess the methods within a project and not necessarily feed back to help the project improve. Formative evaluations explore the progress on the way to realising programme objectives and may be used to make judgments about possible programme improvements. Formative evaluations are carried out as the programme is on-going so that modifications can be made. The clear advantage of this approach is that it provides developmental feedback to help improve practice in the short term. The disadvantage is the time that it takes to collect such data and continually feed it back into programme design.

Summative evaluations

Summative evaluations concentrate on the effectiveness and impact of a programme and are often tied up with assessing the project's final **impact**. Summative evaluations aim to summarise the whole process. They are not concerned with impact alone but also ascertain whether a project achieved its aims and outcomes and how effective the project was in working towards those goals. This type of evaluation does not provide feedback to the project in order to help it improve, as in formative evaluation; rather it tries to give a pure evaluation of outcomes, the effectiveness of the process of the project in working towards outcomes, as well as its impact. Whilst not tied to any particular data collection method, summative evaluations often use distance travelled tools to show progress. There is more on this in Chapter 7.

Vignette 4.2   The Aboriginal Youth Suicide Prevention Strategy (BIM Larsson and Associates, 2008)

The Aboriginal Youth Suicide Prevention Strategy (AYSPS) is an initiative established in response to the Government of Alberta's Children and Youth Initiatives. The focus of the evaluation was to determine to what degree the AYSPS had reached its stated objective: supporting Aboriginal communities to identify strengths and build upon their capacity to prevent youth suicide.

The evaluation used the following methodology:

- Youth survey (n = 171)
- Administrative review of the community action plans (n = 9)
- Eleven focus groups (n = 109): 15 elders, 62 youth and 32 community members
- In-depth interviews (n=25): 12 working group members, 13 community coordinators and staff
- Youth stories (n = 2).

These were all conducted at the end of the project. The findings showed that AYSPS had met its stated goals and objectives. The findings were statistically significant and showed:

- Youth in the communities feel more hopeful about their future.
- Youth report feeling more connected to their culture and their community.
- Youth report that they now have plans for their future, which they did not have to the same degree two years ago.
- There is an increase in cultural awareness and practice within the communities.

Reflecting on this vignette we can see a mixed methods approach to collecting data at the end of a programme in order to ascertain its overall impact. A survey was used to collect quantitative and wide-scale data on the impact of the programme and the focus groups and interviews allowed the evaluators to probe further into the survey results, understanding the exact nature of the changes that had happened as a result of the programme. The programme did not compare evidence of hopes, aspirations, plans and connectivity at the start and at the end of the programme. It assumed that the young people would be able to reflect on and describe the changes that had happened for themselves, rather than their being measured by an objective test or scale. As such this evaluation is a post-positivistic summative outcome evaluation.

These types of evaluation discussed so far are summarised in Figure 4.1. It is possible to have an evaluation which incorporates both formative and summative elements. In this instance, the summative evaluation would be more of a final assessment, including the formative elements. As discussed, your evaluation might also be situated between all of these 'boxes' providing evidence of both process and outcome in a formative and summative way.

Pause for Thought

Think of a project that you have been involved in:

- Which evaluative approach would be the best focus for an evaluation and why?

On-going	
Process evaluation	**Formative evaluation**
Evaluates how the project outcomes were worked towards and the effectiveness of this process	Provides feedback to the project as to the effectiveness of the methods used to achieve outcomes, in order to inform project changes
Impact (outcome) evaluation	**Summative evaluation**
Evaluates the impact resulting from the project and what has changed as a result	Summarises what outcomes the project achieved, the impact of this, what has changed as a result, how it did this, and the effectiveness of this process and any changes made
Final	

Figure 4.1   Evaluation approaches with different foci: Process, impact, formative and summative evaluations

As we have already argued, evaluations are essentially indistinguishable from other forms of research in terms of design, data collection techniques and methods of analysis (Robson, 2002: 174), and so an evaluator needs to have an understanding of a variety of methods – both quantitative and qualitative. However, it should already been clear from our discussion of different types of evaluations, that certain methods are more appropriate to the type of evaluation being planned. Smart (2007) claims that a summative, banking approach is normally associated with a programme evaluation and quantitative methods (such as experimental or quasi-experimental design), while a formative, dialogical, approach is more associated with practice evaluation and qualitative methods. However, we will argue (Gaskell and Bauer, 2000; Robson, 2002) that in planning an evaluation the method of choice must be the one best suited to the question you want to answer, and the needs of the young people that you are working with. It is entirely feasible that qualitative and quantitative methods be used in combination as described in the mixed methods chapter. In the following chapters, we will introduce some basic research methods and demonstrate how they can be used in evaluation practice, however, we shall now give a little more information on each of these types of evaluation.

Deciding on Power and Paradigm

In Chapter 2 we took a look at the difference between positivist and post-positivist paradigms in evaluation. These paradigms were summarised in Table 2.2 and represent two significantly different views of evaluation. These differences have a great effect on the design of the evaluation. We have also made reference to the distribution of power in evaluation. The extent to which the evaluator or the participants are empowered to make decisions also exerts a strong influence on the evaluation design. As a result, we have developed a power and paradigm matrix. The matrix shows that the extent to which the evaluation is positivist or post-positivist, and the extent to which the power is held by the evaluator or by the participants determines one of four types of evaluation. The matrix is shown in Figure 4.2.

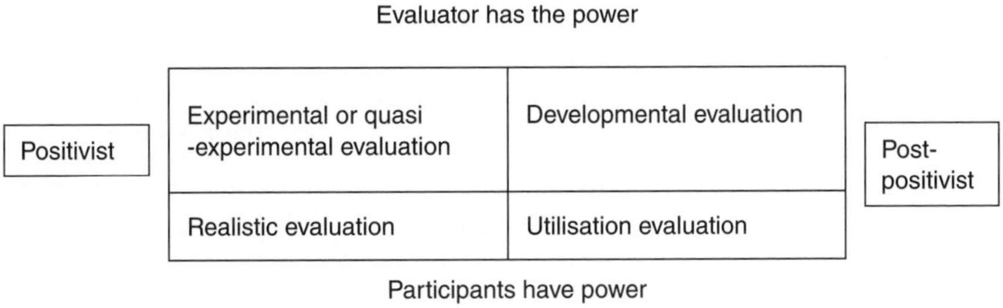

Evaluator has the power

	Experimental or quasi-experimental evaluation	Developmental evaluation	
Positivist			Post-positivist
	Realistic evaluation	Utilisation evaluation	

Participants have power

Figure 4.2   The power and paradigm matrix defining four types of evaluation

---

Pause for Thought

Think about a project that you have been involved in:

- What paradigm would an evaluation of this project best fit?
- Who would have the power in this process?

Four Types of Evaluation

We have already identified our different approaches to evaluation depending on the foci, now we identify four key types of evaluation dependent on power and paradigm.

Experimental, quasi-experimental designs

The experimental method provides the basic foundation for most evaluation designs and is used to observe the impact of the 'intervention or treatment' on participants. A typical experiment involves exposing a group of participants (usually known as the 'experimental' or 'treatment' group) to a programme, intervention or way of working and comparing the 'results' of this group to a '**control**' group (that is, a similar group of young people who have not experienced the programme, intervention or way of working). Evaluations that use this format are based on the logic of natural science experiments and the theory of causation, trying to show that the programme or project has caused positive change. The classic experimental design and its components (e.g. experimental and control groups, independent and dependent variables, randomisation, control) all feature in this method.

The most basic experiment begins by testing the impact of an **independent variable** (IV) (e.g. health awareness project) on a **dependent variable** (DV) (e.g. health behaviour) by comparing its effect on a group of young people who experienced the treatment (Experimental Group) with a group that did not (Control Group).

Table 4.1   The format of a basic experiment

	Control Group	Experimental Group
Independent variable (IV)	No treatment	Treatment (i.e. attends the session)
Dependent variable (DV)	Health behaviour	Health behaviour

A second characteristic of the experimental approach is its attempt to control all those other things that could affect the dependent variable (e.g. health behaviour) whilst the independent variable (e.g. health awareness programme) is being implemented – things that might make it difficult for the evaluator to see if the IV has had the intended impact. So, for example, in the above there might be a whole range of things that could have an impact on 'health behaviour' whilst the intervention is underway – such as public health campaigns, school based educational programmes, what happens to have been on TV – and make it difficult for the evaluator to assess whether it was the health awareness programme that was responsible for any effects seen. The job of the evaluator is to identify as many of these possible clouding variables and 'control' them. There are two key areas that the experimenter tries to exert control over – the environment and the participant. One of the most important things that are likely to affect a treatment's impact is the different ways in which participants respond and behave. There are all sorts of things that people bring to an experiment that can influence what is going on – their personalities, knowledge, mood state – unfortunately, these are things an experimenter can't always predict or control. Although the experimenter usually does try to control some participant variables by making sure that participants are matched, for example, on key variables such as age, education and social background, totally control is impossible. One way experimenters try to overcome this is through the random allocation of participants into conditions (sometimes known as **randomised control trials**).

A good experimental design tries to control all those things that could affect the purity of the IV/DV relationship. Unfortunately, the more that is controlled the less likely the experiment reflects what is going on in the real world! As you can imagine, setting up experiments and controlling variables in the real world is problematic for a variety of reasons. It is partly because of these difficulties that alternative experimental designs are used. **Quasi-experimental** means 'sort of experimental'. One key difference between 'pure' experiments and 'quasi' experiments is that there is less pressure to control variables and there is no attempt to randomly distribute participants into treatment groups. Instead, quasi-experiments work with the basic principles of experiments, by exposing participants to control or experimental treatments and observing impact, but instead of randomly distributing participants into groups they just apply the treatment to whatever groups or individuals they have available. One of the key advantages of quasi-experiments is that they give a much more realistic picture of what is happening.

There are a number of different ways that quasi-experiments can be set up. One way is to use a '**non-equivalent** group' design. Basically this means comparing groups that you just happen to have access to. For example, instead of planning to expose (or not expose) groups of young people to a new project, the evaluator works with groups of young people they have access to and who, for example, by their own choice do (or do not) participate in a project. Although, this can cause **selection bias** (i.e. there could be a whole load of reasons why your groups chose to participate that could impact on your results) the quasi-experimental approach would tolerate that. Alternatively, a quasi-experimental evaluation might use a **pre-test–post-test design.** In this approach, a single group of participants is measured on the dependent variable both before and after the manipulation of the treatment. For example, a group of young people could be given a test on their attitudes to alcohol as a pre-test. They could then have some health talks as the 'treatment or intervention' and at a later date have a further test to see how their attitudes have changed. A change in scores would show whether the change in attitude was due to the intervention. The obvious problem with the pre-test–post-test design is that it is possible that something other than the health intervention could have been responsible for the young people's change of attitude, such as a friend ending up in accident and emergency from drinking too much. It is even possible that having taken the pre-test influenced their scores on the post-test. However, these designs do give us an idea of whether or not the treatment is working and in the 'real-world'.

An example of a pre-test–post-test evaluation **data set** is shown in Table 4.2.

Table 4.2   An example of an experimental evaluation data set

	Pre-test Attitude	Experienced the Intervention	Post-test
Experimental group	Negative	Yes	Positive
Control group	Negative	No	Negative

The differences between experiments and quasi-experiments can be subtle and exist on a continuum rather than under definitive labels, which is why we have placed them together on the matrix (Figure 4.2). At one end of this continuum are ideal experiments in which only the independent variable differs across conditions, so that it is perfectly clear that changes in the dependent variable were caused by the independent variable. But as we move from ideal experiments to quasi-experiments, there are more and more variables that differ across conditions, which make it increasingly difficult to see whether it was the independent variable that was responsible for changes in the dependent variable.

The experimental method provides the basic structure for many evaluation designs. However, there are a number of concerns that we believe are associated with these forms of design that go beyond the practicalities of planning and implementation. These evaluations bring with them the need for control over the participants in a mechanistic way with very little opportunity for involvement. We don't think that experimental based evaluations need to be this way and hope to suggest some alternatives to how evaluations can be designed and implemented but at the same time be meaningful, participatory and empowering for the users.

Whatever your philosophical view on experimental evaluations, there are a number of ethical and practical difficulties that need considering before adopting them. Ethically it might be difficult to provide an intervention to half of a youth group and not to the other, especially when it is done randomly. This raises questions of the rights of all the young people to that provision, and they may feel the random allocation is unjust. The context that you are conducting the evaluation in may also make it impossible to separate out independent variables. If the young people that come to your youth project are very diverse, it could be difficult to separate out variables such as wealth without being accused of prejudice. The role of the evaluator is also tricky to manage in experiments, as you may need to negotiate a dual role as a helpful, supportive youth worker, and an objective, dispassionate test evaluator. This does not mean that experimental evaluations do not have value, it just highlights that there are pros and cons to all of the evaluation approaches.

Vignette 4.3   Family-focused Juvenile Re-entry Services: A Quasi-experimental Design Evaluation of Recidivism Outcomes (Winokur Early et al., 2013)

This study evaluated the effectiveness of a new programme, PLL Re-entry, in terms of reducing recidivism. The study was quasi-experimental as it compared the outcomes of youth receiving the PLL Re-entry Programme (treatment group) with those of a matched sample of youth who received standard aftercare programming (comparison group) in the study site. The young people were juvenile offenders aged 14–17.

The analysis examined 354 cases that were matched to standard re-entry cases yielding 153 pairs of treatment and comparison re-entry cases. A number of variables were identified that could influence the findings:

- Participation in the family-focused juvenile re-entry programme versus standard aftercare probation services
- Demographic and offender characteristics of gender
- Race and ethnicity
- Average age at release from re-entry services
- Most serious current offence
- Number of prior juvenile adjudications and most serious previous adjudicated offence.

The findings from this evaluation were compelling:

> Results from the current research indicate that in addition to potential cost savings, the family focused re-entry program also reduced recidivism compared with standard aftercare programming in the study site. ... compared with the matched standard re-entry sample, youth receiving PLL Re-entry had lower rates of subsequent justice system involvement on all five indicators of recidivism prevalence and seriousness measured. We found significant treatment and comparison group differences in rates of re-adjudication in the intent-to-treat analyses, with the observed rate for the matched re-entry sample more than 51% higher than that of the treatment sample. The prevalence of re-arrest was lower for PLL cases than it was for the matched comparison group, as was the rate of felony arrests. (Winokur Early et al. 2013: 15)

Reflecting on this shows the power that statistical data can have in an experimental evaluation to convince stakeholders of the change that has been achieved. The attribution of outcomes to the programme is clear, and the statistics paint a distinct picture. What is missing from the quasi-experimental approach is data on how the programme achieved those outcomes and how the programme was experienced by the participants, as those factors cannot be 'tested' for.

Realistic evaluation

Pawson and Tilley (1997) developed 'realistic evaluation'. This approach was centred on finding not only what outcomes were produced from interventions but also 'how they are produced, and what is significant about the varying conditions in which the interventions take place' (Tilley, 2000: 101). Realistic evaluations place value on multiple interpretations of experience (Squirrell, 2012: 11). Tilley was critical of quasi-experimental models of evaluation, suggesting they fail to effectively identify why interventions work differently across different contexts. As a result, realistic evaluations seek the contextual conditions that make interventions effective, therefore developing lessons about how they produce outcomes to inform policy decisions. The approach is still positivistic in that it seeks to prove how effective a project is in definitive terms, and power is attributed to the context and participants as variables. There are four stages to a realistic evaluation, and these show the intrinsic positivistic ontology, epistemology and methodology:

1. Develop a hypothesis
2. Collect data
3. Analyse the data
4. Test the theory. (from Squirrell, 2012: 11–12)

Pawson and Tilley (1998) outlined three investigative areas that need to be addressed when evaluating the impact of an intervention within any given context. These are:

- *The mechanism*: what is it about a measure which may lead it to have a particular outcome in a given context?
- *The context*: what conditions are needed for a measure to trigger mechanisms to produce particular outcomes patterns?
- *The outcomes pattern*: what are the practical effects produced by causal mechanisms being triggered in a given context? (Pawson and Tilley, 1998: 145)

This method leads to '**context, mechanism, outcome pattern configurations**' (CMOCs) that allows the evaluator to understand 'what works for whom in what circumstances' (Tilley, 2000). The CMOCs occur through consultation with relevant stakeholders responsible for implementing, operating and participating in interventions. It is this aspect of the model that makes it more participative than the experimental approach. Realistic evaluation allows evaluators to understand what aspects of an intervention make it effective or ineffective and what contextual factors are needed to replicate the intervention in other areas. Evidence based practice also endorses replication of successful programmes, but has frequently neglected the issue of context, leading to successful programmes from America failing when imported into the UK. For example, restorative justice approaches were developed in Maori culture and were not directly importable into the UK as communities in the UK do not have the same value system as Maori cultures, so the practice needed developing before it could be successful here.

One of the key strengths of realistic evaluation is its ability to take the lessons learnt from one evaluation and apply them across a range of different contexts, ensuring on-going learning. One of the drawbacks of the approach is that a realistic evaluation can be very resource intensive.

Vignette 4.4   Realist Evaluation of Aberlour Housing Support Service: What Works and in Which Circumstances (Mansoor et al., 2010)

Working in partnership with other agencies, Aberlour Child Care Trust's Moray Youth Action Housing project provided support to vulnerable young people between the ages of 16 and 25 years. The main purpose of the project was to help young people remain in the community by helping them maintain their tenancies and to seek employment and training.

The efficacy of the project was measured by using a specially designed self-report measure with nine domains of self-scored questions. The service users completed this questionnaire on a monthly basis. As Mansoor et al. (2010: 4) state:

The answers given by individual service users on the questionnaires indicate which domains (life areas) need strengthening and inform if other measures should be used in conjunction, to track the effectiveness of specific work that is being undertaken.

When completed at regular intervals, individual single-system design graphs are prepared and shared with the young people by the support workers. They are then shared with individual service users, who look forward to their arrival to see evidence of personal progress.

The evaluation considered the first and last questionnaire scores from 125 young people receiving the intervention during the period of March 2003 to October 2007.

Change was not recorded across all nine domains of the survey, however, 69% of the young people improved in seven domains and the average change improved from 115.36 to 106.56 with a large effect size. In addition, the identified CMOCs showed that:

older clients tended to improve more than younger clients ($r = .193$, $n = 124$, $p = .032$), and that those who were involved with the Moray Youth Justice Team (i.e., persistent offenders) were less likely to improve on the total domains score ($r = .213$, $n = 124$, $p = .017$). It was also found that those who were not involved with youth justice team at time of referral were 5 times more likely to improve in their total score across all domains. (Mansoor et al., 2010: 6)

Reflecting on this we can see the evaluation provides important detail that goes beyond the overall impact. The realistic evaluative approach and the development of CMOCs has identified exactly what preconditions led to successful outcomes, and the extent to which those factors were important. On this basis, the project can plan improvements and demonstrates the advantages of the realistic approach.

Developmental evaluation

Developmental evaluation (DE) is an evaluation approach that is post–positivistic. It helps people to develop social change initiatives in complex or uncertain environments. Developmental evaluators sometimes liken their approach to the role of evaluation and development in the private sector product development process because it facilitates real-time, or close to real-time, feedback to programme staff thus facilitating a continuous development loop. In many respects it is the antithesis of the structured experimental and realistic approaches described above, rejecting specificity, measurability and clarity as limiting factors (Squirrell, 2012: 28). Within this approach, the evaluator works in the 'here and now', using whatever tools suit the given situation. This demands confidence, communication skills, boundaries, critical thinking and the ability to handle uncertainty.

Patton is careful to describe this approach as responsive to context. As such it is not intended as the solution to every situation, rather it is particularly suited to innovation, radical programme re-design, replication, complex issues and crises. In these situations, DE can help by: framing concepts, testing quick iterations, tracking developments and surfacing issues (Patton, 2010). As Patton says himself:

> Developmental Evaluation supports innovation development to guide adaptation to emergent and dynamic realities in complex environments. Innovations can take the form of new projects, programs, products, organizational changes, policy reforms, and system interventions. A complex system is characterized by a large number of interacting and interdependent elements in which there is no central control. Patterns of change emerge from rapid, real-time interactions that generate learning, evolution, and development ... Complex environments for social interventions and innovations are those in which what to do to solve problems is uncertain and key stakeholders are in conflict about how to proceed. (Patton, 2010: 30)

This stands in stark contrast to the planned and methodical experimental approach. Its flexibility and dynamic nature highlight its use in certain situations, and also its drawbacks. Patton Quinn positioned the approach between formative and summative evaluation types as it provides real-time and end of project findings. The advantage of the approach is its dynamic flexibility, the obvious disadvantage of this can be its unpredictability, the time it may take, and the skill level needed to manage the process, as shown in the vignette below.

Vignette 4.5   Bill & Melinda Gates Foundation's Community Partnerships (The OMG Centre, 2014)

This foundation supports learning in US secondary schools. The goal of the developmental evaluation was to understand what it really takes for a community to coalesce around attainment in schools and then to influence partners to more effectively and efficiently support college success for low-income young people.

In order to do this, the developmental evaluation team (The OMG Centre) maintained a close relationship with schools in the seven partnerships in order to understand what had changed, developing ever more sophisticated interview questions. They used interviews, focus groups, day workshops, telephone calls, data sharing and observations to inform the evaluation. The results created a developmental narrative of change. The project concluded with the production of a **theory of change** that was then used by the foundation as a blueprint for future school partnerships. This included the following ingredients of success: building commitment, using data, aligning policies and practices, and building and sustaining partnerships. As the OMG team commented, this enabled them 'to understand how local innovation occurred, and how communities tackled a complex systems change agenda'. (The OMG Centre, 2014: 12)

Reflecting on this, the true test of the success of the developmental evaluation was not the output of the theory of change demonstrated here; rather, the test should have been the extent to which that theory of change informed other programmes.

Utilisation evaluation

Utilisation focused evaluation places the stakeholders or users of the evaluation at its heart. The evaluator supports others to make decisions rather than passing judgement him or herself. Patton (1986) invented utilisation evaluation. He said that the utilisation part of the name is about making sure that the findings are understandable to a wide range of stakeholders, so that they can do something with the findings in the real world. This type of evaluation therefore displaces some of the evaluators' power, framing the participants and stakeholders as equally, if not more, important. The practicalities of getting the evaluation done are allowed to take precedence over a robust and pure methodology, for example getting the findings ready for a key meeting would take precedence over getting a representative sample involved. It also ensures an applied, real-world focus to the findings. This displacement of power and the focus on practical concerns have led some (Scriven, 1991) to critique it as insubstantial and 'other' than an evaluation. This type of evaluation does not demand involvement for its own sake. Involvement is driven by the belief that involvement creates ownership and comprehension, making it more likely that the findings will be useable. Patton (1996) pointed out that the impact from the process of engagement often lasts longer than the findings do. Utilisation evaluation did not put aside methodological purity easily, but having done so, it does keep practical, utilisable approaches and findings as the most important deciding factor in the design of the evaluation. The advantage of this approach is therefore its practicality.

Vignette 4.6   Improving Bradenton's After-school Programmes Through Utilization Focused Evaluation (Loflin, 2003)

Building on existing local capacity, the Knight Foundation and a local advisory group invested $1.75 million in after-school programmes in Bradenton, Florida over five years to improve positive youth development for students at two middle schools. The goals of the programmes were to: (1) increase youth school engagement; (2) decrease youth negative and violent behaviours; and (3) increase youth civic engagement.

Philliber Research Associates (PRA) were contracted to evaluate each after-school programme. A collaborative approach by the providers of the after-school

(Continued)

(Continued)

programmes formulated a utilization focused evaluation plan that included a school-wide survey administered to all middle school students at the beginning and end of the school year for five years. The survey collected information on: demographics/family status, school engagement indicators, risky behaviours, self-concept, current after-school involvement, and other extracurricular involvement. Additionally, academic performance data and attendance data for each child attending the after-school programme was collected. Collating data at each year end was a simple task with little additional time demands, and the findings were fed into the design of the after-school programme.

Reflecting on this we can see that the evaluation data was simple to collect. Attendance and attainment data already existed, and an annual survey was simple to administer electronically to all students. This illustrates the formative and summative use of the utilisation based method, but begs the question, what else could have been achieved with a more deliberate and less convenience based approach? What outcomes were missed by merely measuring attainment and attendance?

Participative evaluation

The most post-positivist and power sharing form of evaluation is participative evaluation – we see this as so important and significant an approach in evaluations of work with young people that we have dedicated the whole of the next chapter to it. This approach privileges the views of young people, not only as informants, but also as evaluation designers, and as data analysts. As such it is a huge shift from positivism. Participatory evaluation is liberating and emancipatory. Because of the participative nature of the evaluation, it is also often flexible and unpredictable. At the heart of this approach is the value that is placed on the participants' understanding of their own lives, and of the evaluation process, and the gains that all the stakeholders can accrue through the participation. As you read the more detailed information in the next chapter, please bear in mind that it would sit alongside utilisation evaluation in the power and paradigm matrix.

Pause for Thought

Think about a project that you have been involved in:

- How would each of these four types of evaluation fit the project?

The questions that we pose throughout the chapters are designed to increasingly refinine your approach and guiding what you do. It's as if the notion of evaluation is funnelled down, becoming sharper and more focussed as you answer each question. The Step Up case study on the following page exemplifies this process in practice.

Step Up Case Study

The evaluation methodology described in Chapter 2 for Step Up positioned the evaluation as post-positivist. Documentary evidence of data that had naturally occurred was combined with data collection tools that fitted into the programme as activities. The data included:

- Predicted grades at GCSE
- School attendance data
- Session plans and evaluations
- Interview transcripts
- Client satisfaction forms
- Young people's experiences of being looked after
- Journey maps
- Pen portraits.

The inclusion of the young people's views and experiences in the evaluation positions it as participatory to some extent, and reinforces its post-positivist positioning. As such, it is located on the paradigm–power matrix in the participatory box, although it has also employed some scientific measures in using attendance and attainment data in a pre-test–post-test approach. It was participatory in that young people were offered some choice around the activities that they engaged in to evaluate the project, and their views and experiences were placed centrally in the evaluation. They were not, however, involved in the design of the overall evaluation (only data collection tools) and nor were they involved in any data analysis.

The case study shows only a limited involvement of young people in the project evaluation. There were no opportunities, due to limited time, to train the young people in evaluation techniques, or to involve them in the design process in any way. As such, participation was restricted to choice of data collection tools, as is perhaps common in many projects. So much more could have been gained by the young people if they had been more extensively engaged.

Summary

This chapter has introduced you to some more key terminology in evaluation. It has introduced four different foci of evaluations: process, outcome, formative and summative, and four different types of evaluation, depending on the power and paradigm you are working in: quasi-experimental, developmental, realistic, utilisation and participatory evaluation. Creative methods can be utilised in all of these types of evaluation. We have created questions that you need to pose yourself to help you decide on which of these types of evaluation you will adopt and signposted you to other evaluation design guides. After all this decision making, you will probably have a heightened awareness of the importance of reflective practice. After this the decisions become simpler and more fun, as we progress towards choices about data collection tools!

Key Points

1. It is critical that purpose, paradigm and power inform your decision on which type of evaluation you will use.
2. Having decided on the best type of evaluation, you then need to decide what approach you will use – whether your evaluation will be impact or process based and formative or summative, or both.
3. These decisions are all grounded in the evaluation questions and the purpose of the evaluation, highlighting again the importance of clarity when you start any evaluation process.
4. Deciding on the type of evaluation to use is a highly reflective exercise, and youth workers are ideally placed to carry this out.

Further Reading

Dozois, E. et al. (2010) *A Practitioner's Guide to Developmental Evaluation* guides you through the process of developmental evaluation.

Kirkpatrick and Kirkpatrick's (2006) *Evaluating Programmes: The Four Levels* famously attempted to develop more meaningful evaluations, rather than simply reactionary ones. Kirkpatrick's four levels of reaction to programmes include: changes in learning and knowledge; skills and competence; behaviour, and end results.

Kumar, R. (2014) *Research Methodology: A Step-by-Step Guide for Beginners* breaks the process of designing and doing a research project into eight manageable steps. It is written specifically for students with no previous experience.

Pawson, R. and Tilley, N. (1997) *Realistic Evaluation* provides a seminal and simple guide to carrying out realistic evaluations.

Sani, F. and Todman, J. (2005) *Experimental Design and Statistics for Psychology: A First Course* provides a concise, straightforward and accessible introduction to the design of psychology experiments and the statistical tests used to make sense of their results.

Saunders, M. (2000) 'Beginning a valuation via RUFDATA' provides a clear set of decisions in the design of an evaluation. He called this approach RUFDATA.

5

POWER

Chapter Overview

- Who holds power?
- What is power?
- What is participatory evaluation?

Introduction

Power was introduced as a key theme in the ethics chapter above. Here the theme is explored in more depth. In any evaluation setting, power is held variously by commissioners, the organisation, practitioners, evaluators and young people. Tensions may exist between them. Commissioners of services may exert their power over the evaluation. For example, in the UK, youth work contracts are often provided on a 'payment by results' basis. This means that the work is only paid for if the delivery team can evidence the outcomes achieved. In this instance the contract arrangements mean that the 'evaluator' is under pressure to show as many outcomes as possible, potentially influencing the delivery and the evaluation. Organisations may also influence the evaluation process, as they may have very set views on what is evaluated and how data is used, for example demanding that set forms are used to elicit data from young people for organisational benefit. Practitioner evaluators also have control over the way the evaluation is carried out; they decide how much choice to offer the young people in the evaluation design, and they may also have a 'stake' in what the evaluation shows, perhaps not wishing to prove their own project ineffective. Young people also have a lot of power, they can agree or refuse to participate in the evaluation process regardless of whether they are given a choice or not, and they obviously have control over what they chose to tell you. Young people can often be overlooked as holding power, or only granted the power of consent. If we really considered sharing power with young people, we would offer them opportunities to design the evaluation itself. These very brief examples give some insight into the possible power dynamics that exist. These are shown in Figure 5.1.

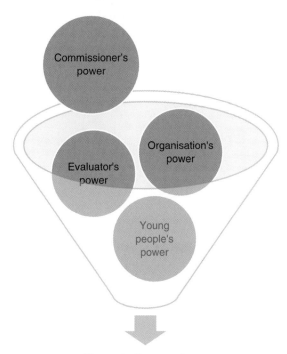

The evaluation experience

Figure 5.1   Sources of power

The stakeholder analysis tools that you were introduced to in Chapter 2 would be very useful at this point to map the power holders in the evaluation process. We recommend that you read this chapter and reflect upon the power dynamics that exist in your setting. To help reveal power, we answer the questions in Table 5.1 each time we embark on a piece of evaluation ensuring that we surface any power dynamics.

Pause for Thought

Think about a project that you have been involved in:

- Complete Table 5.1 for the people engaged in the project.
- Who holds the most power?
- Which areas pose no problems to you?
- Which areas are problematic?
- How will you tackle these areas?

Table 5.1 Questioning power in evaluation design

	Commissioner	Organisation	Practitioner Evaluator	Young People
Commissioner		What control or influence could the organisation have with the commissioner to contract for the type of evaluation that they want? What is at stake for them?	What control or influence could the practitioner have with the commissioner? What will they gain from the evaluation, if anything? What is at stake?	What control or influence could the young people have over the commissioner? What will they gain from the evaluation, if anything? What is at stake?
Organisation	How could the commissioner control what the organisation does to evaluate this project? What will they gain from the evaluation, if anything? What is at stake?		How could the practitioner influence the evaluation practice of the organisation? What will they gain from the evaluation, if anything? What is at stake?	What control or influence could the young people have over the organisation? What will they gain from the evaluation, if anything? What is at stake?
Practitioner evaluator	How could the commissioner influence what the practitioner does? What will they gain from the evaluation, if anything? What is at stake?	How could the organisation control the evaluation by the practitioner? What will they gain from the evaluation, if anything? What is at stake?		How could the young people control or influence the practitioner? What will they gain from the evaluation, if anything? What is at stake?
Young people	How could the commissioner control how the young people engage? What will they gain from the evaluation, if anything? What is at stake?	What influence could the organisation have on the young people? What will they gain from the evaluation, if anything? What is at stake?	What influence or control could the practitioners have over the young people? What will they gain from the evaluation, if anything? What is at stake?	

Before we have a more detailed discussion of power, read and contrast the way that power is dealt with in these two vignettes. Consider who holds the power, who is exerting power, and what the impact could be.

Vignette 5.1   The UK National Citizenship Service (NatCen, 2011)

The National Citizenship Service (NCS) was a flagship eight-week personal development programme planned and commissioned by the UK Government from 2010 for 30,000 young people. The UK Government had a stake in showing that it was a successful policy and investment. They commissioned NatCen, a national evaluation company; to evaluate the programme. The evaluation involved every young person on every programme nationwide filling in the same evaluation form, regardless of their context or abilities. The evaluation form elicited quantitative data that was never fed back to the organisations, practitioners or young people involved. Instead, the results were collated into a national evaluation that demonstrated the value of the NCS programme for the UK Government. The commissioner's power prevailed.

Vignette 5.2   WorkStyles (Puma et al., 2009)

WorkStyles is a two-week, intensive, pre-employment training class for newly arrived refugees in the USA. The project team used 'Community-Based Participatory Evaluation Research' to evaluate the programme. The stakeholder included academics from the Morgridge College of Education at the University of Denver, Colorado Refugee Services, the Spring Institute for Intercultural Learning that developed the WorkStyles programme, the WorkStyles project staff and refugees. The power dynamics were explicitly mapped in the project. People from across all the stakeholder groups were involved in the design, conduct and analysis of data for the evaluation. There were benefits for all the participants, and key learning points were drawn out to inform the future of the project, and the future of any community based participatory evaluation research (Puma et al., 2009). Power was explicitly shared.

Reflecting on these vignettes, you might like to consider:

- Who holds the power?
- Who is using their power?
- Who is excluded, or chooses not to use their power?
- What is the impact?

Having seen the implication of power in evaluations, let us now briefly introduce some key thinkers on power.

Key Theories of Power

There are many academics who write about power. Here we will identify some key aspects of the work of Gramsci (1971), Foucault (1979) and Freire (1970) with pointers to how their ideas can illuminate and inform your evaluation practice.

Sources of power: Antonio Gramsci

Gramsci (1971) thought that capitalism had developed a 'manufactured consent', an invisible agreement in society about 'the ways things are around here'. This unconscious agreement about 'the way things are' was what he called '**hegemony**'. This hegemony was often created and perpetuated by the bourgeois, or upper classes, legitimising the world as they saw it. This led to the idea of 'counter-hegemonic' struggles, where alternatives to dominant views of what is normal and legitimate are advanced. We could suggest that the current climate of 'evidencing' work with young people is becoming hegemonic in the West, that is to say, it is becoming an unquestioned notion of 'truth' and of day-to-day work.

Gramsci's work leads us to question the assumptions or taken for granted notions of 'the truth' in projects. It leads us to question the assumption that those projects are needed, that they are delivered the way that they are, that they need evaluating at all, and whether the projects and evaluations conform to some invisible notion of the truth (such as racism and sexism, etc.).

Technologies of power: Michel Foucault

Michel Foucault became interested in forms and mechanisms of power. He analysed power in very specific contexts: mental asylums, sexuality and crime and punishment.

Foucault (1979: 2–5) proposed that there are games of truth in which different versions of 'the truth' compete for dominance. These different versions of the truth can lead to different forms of domination as they exert power. Think for a moment about sexuality – there are notions of what is 'okay' and not 'okay' in different societies, and individuals may or may not behave in accordance with these norms. Which of these accounts is 'the truth'? How does a society's view of 'normal' sexuality impact on people who do not conform to those norms? If we see truth as a game, then we are perhaps more open to thinking of different sets of the 'truth' vying for popularity, and this can encourage us to be more open minded to findings in our evaluations.

Foucault said that power was relational, it existed in the relationships between people, in their ability to convince or control, and in their agreement to conform to various forms of 'the truth', or to disagree and enter power struggles (1982: 341). To legitimatise their 'truth' people would supervise, control and correct/punish others (Foucault, 1979: 70). To what extent is your evaluation practice supervised, controlled or corrected?

Foucault's ideas encourage us to look for the variety of 'truths' that exist for the different stakeholders in our evaluation projects. The purpose of the evaluation might, for example, look very different for the young people, practitioner, manager and trustees of an organisation. Whose will prevail? With an awareness of these different notions of 'the truth', we might then be more alert to the ways in which we relate to the different stakeholders, and the power that those relationships reveal. Revealing and discussing these different ideas of the truth at the start of a project will help avoid issues further down the line.

Empowerment: Paulo Freire

Freire (1972) saw that people in Brazil were oppressed by their lack of literacy as it prevented them from participating fully in society and democracy. He also realised that the upper classes made no attempt to educate the underclasses, perpetuating their powerlessness. From this perspective, Freire framed education as politically transformational as it led to people having more power, or being 'empowered'. Freire's (1972) educational goal was to achieve 'critical consciousness', a level of thinking that developed through three stages:

1. Magical consciousness is passive and unquestioning, with individuals adapting their thinking to reality. This could also be thought of as resignation or fatalism.
2. Naïve consciousness involves assumptions about what is happening, a state where people impose their ideas on reality.
3. Critical consciousness is integrated with reality. This consciousness has the power to transform reality. It involves deep interpretation of problems, causal thinking, testing out ideas and open mindedness (1974: 14–39).

Freire's ideas prompt us to question whether our projects help young people to develop critical consciousness and the extent to which the evaluation process empowers. The WorkStyles vignette described earlier clearly capitalised on this opportunity, raising the critical consciousness of all of the stakeholders in a participatory process, whereas the NatCen evaluation was not interested in sharing its learning to develop the critical consciousness of the young people who participated, rather it was used by the Government to promote the success of its flagship youth programme. Freire (1972) stressed the importance of dialogue as a tool for learning and power sharing. This prompts evaluators to consider how relationships are built between the evaluators and the evaluated, and to what extent there is genuine dialogue or conversation between the two.

Participatory Work with Young People

These ideas are all very well, you may say, but how do we use them in practice? You may recognise some of these theories from anti-oppressive youth work practice, work that does not oppress young people on the grounds of who they are, or what they believe. These ideas are also evident in **'participatory practice'**. Participatory practice has grown since article 12 of the 1989 United Nations Convention on the Rights of the Child (Podd, 2010). Article 12 stressed the importance of children having their views heard and given 'due weight', and to them having the right to participate in decision-making processes that affect their lives. This was then further embedded in the UK by the statutory duties in the Children Act 1989 and the Education Act 2005. Since then, participatory practice has become a pre-requisite in many funding applications and inspection criteria for statutory services (Kirby et al., 2008). Whilst participation encapsulates ideas of social justice, democracy, empowerment and power (Podd, 2010), it is most frequently expressed practically as the extent to which young people are given the power to decide something, and several models exist to help map the level of participation in projects.

Hart's (1992, 1997) Ladder of Participation, shown in Figure 5.2, is the most frequently used mode of participation. This was a young people focused version of Arnstein's ladder of participation (1969) that was developed for community settings. These have both been criticised as hierarchical, with a 'top step' conveying the sense of increased worth (Podd, 2010). Rather, critics suggest that it is important to use the right form of participation for the situation, rather than always using the 'higher' rungs (Beddoes et al., 2010).

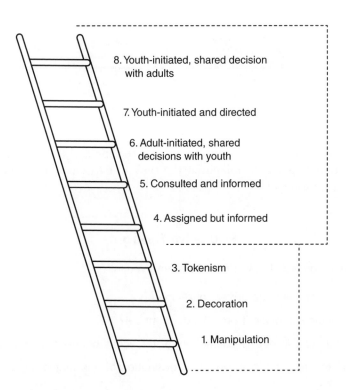

Figure 5.2   Hart's (1992) Ladder of Participation

Manipulation, tokenism and decoration describe projects where young people are not consulted, or asked their views, yet are still used to promote the project at public events, making it appear that they were involved in the project design. Stages four upwards refer to the amount of information, and power that young people are given, up to the stage where young people initiate decision making, but still share that decision with adults.

Treseder (1997) adapted Hart's ladder into a model that did not attach values to the different types of participation (see Figure 5.3).

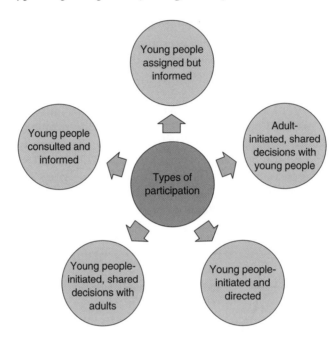

Figure 5.3   Treseder's (1997) approaches to participation

As the types of participation are no longer ranked hierarchically, this model supports a situational approach, matching the type of participation to the wants and skills of the young people.

Pause for Thought

Think about a project that you have been involved in:

• To what extent was the project participatory?

• Where would you place it on Treseder's model?

• Is this the right level of participation for the young people and that project?

• Bearing this in mind, how would an evaluation of this project best map onto the model?

We have considered what participation might look like in a project. Now we turn to look at participation in evaluation. It may seem easy to overlook young people in project design, it is perhaps even easier to ignore them in evaluation design. Participatory evaluation deliberately addresses this issue. Within the underpinning assumptions of non-formal learning are the notions of participation and empowerment (as discussed in Chapter 1). Therefore, young people should have ownership and power in the process of evaluating projects. In this sense, an evaluation should not be 'on' young people and their project, but 'with' young people and 'within' their project. This has been further critiqued, and models are now promoted where evaluation is 'by' young people, for example in Young Inspectors Programmes in the UK where young people conduct inspections and evaluations of youth services. Such approaches are often called '**participatory evaluation**'.

Participatory evaluation aims to level the power differentials between stakeholders from the outset. Participatory evaluation has been most widely used in community development and has also started to flourish in wider contexts. Participatory approaches have also been used for a long time within action research, so much so that participative action research (PAR) is a well-recognised type of research, including evaluation (Reason and Bradbury, 2013). Participative evaluation is most widely used and documented is the USA.

What is Participatory Evaluation?

Participatory evaluation is an applied systematic enquiry that involves evaluators working in partnership with non-evaluator stakeholders (Cousins, 2013: 2). Central to participatory evaluation is giving power and a voice to those who are most marginalised in society, and they are often young people. Power is shared between the participants and the evaluators, who aim to work as facilitators, with shared expertise with the participants. This means more than offering the young people a choice of data collection tools:

> Participatory monitoring and evaluation is not just a matter of using participatory techniques within a conventional monitoring and evaluation setting. It is about radically rethinking who initiates and undertakes the process, and who learns or benefits from the findings. (Institute of Development Studies, 1998: 2)

Young people can be involved in the design, selection of participants, conduct, analysis and presentation of findings. There are a number of benefits to participatory evaluation over non-participatory evaluation, as shown in the following list:

- Engaging disinterested community members
- Capacity building in the community leading to sustainable change
- Increased critical consciousness in the community
- Avoids evaluator assumptions
- Appreciation of other people's views

- Developing evaluation skills
- Action
- Develops collective ownership of issues
- An empowering and emancipatory process.

Mary Kellett (2011) perhaps best describes the far reaching benefits of participatory work:

> The impact of children's participation should not be overlooked. This is not impact in the sense of measurable outcomes to satisfy a tick-box mind set, but impact as efficacy in relation to children's self-development, skill expansion and active citizenship. (2011: 188)

Involving young people in evaluations is therefore non-formal learning itself, developing skills enacted in evaluation, and gaining the value and worth bestowed by the act of involvement, all of which create agency. Squirrell (2012) describes this as a positive cycle of development.

There are also, however, disadvantages to working in a participatory way, and these need to be acknowledged. The first disadvantage is the additional time it will take and the costs that may incur. It may be that the young people would need some information or training before they can be meaningfully involved, increasing the project costs. Other stakeholders, such as trustees, may also need some training in working with young people, before it is possible for them to come together to jointly discuss the evaluation design. The additional time and costs are often reasons for participatory approaches being abandoned. It may additionally be difficult to get buy-in to the process from all stakeholders and to develop trust amongst the group. It may also take more management time to ensure that everyone is involved, not just 'leaders' of various groups. And finally, funders and policy makers may not understand or believe in participatory evaluation.

Participatory evaluation involves participation in every stage of the evaluation. This can be challenging, as designing evaluations has usually been the territory of evaluators and commissioners. To evaluate in a fully participatory way this would include all the stakeholders in:

- Identifying relevant questions
- Planning the evaluation design
- Selecting appropriate measures and data collection method
- gathering and analysing data
- Reaching consensus about findings, conclusions and recommendations
- Disseminating results and preparing an action plan to improve programme performance. (Institute of Developmental Studies, 1998)

We can create a matrix, allowing us to identify the extent of involvement offered to the young people in each of these parts of the evaluation as shown in Table 5.2.

Table 5.2 Levels of participation in each stage of the evaluation process

	Identify questions	Plan the design	Select data collection tools	Gather and analyse data	Disseminate
Assigned but informed					
Consulted and informed					
Adult initiated but decisions shared					
Youth initiated but decisions shared					
Youth initiated and directed					

Pause for Thought

Think about a project you have been involved in:

- Use the matrix in Table 5.2 to map the levels of participation in an evaluation of the project.
- What are the participative strengths?
- Where are the weaknesses?
- Could you do anything to address the weaknesses?

To what extent have you ever considered participatory evaluation when you planned a programme?

- Can you use a participatory evaluation if the aims or evaluation questions have been pre-determined by an external body?

We started by considering how some ideas become 'hegemonic' or taken for granted, and the ways in which games of truth are played and regulated through supervision, control and correction. We thought about the ways in which evaluations can be used to enhance critical consciousness and explored different models of participation. These all inform the practice of non-formal learning in youth projects through anti-oppressive practice, and should also inform the evaluation of these projects. We have described some practical ways in which this can be achieved, and accounted for the difficulties in doing so. Now we will return to our case study of 'Step Up' in order to assess how participatory that evaluation design was.

Step Up Case Study

The Step Up project had a strong case for being participatory, and yet did not make full use of this opportunity.

The young people who were participants in the Step Up project were all in care. Such young people often lack power. They may not, for example, have the power to decide who to live with or where to live. Such young people could be argued to need opportunities to exert power in order to develop empowerment and self-efficacy. The commissioners of the programme wanted to measure the effectiveness of the programme in terms of school attainment data. The school that the young people attended also wanted to measure attainment. Brathay Trust, who delivered the programme, were more interested in the well-being of the young people, and the young people themselves had no voice in the evaluation, perhaps reinforcing their powerlessness. In the end an evaluation was written that adopted a mixed methods approach, combining the quantitative attainment data with qualitative experiences from the young people, giving them as much voice as possible, but there was no scope for the young people to design the evaluation in any way; it was done to them.

The lack of participation in this instance was largely due to the programme being planned and contracted without the involvement of the evaluation team. This is a common occurrence. Evaluation is often 'added on' to programmes rather than being built into them from the start.

This is in stark contrast to the final vignette in this chapter, where young people with learning disabilities in New Zealand designed and conducted evaluations.

Vignette 5.3   Participative Research with Disabled and Non-disabled Young People (Gladstone, 2010)

Gladstone developed a research team that comprised disabled and non-disabled researchers who came together through a shared goal to understand what kind of life young people with intellectual disabilities want when they leave school. The aims of the research were to:

- Improve post-school outcomes for students and young people with intellectual disabilities.
- Explore student self-determination through the process of transition from school to post-school life.
- Achieve meaningful involvement of young people with intellectual disability in the research process.

Researcher training was provided for an initial six weeks, and then throughout the project for the inquiry team. The young people then decided to run focus groups throughout the year, and to develop a questionnaire for all school leavers. To enable the disabled members of the research team to conduct the focus groups the team developed a focus group protocol that included word/symbol cue cards drawn by a graphic designer, a note taker and support worker and digital recorder for each focus group.

The compelling results about the aspirations of disabled school leavers were reported to the New Zealand Government and presented at conferences by the inquiry team. Gladstone (2010) comments that participatory evaluation with disabled young people; 'is fraught with challenges ethically, procedurally and methodologically', overcoming them, however, led to; 'meaningful and active participation of young people with intellectual disability as co-researchers within a team'.

Reflecting on this it is inspiring to see that participation is possible at all levels with many different types of young people as long as they are provided with the right resources. Providing a voice for groups who are perhaps marginalised and excluded is a potent rationale for evaluation and research. As such, it may well be that writing participatory evaluation designs may increase project funding rather than eating into funds allocated for the project delivery alone.

Creative Methods and Participatory Evaluation Practice

Engaging young people in evaluations in a way that levels the power may mean being more creative. Sitting around a table, with heaps of papers, completing questionnaires and engaging in debate may not include all young people or be meaningful to them. This places a demand on the evaluators to find more creative ways to engage with young people. It could be that graffiti walls are a more useful way to collect ideas and views – either of the young people designing the evaluation, or of young people involved in the evaluation. Other options include using digital narratives, Big Brother diary rooms, social mapping, drawings, drama etc. We believe that this is an important skill for evaluators, and one that youth workers are well equipped to carry out as they are well acquainted with the likes and dislikes of young people and how to engage them. There is also a range of toolkits accessible online for participatory evaluators and community development workers should you want ideas beyond those provided in our toolkit.

Summary

This chapter has introduced a range of powerful stakeholders who might influence the evaluation. In considering power we have discussed sources of power, technologies of power and empowerment to help you identify where power might be at play. Creative methods are ideally suited to working in a participatory way.

We have presented participatory evaluation as an approach that openly and explicitly places power with the evaluation participants, and describe it as well aligned to youth work values. The chapter has provided practical tips and key questions to help you identify and think of the implications of power in your own setting. The importance of participatory evaluation globally is perhaps best summarised by its inclusion as a key means of achieving the Millennium Development Goals by 2015 (Gawler, 2005).

Key Points

1. Planning and conducting evaluations demands an awareness of power.
2. Issues of power need to be tackled openly; don't leave them hidden.
3. Creative methods are useful tools to enable participatory evaluation.
4. Factor the additional costs and time involved in participatory evaluation into costings, bids and tenders.
5. Being reflective is critical to enable you to identify power in its most subtle and insidious forms.

Further Reading

Sercombe, H. (2010) *Youth Work Ethics* has a clear chapter on theories of power in a youth work context.

Fox, J. and Cater, M. (2011) 'Participatory evaluation: Factors to consider when involving youth' is an easy to read article showing a critical perspective on the increasing involvement of young people in participatory evaluation. The authors also identify the factors to consider when designing a youth-led evaluation project.

Gawler, M. (2005) *Useful Tools for Engaging Young People in Participatory Evaluation* provides a practical overview and toolkit for anyone wanting to carry out participatory evaluation with young people.

NECF and Horsley, K. (2009) *The Evaluator's Cookbook: Participatory Evaluation Exercises* provides a well-known resource with numerous creative and participative tools for evaluations.

Participation Works (2014) provide an online resource to support organisations to effectively involve children and young people in the development, delivery and evaluation of services that affect their lives.

6

PLANNING EVALUATIONS – AN OVERVIEW

Chapter Overview

- How to work through the stages of planning an evaluation, summarising everything that you have read in the first part of the book

- Introduction to the theory of change planning framework

- Development of the theme of reflective practice, and its importance in planning evaluations.

How to Plan an Evaluation

Each chapter in the first part of the book introduced the theory and practice of different aspects of evaluation practice. In this chapter we draw these together into some simple steps to work through each time you plan an evaluation. The steps are represented sequentially in Figure 6.1, and we will explain each stage in a little more detail, or you can revisit the first five chapters for more depth of information on them if you need to.

This planning process can perhaps be best demonstrated by looking at the Step Up project, and seeing what choices were made here.

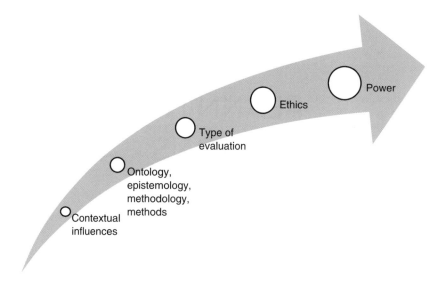

Figure 6.1   The stages of planning an evaluation

 Step Up Case Study

The Step Up design process is used to illuminate the design choices made at each stage of the evaluation planning process, setting the scene for the following discussion.

Stage One: Contextual Influences

The Step Up project was run by Brathay Trust. They are an organisation that values young people as experts on their own lives, and who work in a participative way. This stood in contrast to some extent to the context that they were operating in that demanded quantifiable and 'proven' evidence of impact. The commissioners of the programme wanted to know that it had worked so that they could justify the expenditure on the programme. Brathay wanted to know that it worked so that they could show the commissioners that they had done a good job and potentially get another commission. Brathay also wanted the young people to know if they had learnt, and to what extent. The evaluator had a preference for post-positivistic participatory approaches to evaluation.

Stage Two: Ontology, Epistemology, Methodology and Methods

The Step Up evaluation was planned from a post-positivistic perspective as it wanted to understand whether the project improved attendance and attainment, and in what ways it improved them, and young people and practitioners hold that knowledge. Ontologically and epistemologically this is post-positivist, and this dictated the methodology which would involve the practitioner working with the young people and practitioners to explore what was happening and why. Quantitative methods were needed to quantify improvements in attainment and attendance and qualitative methods were needed to explain how these had come about. This dictated a mixed methods approach and associated statistical and thematic analysis.

Stage Three: Type of Evaluation

This evaluation was designed as a summative process and impact evaluation as it sought to understand changes in outcomes at the end of the project and the mechanisms that had led to those changes. The evaluation type had to be partially participatory, as young people are involved in giving their views on the gains that they have made and the ways that they have made them. Despite this, there are also some experimental methods employed in pre-test–post-test measures of attendance and attainment. The Step Up evaluation was therefore a hybrid approach using mixed methods drawn from participative and experimental types of evaluation.

Stage Four: Ethics

The ethical issues that were identified through the completion of an ethical checklist included how to keep identities confidential when the group was so well defined in the school, how to ensure that the young people used their right to consent and withdraw when they are in a compliant school setting, and how to deal with any potential disclosures that they might make as part of the experience.

The Step Up evaluation involved the evaluators exercising their power over the young people. They were not given voice in the evaluation design, the evaluation questions, the analysis or dissemination and were only allowed to choose from a given range of data collection tools.

Hopefully you can see that each chapter helps you to scaffold a paragraph about your evaluation design. It is vital that you are aware of the choices that are being made about the design, and that you can reflect on how congruent they are with one another, with young people and with your practice. It is also excellent practice to publish this 'methodology' at the start of your evaluation so that the reader can understand the choices made.

Having seen what these stages look like in practice with the Step Up case study, we will now guide you through each one for yourself.

Stage one: Contextual influences

The first step in planning an evaluation is to identify how the context that you are operating in influences you. If the evaluation design was a play, then this stage is creating the scenery, the backdrop against which all the action takes place.

The way it looks will influence the way the audience sees the action, and so the contextual influences affect the way in which the reader will interpret your evaluation. This involves mapping the organisations beliefs, values and practice regarding evaluation, the values of the organisation regarding young people, the reason why a range of stakeholders want the evaluation, and any tensions that you might find between these factors. This sets the scene, as it were, for the rest of your thinking around evaluation. You may notice that these factors are all external to you, they are pre-existing contextual factors. Your beliefs and values, and your reasons for evaluating may align, or contrast with the contextual influences. This highlights the role of reflective practice, in that you constantly need to be aware of what is being demanded, and what you 'want' to do. What you actually do will depend on you managing these two factors, and thinking through the relative importance of the two positions in each stage of the planning. For example, you may want to work in a highly participative way, but only a monitoring attendance report is needed and so there is no scope for the evaluation to be meaningfully participative.

- What are your organisations beliefs, values and practice regarding evaluation?
- Are these different from the national climate, and is that problematic?
- What are the values of the organisation regarding young people?
- What views do you have about evaluation with young people?
- Who are the stakeholders?
- Why does each stakeholder want the evaluation, what do they think its purpose is?
- Are there any tensions between these factors?

You do not need to arrive at any decisions at this point, simply map all the different factors that influence you, perhaps in a mind map, so that you are aware of them as you make decisions in each of the next four stages.

Stage two: Methodology

In stage two, you need to weigh up, on balance what the beliefs will be that underpin your evaluation. It may well be that there is no tension between them, in which case this stage should be straightforward. This will guide your paradigmatic choice. Remember that the paradigm that you chose incudes your beliefs about the nature of reality and what you want to know (ontology), about how knowledge is created and who creates it (epistemology), how you will find that knowledge out (the methodology), and what data (qualitative or quantitative) will give us that knowledge (methods). This framework is summarised in Table 2.2. Whilst there are a number of questions to answer, the end result is a choice between two main ways of operating – a positivistic, or scientific way of working, or a post-positivistic or interpretivist way of working. The former focuses on proving an objective truth, and the second focuses on understanding a range of truths from different perspectives. Despite the complexity of the language and concepts, the key question in stage two is, given the contextual influences:

- Am I working within a positivistic paradigm or in a post-positivistic paradigm?

The sub-questions from Chapter 2 that will help you to answer include:

- What do you want to know (ontology) – does the evaluation seek an objective fact or a subjective phenomenon?
- What is the nature of this knowledge (epistemology) – can the evaluation question be proved objectively or is it a socially constructed question?
- How will you find this out (methodology) – can the evaluator construct the answer, or is it owned by the young people and practitioners?
- How will you find this out (methods) – will the answer to your evaluation question be demonstrated by qualitative or quantitative data (or both using mixed methods)?

Answering these questions will demand that you are highly reflective, aware of your own beliefs, values and preferences, and able to reflect on the beliefs, values and preferences that come from the context that you operate in. The type of evaluation that you choose may suit both sets of values, or your own, your organisations, or the national contextual values. There is no hard and fast rule about which is the best one to work to – that difficult decision sits with you. It is useful at this point to jot down which paradigm you have decided to work within and to give a rationale for that choice that you can return to later if you start to doubt what you are doing, or if questioned by the stakeholders.

Stage three: Type of evaluation

Having decided which paradigm you are working within, the next step is to decide on the specific type of evaluation that you will use. These types were discussed in Chapter 4, and you can refer back to that chapter for more detail to guide your decision making.

The first decision is whether you are evaluating the outcome or impact of the work that you have been doing with the young people, or whether you are evaluating the process of working with them. You may also be evaluating both of these at the same time. Outcome and impact evaluations typically measure changes in outcomes and may use distance travelled tools. Process evaluations typically account for how the project was delivered and may use observational techniques and monitoring records. These could both be carried out within the positivistic or post-positivistic paradigm.

The second decision in stage three is to work out whether you are going to do a formative or summative evaluation. Formative evaluations are carried out as the project develops in order to provide project improvement feedback whilst the project is still happening. Summative evaluations in contrast happen at the end of a project, and summarise what was achieved (summative impact) or how it was achieved (summative process). These could both be carried out within the positivistic or post-positivistic paradigm.

We now have two design questions to answer at this stage:

- Is the evaluation a process or impact evaluation, or does it need to demonstrate both?
- Is the evaluation formative or summative?

Whilst the answers to these two questions are not dependent on the paradigm, the third decision is. The third decision relates to where you think the power is placed in the evaluation, and what paradigm you have chosen – you can refer back to the power and paradigm matrix in Figure 4.2 if you like. This provides us with one decision to make that has four possible answers. The question is:

- What type of evaluation shall I use?

If you have opted for a positivistic paradigm, then the answer to this question is a choice between an experimental design or realistic design, depending on whether the power sits with the evaluator or participants.

  If you have opted for a post-positivistic paradigm then the answer to this question is a choice between a developmental design or utilisation design, again depending on whether the power sits with the evaluators or participants. If you opt for a post-positivistic, power with the participant stance, then we also have a further question, which relates to the whole of Chapter 5, which is whether your evaluation is participative, and if so, to what extent it is participative.

- If your evaluation is post-positivistic and places power with the participants, then how participative will it be?

An explanation of participative evaluation, and more refined questions are found in Chapter 5.

Stage four: Ethics

Now that you are aware of the main decisions regarding your evaluation design, and before you design data collection tools, you need to consider any ethical issues. This leads to a single, simple question with multiple and perhaps complex answers:

- What ethical issues arise in the evaluation that you have designed?

Chapter 3 has more detail on exactly what range of ethical issues may emerge for you and it suggests some ways that people manage them. You will need to reflect on the purpose of the evaluation and the needs of the young people and try to hold them in balance. This is another key area where reflective practice is essential. The nature of the ethical issues will also be influenced by the paradigm that you are working in. Experimental approaches, for example, throw up very different ethical issues (for example, whether equity is being denied access to an intervention to help prove that it works) than a participative design might (for example, whether the young people understand enough about evaluation to be able to carry it out).

Stage five: Power

Chapter 5 guided you through the various ways in which people hold power. You need to map the stakeholders and the power that they hold over other stakeholders and evaluation processes. You will also need to reflect on the level of participation possible at each stage of the evaluation. The extent to which you power share will also depend on the assumptions in stage two – a positivistic evaluation would not seek the views of young people for example.

Alignment of Design Choices

You will have noticed that some of the contextual influences might govern all the choices that you make. The project that you are running, for example, might be funded and there may be very prescriptive reporting procedures that govern the evaluation design. If you do have more freedom to design the evaluation to best suit your needs, you may notice that some of the choices that you make early on influence the choices that you make later in the process. Whichever is the case, it is hopefully apparent that there needs to be alignment of choices. If you chose a positivistic paradigm you would not use a participative approach. Conversely, if you chose a post-positivistic approach you would not use an experimental design. When design choices do not align the resulting evaluation process, output is usually poor, as exemplified in the following vignette.

Vignette 6.1   The Exit from Weapon Use Project (Brathay Trust, 2012)

This project worked with young people who were involved in gangs to empower them to leave the gang and stop carrying weapons. This was a major project that worked with small groups of young people over 18 months. The commissioners were interested in statistics that proved that the young people committed fewer offences, carried weapons less, and used substances less. This can perhaps be seen as a negative set of drivers, seeking for evidence in a reduction of negative attributes that are important to the commissioner. The youth work organisation that delivered the programme was interested in demonstrating that the programme was meaningful for the young people, that it had helped them to create a positive sense of identity, and that it had helped them develop skills and set goals that empowered them to enter employment education and training, rather than remaining gang involved. This can be seen as a list of positive attributes that are meaningful for the young people.

These different perspectives were not explored at the time of the work being commissioned. An evaluation was not planned before the project was

(Continued)

(Continued)

delivered, although it was expected by the commissioners. The youth workers thought that they could do all that 'paperwork' at the end.

As a result, there were no measures of offending, weapon use or substance use collected at the start, or monitored or measurable at the end. The youth workers did not have access to the information collected by other statutory services and had not collected it themselves as it would have prevented them from building relationships with the young people.

The youth workers did have stories of change. They could explain the positive changes that had happened for many of the young people, and many of the young people would explain those changes themselves. There were photographs of young people engaged in project work, and the staff could evidence certificates of achievement, but all of these counted for nothing in the eyes of the commissioner.

The project had been successful in terms of achieving positive outcomes for the young people, but there was no evidence of it reducing negative outcomes, and so the commissioner did not deem it effective. This could be the impact of unclear expectations, and of the design choices not stacking up. There were three options here that would have solved the problem:

Option A: Use a quasi-experimental approach to test whether the programme reduced negative outcomes as per the commissioner's positivistic preference.

Option B: Use a participative approach to demonstrate the acquisition of positive outcomes from the perspective of the young people as per the youth workers' preference.

Option C: Run a mixed methods evaluation that captures the quantitative reductions in negative outcomes and the qualitative increases in positive outcomes satisfying all the stakeholders.

Sadly, and logically, the use of qualitative data did not match the positivistic expectations of the commissioners, a preventable situation. This again demonstrates the difficulties of evaluation being 'added in' rather than thought through at the point of project initiation. This situation was then further compounded by the difference in views between the youth workers and commissioners about the nature of evaluation and data. We hope that this story helps you to avoid similar situations.

Hopefully you can see that the questions in each of these stages refine your evaluation design further and further, increasing your clarity about what you are doing. You should now be at the point where you are really eager for those data collection tools, and they are coming in the next chapter! Your experience so far should hopefully look like the funnel in Figure 6.2, with your thinking being refined as we progress down into the spout, progressing from abstract concepts like paradigms to concrete practical ethical issues.

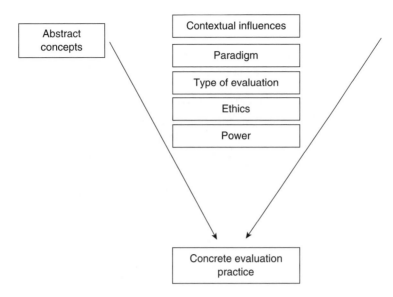

Figure 6.2   Refining the evaluation design

Whilst this is the logical order of thinking, from abstract broad concepts down to narrow practical issues, it is not always how people think. Some of us prefer to start with the known practical world, and progress upwards in our thinking to more abstract terms. If this thinking process feels difficult to you, then you might want to try the next approach that starts with practice, and works its way back up to the more abstract terms. The tool that we want to introduce here is the **theory of change** planning framework. First though, we will show you how the different stages of planning identified above were used in the Step Up Project.

Theory of Change

The theory of change methodology will be introduced and critiqued. A series of questions will then guide the practitioner's thinking through: the strengths and needs of the young people, the outcomes and pedagogical approach of the project, the evaluation questions, the appropriate type of evaluation, indicators and data collection tools (e.g. interviews, surveys, creative tools, photos, videos, etc.). The reader will be encouraged to consider the pros and cons of each method, including the practical and ethical limitations, and examples of key difficulties such a differentiation highlights are discussed.

A theory of change is a **logic model**. This is a pictorial map of a programme or intervention that shows your systematic thinking about the people who will come on the programme, what you will do, and how that will lead to outcomes (Kellogg Foundation, 2004). A logic model can provide the same thing to programmes that involve social and human change that business plans have done for simple, linear organisations. As Ellis et al. (2011) say: 'a theory of change is a description of a social change initiative that shows how early changes relate to more intermediate changes and then to longer-term change'. As the quote shows, a theory of change is a logic model that states that in order to achieve outcome C in a social context, you will put steps A and B into place. The concept emerged from 'realistic' evaluation methodologies in the 1980s. It is now common in the UK in 'social return on investment' measures; it features in the UK Department for Education guidance for youth work (Young Foundation, 2013) and in guidance on youth projects in Greater London through 'Project Oracle' (Mayor of London, 2012).

A theory of change is usually mapped backwards, starting with the impact that you aim to achieve, working back through all the smaller outcomes that are needed to achieve that aim, and linking those to the inputs and activities that are fundamental to achieving them.

The benefits of using a theory of change are that it creates:

- A clear and testable theory about how change will occur
- A visual representation of the change you want to see
- A blueprint for evaluation of the project with measurable indicators of success
- An agreement among stakeholders about what defines success
- A powerful communication tool to capture the complexity of your programme
- A flexible re-design framework.

As we have said, the theory of change starts with your practice, with what you want to do with the young people and helps you to build an evaluation design from that perspective. Here are the steps that are needed to map a theory of change:

Step one: Identify the needs that you are addressing.

Step two: Identify the long-term impact that you aim to achieve to address that need.

Step three: Bridge the gap between the needs and the impact you are aiming for with a series of outcomes and outputs. Map as many as you need to be clear. They should build one upon another, 'outcome A, so that outcome B, so that outcome C, so that ... Impact'. You may have a single column or chain of outcomes, or several columns and rows of outcomes in a network map, depending on how complex your programme is.

Step four: Identify the inputs and activities that are needed to achieve those outcomes.

Step five: Identify how you will measure the outcomes and outputs by creating indicators and targets for each outcome.

Step six: Identify any longer term or distal outcomes that might be achieved once your programme has ended, beyond your programme aims (you may not be able to evidence these, but you will be able to claim that you are contributing to them (Mayne, 2008)).

Step seven: Check the logic and assumptions between each of the building blocks of the theory of change.

This flow is demonstrated in Figure 6.3.

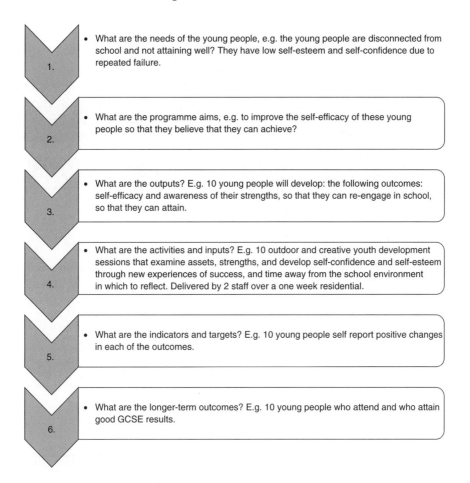

1. • What are the needs of the young people, e.g. the young people are disconnected from school and not attaining well? They have low self-esteem and self-confidence due to repeated failure.

2. • What are the programme aims, e.g. to improve the self-efficacy of these young people so that they believe that they can achieve?

3. • What are the outputs? E.g. 10 young people will develop: the following outcomes: self-efficacy and awareness of their strengths, so that they can re-engage in school, so that they can attain.

4. • What are the activities and inputs? E.g. 10 outdoor and creative youth development sessions that examine assets, strengths, and develop self-confidence and self-esteem through new experiences of success, and time away from the school environment in which to reflect. Delivered by 2 staff over a one week residential.

5. • What are the indicators and targets? E.g. 10 young people self report positive changes in each of the outcomes.

6. • What are the longer-term outcomes? E.g. 10 young people who attend and who attain good GCSE results.

Figure 6.3   Creating a theory of change

These questions flow in a logical order to help you create the theory of change map, but you will notice that the theory of change map is not presented in the same order as the questions. The theory of change is mapping what needs to happen in the gap between the current abilities (and needs) of the young people and the planned aims of the programme. This mapping is shown in Figure 6.4. The numbers in the boxes refer to the question numbers from Figure 6.3, so you can see where to place the answers that you have generated to those questions. Don't be constrained by the number of boxes shown. One activity might contribute to more than one outcome, so be prepared to have multiple boxes and arrows to capture the complexity of what you do – this is a simple example to help you grasp the principles.

Criticisms of the theory of change

In response to the growing interest in and demand for theories of change, a critique is also emerging. The first criticism is that it is often poorly defined, meaning that it is hard to ascertain its quality. In addition, the term 'theory' is contentious. Other

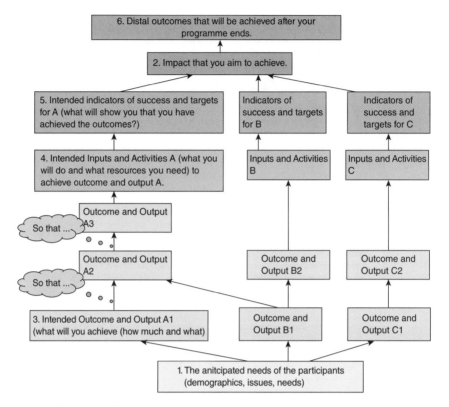

Figure 6.4   The theory of change map

terms like 'change pathway' or 'practice map' may resonate better. A strength of the tool is its ability to capture complexity, but this may also be a weakness, as large elaborate examples can be discouraging for newcomers – and can look like rigid plans. Those who have not been involved in articulating a theory of change may feel disconnected, feeding imbalances in understandings within the larger group and partial views. Mandating a theory of change may also turn it from a participatory practice tool into a bureaucratic exercise. Despite these criticisms, we have found it a very useful tool to help a range of organisations to develop an approach to evaluation.

From theory of change to evaluation design

The theory of change clearly maps what you hope to achieve, and all the steps that are needed to achieve the goals or aims that you have in mind. It makes the project process really explicit. From that practical base point, you can then plan upwards, answering the evaluation design questions in the opposite order, working from the theory of change, through ethical issues, through the type of evaluation that you will use, up through the methodology and then specifying the contextual challenges that created the practice and evaluation in the first place. The questions are identical. You are just answering them in the opposite order, starting with practice and working up to abstract concepts. This is shown in the Figure 6.5.

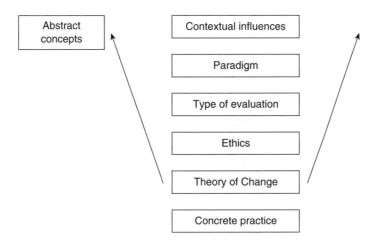

Figure 6.5   Refining the evaluation design with a theory of change as the start

This has probably triggered you to question whether it matters which way round you tackle the questions. It doesn't matter at all as long as you have answered all the questions and checked the logic before you start evaluating. In fact it is useful if you think through your questions in both directions before you start so that you can be certain it all stacks up. If you have worked from the top down as in Figure 6.2, you might now want to do a theory of change as a further refinement of your thinking.

We will now look at the process of planning an evaluation starting with a theory of change so that you can see how it works in practice. You will note that the steps are reversed.

(a) Ethical issues

- What are the ethical issues?

  A checklist of common ethical issues was completed including; consent, anonymity, protection from harm and participant validation. These were all resolved simply. One ethical issue stood out from this theory of change in that Brathay were running participative programmes and yet wanted to find out impact information predominantly for its own benefit. This tension would have to be reconciled by using participatory and creative techniques in the evaluation that would benefit the young people as well as the organisation as they would contribute to the learning process and empower the young people as well as helping the organisation show impact.

(b) Type of evaluation

- What type of evaluation shall I use?
- Is the evaluation formative or summative?
- Is the evaluation a process or impact evaluation, or does it need to demonstrate both?

The evaluation was obviously going to be participative in nature in order to correlate with Brathay's participative programmes. Within the Brathay context, this meant that outcomes were negotiated with the young people whenever possible. Young people were given as many activity choices as possible, and they were also provided with choices as to how they reflect on their learning, or in other words, how they evaluated their learning. This represents the extent of the participation in the programmes and evaluation.

The evaluation could only be conducted at the end of the programmes if it was to draw on the young people's views of what they have learnt, and so the evaluation would be summative, and as it was seeking to understand the extent to which aims and outcomes had been achieved it would be an impact evaluation.

(c) Methodology

- How will you find this out (methods) – will the answer to your evaluation question be demonstrated by qualitative or quantitative data (or both)?
- How will you find this out (methodology) – can the evaluator construct the answer, or is it owned by the young people and practitioners?
- What is the nature of this knowledge (epistemology) – can the evaluation question be proved objectively or is it a socially constructed question?
- What do you want to know (ontology) – does the evaluation seek an objective fact or a subjective phenomenon?
- Am I working within a positivistic paradigm or in a post-positivistic paradigm?

The evaluation was seeking to explore what the young people thought about their learning and it would probably use a combination of qualitative and quantitative data. The understanding of whether, and to what extent, learning had taken place was owned by the young people. Because the young people own this knowledge, it is entirely subjective and socially constructed by their understanding of who they are, what learning is, and what changes took place for them on the programme. This means that Brathay are seeking to explore a subjective phenomenon as clearly as possible. With such clearly post-positivistic epistemology and ontology, the paradigm can only be post-positivist. This means that Brathay will not measure or test young people, or impose practitioners or evaluators knowledge above that of the young people themselves.

(d) Contextual influences

- What are your organisations beliefs, values and practice regarding evaluation?
- Are these different from the national climate, and is that problematic?
- What are the values of the organisation regarding young people?
- What views do you have about evaluation with young people?
- Who are the stakeholders?
- Why does each stakeholder want the evaluation, what do they think its purpose is?
- Are there any tensions between these factors?

These values, beliefs and practices do stand in contrast to the current evidence based climate in the UK, and this is creating tension for Brathay as an organisation, as documented in Table 1.3.

We hope that you can see from the case study and Vignettes 6.1 and 6.2 that it is quite possible to plan an evaluation design from the bottom up or from the top down. The important thing is that the evaluation is planned and thought through before it happens.

Pause for Thought

Think about a project that you have been involved in:

- Plan an evaluation for it using either the paradigm to theory of change approach, or the theory of change to paradigm approach. Use this chapter as a guide to each stage of planning.

Whilst theories of change are valuable maps to enable practitioners to plan and evaluate programmes, they perhaps give too much focus on the changes that young people need to achieve. The assumption that young people must change is not unique to theories of change as it spans many programme designs and evaluations. This focus on individual change obscures the necessity for organisational, system and policy changes needed to enable more young people to flourish. Youth work seeks to empower young people from a 'rights based' approach to participate in and contribute to democracy and ultimately social justice. We therefore need to ensure that our evaluations do not unwittingly contribute to on-going oppression of young people and that, instead, they point out the changes needed in society to enable young people to flourish as well as the changes young people can make to enable societies to flourish! For this reason we encourage you to write findings for a broad set of stakeholders, including implications for the project, organisation and policy.

Reflective Practice

In Chapter 2 we introduced reflective practice and suggested the ways in which it can help support your evaluation practice. We suggested a reflective evaluation cycle that had four parts:

- Posing yourself critical questions about your practice
- Reflecting on your thoughts, feelings, actions and behaviours
- Reflecting on your observations, recollections and perspectives – how you can interpret them
- Deciding what impact your reflections should have on your learning.

Now that you understand more about the different aspects of evaluation design, we can now refine the first two of these questions further. The second two have a role in the write up and publication of the evaluation. The questions that arise when the reflective cycle is applied to each stage of evaluation design are shown below.

(a) Contextual influences

  • To what extent do you agree with the organisational and national context that you work in?
  • How does the context influence your evaluation practice?

(b) Methodology

  • To what extent do you plan a methodology that you are comfortable with, or that you prefer, and is that OK?
  • To what extent does the context influence the methodology, and is that OK?

(c) Type of evaluation

  • To what extent do you use types of evaluation that you are comfortable with, or that you prefer, and is that OK?
  • To what extent does the context influence the type of evaluation, and is that OK?

(d) Ethics

  • To what extent are the ethical issues that you identify representative of your views rather than those of the young people themselves?
  • To what extent does the context influence the ethics, and is that OK?

Answering these reflective questions is important for two reasons. Firstly they ensure that you identify any bias that there might be in the evaluation coming from a range of stakeholders – in identifying them you can either then address them in the design, or if that is not possible, highlight them in the evaluation report. Secondly, it is through reflective practice that your evaluation practice will improve. The more you question what you do and why you do it, the more you learn about evaluation, and the more you hone your skills, as opposed to rolling out the same thing each time unquestioningly.

At this planning point in the evaluation process this could be called 'reflection-pre-action'. Your reflections will not end here. You will also reflect on the process as you carry out the evaluation, what Schön (1983) called 'reflection-in-action', and looking back on the whole process at the end – 'reflection-on-action'. These are not onerous or lengthy tasks, but they do require some conscious focused mental effort. We highly recommend capturing your reflections as you go along as they may well help your interpretation and write up of the evaluation report, and they will certainly help you when you next design an evaluation. Reflective logs or reflective journals are a common part of much professional practice, and evaluators regularly use this device. The reason that reflective practice is used so widely in professional practice (including for example, education, youth work and nursing) is that these jobs are hard to make routine or simple. They all involve complex decision-making processes and a degree of uncertainty. This demands that people carrying out these jobs develop professional judgement, and this is aided by reflective practice. There are many other benefits that have been attributed to reflective practice:

- Increased learning from an experience
- Promotion of deep learning
- Identification of personal and professional strengths and areas for improvement
- Identification of personal and professional needs
- Acquisition of new knowledge and skills
- Further understanding of own beliefs, attitudes and values
- Encouragement of self-motivation and self-directed learning
- Possible improvements of personal and professional confidence. (Davies, 2012)

At times these benefits have perhaps been oversold, and we believe that it is also important to acknowledge the limitations of reflective practice:

- Not all practitioners may understand the reflective process.
- Some people may feel uncomfortable challenging and evaluating their own practice.
- It could be time consuming.
- There may be confusion as to which situations/experiences to reflect upon
- Reflection alone may not be adequate to resolve professional problems. (Price, 2004)

Reflective practice is therefore a tool in your toolbox alongside reading (this book), training, shadowing, mentoring and other professional learning tools.

Summary

In this chapter we have summarised all the steps for planning an evaluation that were presented in the first half of this book. We have presented the planning process as logical and sequential, and suggested that it can be completed working from abstract ideas down to practice, or vice versa. The most important thing about evaluation planning is that it happens before the project starts, and that the decisions align. We have introduced theory of change as a useful tool to aid planning in that it makes the assumptions behind any project explicit and links outcomes to indicators – helping make the assumptions that need to be encompassed within the evaluation design clear. We have also suggested that reflective practice has a strong role to play here at the stage of evaluation design. In the next chapter we detail the data collection tools, particularly creative methods that fit under these choices.

Key Points

1. It is important to plan your evaluation before you deliver the project.
2. Plan logically from step to step, either planning up or down the stages of evaluation design.
3. The design should be logical, one step leading to another.
4. It is important to reflect throughout the evaluation design process in order to identify any potential for the context, or for your views, to overly influence the evaluation design.
5. Keeping a reflective journal can help you keep track of your design choices, and help you learn and grow your skills.

Further Reading

Better Evaluation (2014) is a website designed to support people planning and conducting evaluation internationally. They have an easy to use visual tool to support you when you plan evaluations.

Bolton, G. (2010) *Reflective Practice: Writing and Professional Development* gives a very accessible demonstration of the value of written reflective practice across contexts.

Buck, A., Sobiechowska, P. and Winter, R. (2002) *Professional Experience and the Investigative Imagination: The Art of Reflective Writing* explains how creative writing can be used successfully in the context of professional learning. The authors include a set of distance-learning materials that you can use yourself.

Charities Evaluation Services (2014) is an online resource offering a range of downloadable tools to support evaluation design.

Thompson, S. and Thompson, N. (2008) *The Critically Reflective Practitioner* provides a succinct and insightful guide to reflective practice. It is designed for students and practitioners of social work, healthcare and related fields.

7

COLLECTING DATA
TO EVALUATE

Chapter Overview

- Introduction to a range of data collection tools

- Explanation of the advantages and disadvantages of a range of data collection tools

- Demonstration of the application of data collection tools in a range of vignettes

- Discussion on how to decide which data collection tools to use.

How to Choose Data Collection Tools

In this chapter we introduce a number of different ways in which evaluation data can be collected. As we have seen in the previous chapters, evaluations can be used for a variety of different reasons. They can be used to evaluate the outcomes of projects, their impact, the distance the recipients have travelled or the success (or not) of a project's process. Additionally, evaluators can be interested in studying very different types of outcomes (e.g. soft outcomes such as self-esteem or hard outcomes such as the reduction in offences) which by their very nature generate different kinds of data. To a large extent, the data collection tools chosen are determined by the type of evaluation being undertaken and the nature of the outcomes. So, for example, an impact evaluation which aims to establish how effective a project has been on school attendance will benefit from data collection tools which gather numerical data of recorded incidents of school attendance before and after the project. On the other hand, a process evaluation set up to investigate why a particular project is successful in reducing school truancy and aims to identify, for example 'what works' and 'why' would benefit from data collection tools such as in-depth interviews or focus groups with young people which aim to gather detailed data about their feelings and experiences of being part of the project.

In this chapter we begin by introducing a variety of data collection tools. We will then consider how these can be used in evaluation planning and discuss their strengths and limitations.

Qualitative versus Quantitative Data Collection Tools

One of the most straightforward ways of differentiating between the wide variety of data collection tools available is by dividing them into **qualitative** or **quantitative** techniques. Very simply, quantitative data collection techniques aim to collect data in the form of numbers whilst qualitative methods aim to collect rich, descriptive data often which takes the form of words or narrative.

Typical quantitative methods include data collected from **experiments** or **quasi-experiments**, **structured questionnaires** and **surveys**. Qualitative methods, on the other hand, include detailed, descriptive data drawn from **in-depth interviews**, **focus groups**, **group interviews** and **diaries**. Qualitative methods allow participants to talk freely and enable them to share ideas, thoughts and feelings. They enable the evaluator to look at the world in depth and aim to uncover reality as seen from the eyes of the research participants themselves, or in other words 'by examining life worlds from the inside out' (Flick, 2009).

On occasions, the actual data collection method used in an evaluation might be identical but the way the responses are measured differs and determines whether they are categorised as qualitative or quantitative methods. For example, a practitioner might be interested in finding out how useful a course they have delivered has been and decide to use a questionnaire. If they use a qualitative method of data collection, they might use a set of very 'open ended' questions which encourage participants to talk about what they have enjoyed the most and/or the least. However, if a quantitative approach is taken to the questionnaire, participants might be asked to rate the course on a scale of one to ten, from not enjoyable at all (1) to highly enjoyable (10).

The main differences between the two approaches to data collection are shown in Table 7.1.

There has traditionally been a binary view of qualitative and quantitative tools, that they should be one or the other, but as you can see from Table 7.1 tools can be both qualitative and quantitative depending on the kind of data that they generate. Quantitative data can be collected in a rich, creative way just as qualitative data could be collected on a survey form. As we have already seen in Chapter 6, thinking about the data that you want, based on your evaluation questions, comes before deciding on the tools to acquire that data. That is why this chapter comes so late in the book.

Having introduced the two broad categories of data collection tools we will now describe each type in more detail.

Table 7.1   Qualitative and quantitative data collection tools

	Qualitative Data Collection	Quantitative Data Collection
The kind of description they provide	General and detailed description Similarity and difference in themes, types, kinds, by word	Numerical description Quantification, similarity and difference in number
Cases	A few in-depth cases	As large a scale as possible, many cases
Used for	Understanding meaning	Describing and explaining scale
Common tools	Open ended questionnaires	Numerically scored questionnaires / surveys
	Narrative interview questions	Numeric interview questions
	Narrative focus group questions	Numeric focus group questions
	Qualitative observations	Numeric observations
	Narrative creative methods	Numeric creative methods
	Diaries	Assessments
	Videos and pictures	

What Characterises Quantitative Data Collection

There are many different ways of collecting quantitative data. The key feature of quantitative methods is that they collect numerical data. However, there are a number of different ways in which numbers can be used. One very simple way of collecting numerical data might be to ask participants to rate a course on a scale of one to ten. The numbers are used to represent participants' feelings and allow the evaluator to very quickly gain a sense of how well a course is received – are people scoring it high or low? Another way of collecting quantitative data might involve simply counting the frequency of an event and comparing it with some other measure. For example, a practitioner might be interested in counting the number of incidents of youth nuisance that are recorded after an intervention and comparing this count with the number of incidents before the intervention. If a difference is found this might enable the evaluator to work out if the intervention is having a positive or negative effect on youth nuisance – or, in fact, if it is having any effect at all. Often numerical data is collected as it allows us to undertake a 'statistical analysis' of our results. This sounds very complicated but in actual fact is quite straightforward. There are a range of statistical tests that allow us to interrogate our results in more depth. We might find that our intervention has reduced the number of recorded incidents of youth nuisance. However, it might be difficult for us to judge how much of a reduction is needed before we can say with confidence that our intervention was responsible. A statistical test enables us to work out whether our results are 'just the result of chance' or something more meaningful. We will discuss some simple statistical procedures later on in the book; however the key to understanding the different kinds of tests is recognising the different ways in which numbers can be used. We will introduce some of these below.

One common feature of all the techniques so far discussed is that they all use numbers to record responses and observations. However, the ways the numbers have been used in each example, differ. These differences are known as types of scaling. The most widely used methods of scaling are nominal, ordinal and interval.

Nominal scales

The nominal level of measurement works with **variables** that are 'categorical' and can produce **frequency counts**. For certain characteristics (e.g. male or female, employed or unemployed, smoker or non-smoker, passive or active) people or their behaviour is placed in a category by the pure fact that they possess or reflect that particular variable. Categories cannot overlap. Categories are then given numbers (for example, 1 for a yes, two for a no). In evaluations using this form of scale, responses (for example, to a question) or behaviour (in an observation) are noted and placed into the identified categories by their number. The number of responses in each category can then be counted. This provides a quantitative measure of both the frequency of responses in each category and generates numbers that can be used for further analysis. Examples of this are provided below:

Question: If the local sports centre was open until 10pm, would you use it?

Yes (1) ___   No (2) ____   Don't know (3) ____

Similarly, an evaluator might be interested in observing and recording the social behaviour of young people in a skate park to collect data about anti-social behaviour. In this example, the evaluator might produce an observation chart including the categories of 'anti-social', pro-social and neutral behaviour.

By observing the young people in the park, observed behaviours are categorised, entered on the observation sheet as a number and then counted: e.g., Anti-Social (1), Pro-Social (2), Neutral (3).

Such data is very simple to collect and make sense of. It also allows the evaluator to draw some themes from the data, such as who would come to the centre if they did open later or whether behaviour in the park is a problem. Also, by allocating categories numbers, this enables the evaluator to carry out some simple analysis, such as frequency counts or working out which is the most common score – e.g. the **mode** (this is a measure of **central tendency**; we will talk more about this in Chapter 9). Allocating categories numbers also gives you the basis for carrying out certain types of **statistical analysis**, or would allow you to use a computer program to analyse or display your data. We will discuss descriptive data analysis in the Chapter 9.

Often **pie charts**, **bar charts** and **frequency distributions** are used to visually depict the results of frequency counts. There are examples of these in the next chapter.

Ordinal scales

This type of scaling is used when there are no clearly defined 'categories' such as male or female, and the issue or question answer can be positioned on a continuum instead, e.g. how happy you are today. The most common use of this form of scale is in **psychometric tests** which aim to investigate people's attitudes or opinions. In Table 7.2 there are some examples of questions that use ordinal scaling. In the examples we have used in Table 7.2 a number is assigned to each point on the scale (the participant doesn't always see the numbers). These numbers enable us to carry out a quantitative analysis of our data.

Question1: On a scale of 1 to 10 (with 1 being the lowest and 10 the highest) how happy do you feel right now?

Or

Question 2: On the scale below indicate how much you agree with the statement (this is known as a **Likert scale**).

Table 7.2   Likert scale

	Strongly Disagree	Disagree	Neutral	Agree	Strongly Agree
I am happy					

Or

Question 3: Rate the characteristics of police officers by ticking the boxes that you think apply to them (this is known as a **semantic differential scale**).

Table 7.3   Semantic differential scale

Police officers are:	Honest		Tough		Energetic	
	Dishonest		Tender		Lazy	

Or

Question 4: How is your mood today? Indicate on the dotted line the level of your mood today (this is known as **a visual analogue scale**).

Low ————————————High

Or:

Using the sticky faces, choose the one that you feel most closely reflects your mood right now.

Figure 7.1   Visual analogue scale

This last example, shows how data collection tools can be creative and engaging, yet still provide accurate data. The faces in this example can be attributed a value so that the data can still be numerically analysed. This is discussed in more detail later in this chapter.

Interval scales

An interval scale uses equal units. For example, time, weight and temperature are all measured in equal units. Interval scales measure the same amounts for the same scale units. If you were timing how fast a participant completed a task before and after an intervention, is would be likely that you would be using an interval scale. Here are some examples of interval scales.

- Amount of cannabis used each week by the participant in grams (e.g. for a drug rehabilitation programme)
- Time taken to complete benefit forms each week in minutes (e.g. for a life skills programme)
- Weight gained/lost each week in kilos (e.g. for an eating disorder programme).

To summarise, in quantitative methods, there are three types of measurement, nominal, ordinal and interval scales and each use numbers in different ways, as shown in Table 7.4.

Table 7.4   Types of scales

Scale	Description	Type of Number Generated
Nominal	Only tells us that you are in one category, not another	Frequency counts
Ordinal	Tells us your position in a group but not the distance between you and any other person in the group	Ratings
Interval	Tells us how many intervals on the scale each person is from anyone else	Measurements on a scale

Pause for Thought

Think of evaluations that you have been involved in or read about:

- Were any of these data collection tools used?
- Were they appropriate?

What Characterises Qualitative Data Collection

Evaluators who use qualitative data collection methods are much more interested in collecting detailed descriptions about phenomena and, as you would expect, the best way to collect such data is to ask someone to talk (or write) about their experiences. Hence, the standard unit of measurement in qualitative approaches is words or **narrative**. However, there are lots of other ways that people can express their experiences and for qualitative data to be collected – visually, as in art work, puppetry or mime, or through music or dance. For the qualitative evaluator, there are lots of ways to gather detailed, rich data about people's thoughts, feelings and experiences, the challenge is how to encapsulate that data and make sense of it.

The most common ways of collecting narrative data is through asking questions, either through questionnaires which use open ended questions, interviews or focus groups, and asking participants either to write or talk through their responses. As we explain below there are a range of ways that such data can be prompted. Once the evaluation has been conducted the evaluator is likely to have a vast amount of written (or taped data) that needs to be analysed. Just as quantitative data collection tools use a number of different ways to measure participants' responses, qualitative data collection tools use a variety of units of measurement to analyse 'words' and narrative. Individual words, sentences, paragraphs or whole stories are all potential units of analysis. Silverman (2013) compares these different approaches to analysing narrative to 'chopping wood', 'you can chop sticks, branches or whole trees, or look at the forest as it stands'.

Qualitative data can also be collected in a variety of forms. We most traditionally tend to think about interviews and focus groups when we talk about qualitative data, but surveys can also be used to collect this kind of data. Diaries and arts based methods certainly collect qualitative data – more on this later when we discuss creative methods. Narratives can be used to show distance travelled, but this is currently not a common practice. This narrative data can also be used quantitatively (just to add to your confusion!), for example if you counted the frequency of a word you would be using a quantitative analytical approach rather than a qualitative one, but more of that in Chapter 9.

Pause for Thought

Think of evaluations that you have been involved in or read about:

- Were any of these data collection tools used?
- Were they appropriate?

So, having clearly established that qualitative and quantitative data can both be collected with a range of tools, we will now describe the tools themselves and discuss some of their advantages and disadvantages. Because the mixing of data and data collection tools is common in evaluation practice, we devote the whole of Chapter 8 to discussing it in more depth.

Data Collection Tools

Questionnaires/surveys

Numeric, or quantitative questionnaires seek to find defined answers from a large population. They are the basis of much quantitative evaluation. This approach involves asking a large population a set of standardised questions with answers that are quantifiable (on an ordinal, nominal or interval scale). The focus is on simple measures from large samples, and they usually aim to support or reject a **hypothesis**. They may also be used to identify and measure **variables**, such as the variation of television viewing by age of viewer.

Qualitative questionnaires also seek to find a range of views or beliefs or experiences about the topic under investigation from a relatively large population. This approach involves asking a moderately large population a set of standardised questions that require open written answers. The focus is on gaining a relatively large selection of views to build a picture of what might be happening.

Many surveys combine quantitative and qualitative questions so as to establish the scale of the issue as well as an understanding of the issue – there will be more on this in the next chapter on mixed methods.

There are four key ways of administering questionnaires. They can be sent out by post, emailed as electronic surveys (such as SurveyMonkey or Fluid), or conducted over the telephone or in person, face to face. The major issue with questionnaires is that of response rates. Think of the last time someone rang you to conduct market research – did you answer their questions or put the phone down? Have you ever avoided street based market researchers? Do you ever complete questionnaires sent to you by post? If you are sending the questionnaire to stakeholders who have a good buy in, or who know you well, then you are likely to get a good response rate. The less you know someone, and the less meaningful your questions are to them, the less likely they are to answer them. So, the way that you send out the survey may also influence the number of people that complete it – people without computers, will not, for example, be able to complete an electronic survey for you.

When should you use questionnaires?

This will really depend on the evaluation question or the hypothesis and variables you have identified (e.g. 'I hypothesise that this programme leads to positive change for the young people'). Some additional questions might help you decide whether to use questionnaires or not:

- Can I get the information I need from a questionnaire?
- Is a questionnaire the most appropriate method? (Will your stakeholders fill them in?)

- Are other methods excluded? How much time do you have? (Questionnaires are relatively quick and cheap to administer)
- How many people do you want to get this information from? (Questionnaires are suited to large samples).

Questionnaires are accessible to many people. They can allow you to reach a large geographically dispersed population at a low cost, and they are not dependent on people turning up to an evaluation session. They can be completed remotely. This means that they could be used as follow up, sometime after your programme has ended. An allied benefit is that the respondents can take the time that they need to complete them; they need not be rushed, and this may lead to better quality data – as long as the questionnaire is simple to follow. Questionnaires are generally thought to reduce the potential for evaluator bias, as they are less open to interpretation when designed well. Questionnaires can also be completed anonymously, helping to protect individuals and enabling you to ask more potentially sensitive questions than you might in an interview. The main advantage of questionnaires is that they provide highly structured data and so are easier to analyse than lengthy open interview data. This does not mean that they produce better answers to evaluation questions, in fact their ease of administration and analysis equally serves as a disadvantage in that it leads many evaluators to choose them over other methods as they seem simpler to conduct.

Questionnaires do not work well when there are complex or unclear questions. They rely on all the participants being able to understand what is being asked, in the same way. If they are conducted electronically or by post then there is also no opportunity for participants to seek clarification. This need for clarity means that the questionnaire is restricted to relatively simple questions. The standardisation of the questionnaires means that there is no opportunity to probe further for more detail or explanation, and this can reduce the quality of data captured.

How to design questionnaires

Designing questionnaires generally takes more time than anticipated. It may appear simple, but the process requires care and thought, as you only have one chance at it. There are three main questions to ask at start of design:

- What information do I need to answer my evaluation question?
- What question can I ask that will provide me with data, that when analysed, will give me such information?
- How am I going to analyse data I get from such questions to answer my evaluation question?

You need to try to keep your questionnaire as short as possible, as this will help response rates. You should spend a great deal of time thinking about how best to phrase, set out and structure your questions. Before you begin your evaluation, always pilot your questionnaire first. This means testing out your questionnaire on a group of willing people who are able to give you constructive feedback. This will enable you to check whether your questionnaire makes sense, whether your language is appropriate, and whether your questions address the issues you intended it to, etc.

Open and closed questions

Whether using qualitative or quantitative methods, you will want to consider whether to use open or closed questions in your data collection tools. Here is a clear guide on when to use each. You may want a range of open and closed questions in your data collection tools.

Use closed questions if...

- You require quantitative data
- You have a clear idea of likely responses
- Responses are likely to be simple
- You need to use predetermined responses.

Use open questions if...

- You require qualitative data
- You are unsure of likely responses
- Responses are likely to be complex
- The respondents' own words are important.

Try and begin your questionnaire with straightforward closed questions requiring factual responses (get them into it). Avoid complex or lengthy questions at the start, and group questions on similar themes – don't jump from topic to topic. Leave any personal or 'threatening' questions to the end when they are more used to the questionnaire. Here are some of the most common mistakes in designing questionnaires:

- Ambiguous/complex wording: just because it is clear to you doesn't mean it is to your respondents
- Technical jargon, inappropriate language
- Leading questions: 'How often do you take part in normal healthy sport?'
- Double barrelled questions: 'Do you agree boxing is dangerous and should be banned?'
- Threatening questions that seek sensitive or personal data: 'What offences have you committed recently?'

Because of the difficulty of getting a questionnaire right first time, we suggest that you run a pilot. This means designing the questionnaire and then getting some people, similar to the participants that you will work with, to answer it. This allows you to check the wording and the sequence of the questions, see how long it takes to complete, and allows you to test whether the data that comes back is in fact useful to you.

Vignette 7.1   Youth Volunteering Perceptions and Motivation in South Africa, by the National Youth Development Agency (NYDA) and the Government of Flanders (NYDA, 2012)

This study was to inform the ways in which volunteering was promoted in South Africa. The survey was conducted by the Volunteer Service Enquiry Southern Africa (VOSESA) and was completed by 300 young people. The questionnaire features 132 questions that seek quantitative data on the reasons for and attitudes to volunteering, for example:
'If rich people volunteer they should be financially compensated.

Strongly agree

Agree

Neither agree or disagree

Disagree

Strongly disagree'

The surveys were conducted in person door to door to ensure a higher response rate than a postal survey.
   An excerpt from the executive summary of findings provides a flavour of the type of data and results that were generated with this survey:

A common understanding of volunteering as an unpaid activity that involves work or is charitable emerged from survey respondents. Their understanding of volunteering encompassed 'doing work without receiving and expecting financial compensation' (35 percent), 'helping others' (29 percent), 'assistance, service provision and support within one's community' (12 percent), 'supporting and assisting institutions' (10 percent), 'a means of increasing one's employability' (8 percent), 'activities done out of empathy and love' (1 percent), and 'doing something out of "choice" and free-will' (2 percent). A few respondents (4 percent) lacked an understanding of volunteering. (NYDA, 2012: 11)

This demonstrates that numeric data from this survey allowed the survey team to understand trends in views of the South African youth to volunteering.
   Following this quantitative phase there were six focus groups conducted to further explore the themes that emerged from the quantitative data – we will discuss this in the section on focus groups.
   Reflecting on this we may wonder at how many young people were put off by the 132-item questionnaire, and how much that has skewed the data.

Interviews

Interview methods are usually qualitative, but could also collect quantitative data, and narrative data could be analysed in a quantitative way. The evaluator is central in the process of an interview – interviewers accept that they influence the evaluation by asking questions and relating to the interviewee. There is no attempt to claim that these are impartial and objective or unobtrusive, as the evaluator is asking the participants direct questions.

When to use interviews

Interviews allow you to explore the interpretive issues of 'Why' change has happened and 'How' it happened. Because of the time taken to do interviews they are usually limited to smaller samples. They aim to collect rich data. As ever, it is not as simple as just asking someone questions.

An interview is basically a structured conversation where the evaluator asks each participant the same series of questions. This allows the evaluator to capture the experiences in the respondents' own words. Their answers can provide insight into experiences, practices, beliefs, perceptions, etc. Interviews can produce 'unexpected' data because they are grounded in the respondents' frames of reference rather than that of the evaluator. Because they are carried out face to face they allow the evaluator to also assess body language. Difficult questions can be explained, and the evaluator can use interpersonal skills to build rapport, allowing them to access more detailed or more personal information. There are also some downsides to interviewing. It is a very resource intensive activity, taking time to do, and time to write up and analyse. Interview data may also be perceived to be more open to bias and interpretation as the interviewer may ask questions or interpret data to fit their preconceived ideas. The interview process yields a textual answer to a question. This can be complex data meaning more complex analysis. And, of course, despite the evaluator's best efforts, interviewees may not want to talk to you, so you may not get any, or quality data.

How to design an interview

There are two main types of interviews, structured and semi-structured. The structuring refers to the extent to which you decide upon and fix the questions prior to the interview. This is more like a continuum than a choice. At one extreme there is the fully structured interview, which is rather like a verbal questionnaire, with fixed questions in a set order; at the other extreme is an unstructured interview schedule with only some loosely defined areas for discussion.

Fully fixed interview----semi-structured interview----loosely defined interview

Here is some more information on each to help you decide which to use.

Structured interviews have a list of questions. This set list is aimed at reducing interviewer error by standardising the process. The assumption is that the set list of questions will reveal any variations accurately and will ensure that everyone has the same opportunity to say the same things. This means that these interviews are based on use of a fixed interview schedule so that the same questions are asked in the same way with each interviewee. This also helps the answers to be aggregated and analysed. This seems a very sensible approach, but as with all these tools, there are some potential problems.

As there is a fixed set of questions, the interviewees may tend to answer the questions related to what they think is the most socially desirable answer. This is called **social desirability bias**. For example, young people may feel socially bound to say that they have learnt a lot from your programme, as they suspect that is the answer that you want. A second issue is that the fixed questions mean that the interviewer and interviewees may end up with different understandings of the questions and answers as the fixed schedule does not provide scope for exploration of meanings. Here is an example to demonstrate what we mean:

Interviewer: How often have you offended since you started this programme?

(N.B. the interviewer and interviewee may have different understandings of the term 'offended')

Interviewee: Not often

(N.B. the interviewee and interviewer may have very different views about what 'not much' means)

To overcome some of these issues, many evaluators use semi-structured interviews.

Semi-structured interviews are less about maximising reliability and validity, and more about the formation of ideas from the interviewees' perspectives. The focus in these interviews is on the respondents' point-of-view rather than the interviewer's concerns. Because of this, going 'off the point' is not necessarily dis-couraged. The semi-structured interview schedule will list a range of potential questions, as an aide memoire, but clarification, diversions, additional questions and so on are all allowed in between. In this way the semi-structured interview has flexibility in direction, structure and focus. These interviews tend to feel more like conversations than question and answer sessions, and they produce detailed rather than 'quick to code' data. The semi-structured interview schedule will:

- Create a certain amount of order on topic areas (flow)
- Formulate questions or topics that help you get the info you need without being restrictive
- Help the interviewer avoid loaded terms, jargon, error
- Enable you to record standard elements of demographic information useful for contextualisation.

They will take some preparation. It is hard to remember to follow your semi-structured questions, build rapport, pursue interesting answers from the interviewee and note down your answers. We would suggest that you pilot your schedule and practise using it before the real deal so that you feel as at ease as possible.

Whether you are using structured or semi-structured interview schedules, you will have a second decision to make about data capture. That is whether to write notes or to record answers. Writing notes can be difficult when you are trying to actively listen and ask questions; however, recording the answers will require that you get permission (possibly from parents/carers), and the presence of a digital recorder might put some people off. When you have captured your data you will also have to write up your notes or tapes so that you can analyse the answers to questions, and this can also be a time-consuming process.

Vignette 7.2   The NSPCC Qualitative Study of Children, Young People and 'Sexting' (Ringrose et al., 2012)

Sexting has been conventionally defined as 'exchange of sexual messages or images' (Ringrose et al., 2012) and 'the creating, sharing and forwarding of sexually suggestive nude or nearly nude images' (Lenhart, 2009: 6) through mobile phones and/or the internet.

The small-scale qualitative study was to respond to and enhance understanding of the complex nature of sexting and the role of mobile technologies within peer teen networks. The researchers 'began with an open mind, being ourselves undecided at the outset as to whether "sexting" is a coherent phenomenon that constitutes "a problem" for which policy intervention is required' (Ringrose et al., 2012: 25).

The study was carried out in two London schools and included 22 students. A semi-structured interview schedule was used to allow the team to follow key questions but in a flexible and responsive way given the sensitive nature of the discussions. Here is an excerpt from one of the conversations:
Sexting scenarios: Boys 'owning' girls' bodies

R: Well like say I got a girlfriend I would ask her to write my name on her breast and then send it to me and then I would upload it onto Facebook or Bebo or something like that. But like some people would say who it is, but some people won't.

I: Oh okay. So like would you – are you going out with someone at the moment?

R: Yeah.

I: So have you go pictures of her like that?

R: Yeah.

(Kamal, Year 8, School Two.
Taken from Ringrose et al. (2012: 27))

The study showed overall that sexual threat is often from technology-mediated peer pressure. Sexting is coercive and mainly affects girls. Technology amplifies the issue and reveals wider sexual problems in society. It can affect young children and is culturally specific. This all pointed to the need for resources to tackle the issue.

Reflecting on this we can see the value of the small scale in revealing meaning, although the research does beg the question as to what extent these views are held by children across the UK and beyond.

Focus groups

Focus groups are essentially interviews in a group setting. These can be more convenient than interviews in that you talk to a group of young people all at the same time, so the whole process takes less time. There are of course, equal disadvantages. Managing a focus group means that you will have to manage a group as well as asking your evaluation questions which may be demanding. In a group setting you may also have a greater propensity for the social desirability bias, as young people may not want to say what they really think in front of their friends – conversely, being with friends may give them the courage to say things that they would not on their own in an interview! You will also have to be attentive to how you get individual young people to speak – you may find that one or two young people seem to dominate the focus group and you might need strategies to manage that.

Aside from these considerations, focus groups work in the same way as interviews. You may have a structured or semi-structured schedule as per interviews, and you will also need to decide whether to write notes or record the conversation. You could also write key points on a flip chart to enable the group to reflect on what they have said. These all need transcribing in the same way as the interviews.

There are other considerations too with focus groups and interviews. The setting of the conversation is important. It should provide the right level of informality so that participants feel at ease rather than intimidated. The relationship between the evaluator and participant also needs to be established carefully – if the participants are distrustful of you or do not like you, you are unlikely to get good data. You need to develop a good trusting relationship with them, and have the right level of formality, not too formal, nor too relaxed and informal. You will also need to make decisions about how to record the data. There are two different approaches, one is to write down everything that is said, but it is often hard to write notes at speed whilst maintaining eye contact and the flow of the conversation. The other option is to record what is said on a Dictaphone, but that will (a) need consent from the participant and (b) need to be transcribed at a later date which is a slow and laborious process (taking about three times as long as the initial conversation).

Vignette 7.3   Returning to the Youth Volunteering Perceptions and Motivation in South Africa, by the National Youth Development Agency (NYDA) and the Government of Flanders (NYDA, 2012)

Six focus groups were conducted across South Africa with between eight and 10 participants in each. The focus groups had structured questions to ensure consistency of data. These were concerning their understanding of volunteering, perception of volunteering, involvement, motivations and recommendations to promote youth volunteering. The discussions were between one and two hours long.

An example of the findings shows the insights that they gained from the focus groups which provided them with cultural shades of meaning within the overall trends of the quantitative survey:

The Lenasia group listed community-orientated events, such as volunteering at cultural events in the community, burials, weddings, general community events, soup kitchens and activities to address pollution affecting the community. The Hindi word provided by the group was 'sevakaro', which translates as 'to serve or to be of service'. The Mayfair group also focused on community initiatives,

(Continued)

(Continued)

but differentiated between the forms that volunteering takes in affluent and impoverished communities. Volunteering within affluent communities was seen as 'helping the underprivileged', whilst in underprivileged communities volunteering represented an opportunity for employability. (NYDA, 2012: 15)

Reflecting on this we have clear depth and richness on the data adding to the quantitative survey results that we saw in Vignette 7.1. Together we can see that these create a well-balanced report, we talk more about how to mix methods like this in the next chapter.

Diaries

In order to fully assess the process of change for young people, you might want to ask them to write a diary each day or week that they are on your programme. You could allow the young people to fill in the diary as an optional activity or make it a compulsory part of the programme. The idea with diaries is that they prompt individuals to reflect on a regular basis on the changes that are happening to them, and they can therefore help you understand what is changing and why.

For example: At the end of each day of the programme please fill in the diary sheet:

Date:

What did I do? (Activity):

What did I think about the day? (Thoughts):

How did the day make me feel? (Feelings):

How to design diary tools

You could structure the pages of the diary so that they reflect on key evaluation questions for you over time, or leave them completely open ended – rather like the structured and semi-structured interview schedule choices.

As a diary is a personal document you will need to be very clear about what you will use and how you will use it. The young people may also want their diaries back as they are personal, so you may need to factor that in. You could transcribe key parts of their diary, or the whole document depending on the resources that you have and the quality of the data. As they are individual reflective accounts you need to be prepared for the young people to not engage at all, or engage fully but not answer your questions.

Vignette 7.4   Pakistani Mobile Phone Use (Kamran, 2010)

This research qualitatively investigated the mobile phone calling and texting patterns among young people in Pakistan. Initially, the data was gathered from

77 college students aged 17–21 years, who completed 24-hour mobile phone communication diaries. This was followed by 23 in-depth interviews with the college students to collect detailed background information. Study results revealed congruity of SMS and calling patterns among male and female young people. This research discovered that the majority of young people are extremely high users, fond of texting and low users of voice calls. It also showed that most of their mobile phone communication is peer to peer, and was equally positive and negative in nature. Very low priced prepaid packages offered by the telecom operators in Pakistan motivates high and problematic use of mobile communication among young people. The policy implications for the regulatory body were to educate young people about the appropriate use of mobile phone technology, and the issuance of a code of advertising to the telecom operators in Pakistan.

Reflecting on this perhaps begs the question as to who the findings are for. Was the intention to influence young people's behaviour, the telephone providers', or the policy makers'? Focusing on the audience in report writing will be picked up again in Chapter 10. Open-ended evaluations can often lead to general findings like this. This is why we have advocated that you have clear questions and a clear design in mind before you start, so that you get the data that you want for the audience you are targeting.

Documentary evidence

Every programme is documented in some way. There may be a contract, a programme description, an advert, monitoring sheets, letters, or emails from practitioners and parents/carers. There is usually a wealth of electronic and paper documents to hand. Documentary evidence also includes policy documents, journals and articles, and newspaper or electronic media. These can all be used in your evaluation.

How to use documentary data

Collect together all the documents that you can find that relate to the programme. If they are internal documents you may need to check that you have permission to use them. Read through them with your evaluation questions to hand and decide which are relevant. They may be relevant because they provide positive and negative data for your evaluation questions. Discard all the documents that are not relevant. Anonymise the documents by removing any people's names, job titles or place names that could identify them. When you use them in your data you should refer to them by title and date, by saying for example:

'The data in the *Project Monitoring Form (2010)* shows that the young people on the project gained outcomes week by week'.

Now you can analyse this like any other qualitative data set, as we will discuss in the next chapter. As you can see documents are very convenient to use as they already exist.

Vignette 7.5 The Heartland Alliance Youth Media Program (Heartland Alliance Social Impact Research Center, 2014)

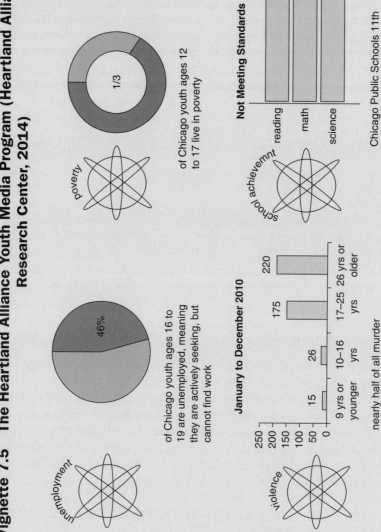

unemployment

46%

of Chicago youth ages 16 to 19 are unemployed, meaning they are actively seeking, but cannot find work

poverty

1/3

of Chicago youth ages 12 to 17 live in poverty

Not Meeting Standards

reading 69%
math 71%
science 75%

school achievemnt

Chicago Public Schools 11th graders are not meeting reading, math, and science standards

violence

January to December 2010

250
200
150
100
50
0

9 yrs or younger — 15
10–16 yrs — 26
17–25 yrs — 175
26 yrs or older — 220

nearly half of all murder victims in Chicago are between the ages of 10 to 25

Figure 7.2   Heartland Alliance data extract (Heartland, 2014)

In this example the Heartland Alliance employed the Social Research Impact Center to evaluate their youth media programme in Chicago. One of the first steps was to establish the context that the programme was operating in. They did this by reviewing and summarising documentary evidence. The results are shown in Figure 7.2 in an accessible format.

Reflecting on this we can quickly gain an overview of the nature of the young people in Chicago; however, this does beg the question of what data is missing. Why are there only four graphs? What is being left out? Have the authors selected all the negative statistics and left the more positive ones?

Assessments

Assessments are essentially questionnaires that have been written by academics and tested rigorously to prove that they do accurately measure what they set out to measure. There are literally hundreds of assessments available to 'measure' young people. Some stakeholders only value these assessment tools and dismiss assessments devised by evaluators in the field. Assessments are really useful tools in that they usually have in-built analysis and are easy to report from; however, a disadvantage can be that they have a lot of questions which may be off putting to young people. A second disadvantage to these data collection tools can be the cost associated with some of them. They also may not measure exactly what you want to measure.

An example of a short and free validated assessment tool is the Rosenberg Self-Esteem Inventory which has been in popular use since 1965. This tool essentially asks young people to score themselves on 10 questions as follows (Rosenberg, 1965).

Instructions: Below is a list of statements dealing with your general feelings about yourself. If you strongly agree, circle SA. If you agree with the statement, circle A. If you disagree, circle D. If you strongly disagree, circle SD.

1. On the whole, I am satisfied with myself. SA A D SD
2. *At times, I think I am no good at all. SA A D SD
3. I feel that I have a number of good qualities. SA A D SD
4. I am able to do things as well as most other people. SA A D SD
5. *I feel I do not have much to be proud of. SA A D SD
6. *I certainly feel useless at times. SA A D SD
7. I feel that I'm a person of worth, at least on an equal plane with others. SA A D SD
8. *I wish I could have more respect for myself. SA A D SD
9. *All in all, I am inclined to feel that I am a failure. SA A D SD
10. I take a positive attitude towards myself. SA A D SD

Scoring: SA = 3, A = 2, D = 1, SD = 0. Items with an asterisk are reverse scored, that is, SA = 0, A = 1...

It is perhaps obvious that this is short, easy to administer, easy to analyse and generally user friendly. For this reason it has become very popular, and is very useful for measuring changes in self-esteem if used at the start and end of a programme. And this is the downside of all such assessment tools, their benefits are limited by what they set out to measure. If your programme is exclusively about self-esteem then this could be an excellent assessment tool for you to use. If self-esteem is only one of a range of outcomes, it may not be as effective for you. It would be difficult for you to have an assessment tool for each outcome that you are working towards. Deciding whether to adopt an assessment tool therefore often comes down to three things: cost, appropriateness to young people, and fit to your programme outcomes.

Vignette 7.6   Mental Toughness and Stress Resilience (Gerber et al., 2013)

The mental toughness questionnaire (MTQ) is increasingly popular in the UK. This evaluation explored whether mentally tough participants are more resilient against stress. A total of 284 high school students (99 males, 185 females) with an average age of 18 participated.

Participants were asked to fill in the 48-item MTQ (Clough et al., 2002), which measures total mental toughness and its eight subcomponents. Answers were given on a 5-point Likert-type scale ranging from 1 (strongly disagree) to 5 (strongly agree). Twenty-two items were reverse scored. Items were summed up to obtain the overall and subscale scores.

Perceived stress was assessed with the 10-item Perceived Stress Scale (PSS). The PSS draws on cognitive-transactional stress theory (Lazarus and Folkman, 1984) and measures the degree to which respondents find their lives unpredictable, uncontrollable and overloading. Answers were given on a 5-point Likert-type scale anchored at 1 (never) to 5 (very often). Four items were reverse scored.

The Beck Depression Inventory (BDI: Beck et al., 1961) was used to assess the severity of depressive symptoms. The BDI consists of 21 items, including a range of affective, behavioural, cognitive and somatic symptoms that are indicative for unipolar depression. Participants were asked to select from four alternative responses that reflect increasing levels of depressive symptomatology. Possible scores ranged from 0 to 63, with higher scores indicating more depressive symptoms.

The findings showed that high mental toughness mitigates depressive symptoms if participants perceive high stress.

Reflecting on this we can see that whilst psychometrics demonstrate scientific results, these may not have immediate use but need translating into everyday practice. We might also wonder how many of the young people that we work with would be inclined to complete a 'test' with this name, and with 40 questions?

Observations

Most data collection methods assume the answers to our questions can be found by simply 'asking' a question. However, although a useful way of gathering data, questionnaires and interviews do come with a 'health warning' as participants' responses might not always be as 'natural' or **ecologically valid** as you might like. It's not necessarily that participants go out of their way to intentionally mislead you (although of course this can happen) but the mere act of 'asking a question' and when, where and how you do it can affect the response given. One way some evaluators try to increase the 'reliability' and 'validity' of the data they collect is to observe people behaving naturally, in their everyday environment. This is reckoned to be more objective.

The key aim of this method of data collection is to observe and record data about behaviour, as it happens, in the natural environment. Observations collect behavioural data as only behaviour can be observed. We cannot observe what someone is thinking or what they believe, only what they say and do. Like questionnaires, observations can also be used for both qualitative and quantitative purposes, and we will explore both here. The rudimentary difference is that a quantitative observation would seek to devise categories of behaviour often before the observation starts and then record and 'count' the number of incidents observed that fall into each category (e.g. each time a young person uses a new skill). On the other hand a qualitative observation would record descriptions of what is happening (e.g. writing down what the young people are doing which may include the use of the new skill). The former would quantify the frequency of the behaviour, the use of the new skill, and the latter would allow you to describe the situations in which the new skill was used, and how often it was used.

Some evaluators believe observations should influence the participants as little as possible, so that they observe behaviour that is as natural as possible. For that reason, they may watch from the sidelines, trying to be as unobtrusive as possible. Other evaluators believe that they cannot fully understand the behaviour that they are observing without taking part fully. They believe that the presence of an observer will inevitably alter the behaviour of the young people, so the best way to observe natural behaviour is to join in. So we have two positions, one where an observer remains on the sidelines as an unobtrusive observer and the other where the observer gets fully involved and becomes a participant.

Unobtrusive Observer --------------------------------------- Participant Observer

If you use this data collection method, you will have to decide which position to adopt. Here are some pointers to help you decide.

Unobtrusive observation allows direct and first-hand observation as the observer can write down what they see in the moment, whereas participant observation relies on the observer remembering and writing down what they saw at the end of their involvement. Advocates claim that unobtrusive observation doesn't affect the behaviour under study and so it would therefore be better for looking at actual rather than perceived behaviour. Disadvantages of this approach are that the behaviour can be misinterpreted/misunderstood from 'outside' without insider's guidance. The peripheral position of the unobtrusive observer prevents them from asking clarifying questions. It is sometimes impossible, as certain situations are so personal that the presence of an observer will always alter behaviour. There are also a number of ethical issues with this type of observation. As it is key to the success of the method that the participants might not know they are being observed, informed consent before the observation might not be possible.

Participant observation allows the evaluator to gain an insider's perspective by taking part themselves, and by allowing them to ask the other participants questions. This means that 'why' questions can be asked, reducing the assumptions made by the observer. Some evaluators claim that participants' behaviour will be less distorted by contact with a participant observer and the observer's involvement will make the participants more willing to share their experiences, etc. Other evaluators, however, claim that it is hard to avoid the bias of your own perspective when a participant, and that we don't always understand our own cultures because we are so submerged in them. Further, data recording can be difficult as much has to be remembered and written up at the end of the activity.

How to design an observational data collection tool

All observational studies would start by identifying the behaviour, or range of behaviours that need to be observed. For example, if you are evaluating the changes in the communication skills of a group of young people, you might create a mind map of all the components of communication, so you are aware of what you will be looking for. Some examples could include:

- Eye contact
- Listening skills
- Turn taking
- Tone of voice
- OTHER…

These are then used to inform the observational schedule; they detail the things you will be observing. They usually always provide a space for 'other' behaviours that you may not have initially thought of, but that you observe and are significant.

A quantitative study would detail each behaviour, and provide a space for the observer to tally the frequency of each, as shown in Table 7.5.

A qualitative observational tool may detail a range of behaviours, or identify a single broad area of behaviours, and provide space for the observer to record pertinent details about the behaviour that is seen, as shown in Table 7.6. This means that you would need to decide what is important to observe about the behaviour.

A third approach which is also qualitative involves writing field notes. This means that you simply record everything that you see without any checklists or structure. Field notes should be descriptive and as detailed as possible to allow you to analyse them at a later date.

Table 7.5   A quantitative observational record sheet

Date:		
Group:		
Observer:		

Behaviour	No. of times the group is observed exhibiting the behaviour	Notes
Being polite		
Turn taking		
Making eye contact		

Table 7.6   A qualitative observational record sheet

Date:		
Group:		
Observer:		
Behaviour being observed: Communication		

Time	Activity	Behaviour
0–5 mins		
6–10 mins		
11–15 mins		

Common mistakes in designing observations include:

- Attempting to observe too many variables
- Not evaluating the effect of the evaluator on the subject
- Not taking a sample of times and/or locations
- Making inadequate field notes and/or over-relying on recall (your memory isn't that good...)

Vignette 7.7   Swedish Family-based Behavioural Intervention Programme for Obese Children: An Observational Study of Child and Parent Lifestyle Interpretations (Teder et al., 2013)

Family-based behavioural intervention programmes (FBIPs) against childhood obesity have shown promising results, but the mediating mechanisms have not been identified. The aim of this study was to examine changes in obese children's lifestyle habits during a 2-year FBIP, according to their own and

(Continued)

(Continued)

parents/carers' reports, the concordance between these reports and the correlations to change in post-intervention body mass indices (BMI).

Twenty-six children were observed over a 2-year FBIP. Weight and height were measured from baseline to 12 months after the end of the programme. Eating habits and physical and sedentary activity were observed and reported separately by children and parents/carers. Data were analysed with regard to concordance between parents/carers' and children's reports and association between the lifestyle reports and change in BMI at the study endpoint using descriptive statistics and parametric and non-parametric tests.

According to both children's and parents/carers' reports, the level of physical activity among the children had increased after the intervention as well as the agreement between the informants' reports. According to the children, eating habits had improved, while the parents/carers' reports showed an improvement only with regard to binge eating. The concordance between children and parents/carers regarding eating habits was slight to fair also after the intervention. No statistically significant associations between changes in lifestyle reports and changes in BMI were observed.

Child and parent reports of physical activity were found to converge and display an improvement in a 2-year FBIP, while the reports on eating habits showed a more refractory pattern. Changes in concordance and agreement between children and parents'/carers' reports did not correlate with weight reduction. Further methods development and studies of the processes during family-based interventions against childhood obesity are warranted.

Reflecting on this heavily quantitative study we can see that evaluation does not always show what you want it to. Here it has shown that the programme was not effective in reducing obesity, and we can only applaud the transparency of the evaluators in publishing the results.

Creative Methods

Many young people that we work with on a regular basis will not fill in questionnaires. These young people may have had negative experiences at school and may have negative attitudes to writing, or may have limited literacy. They may also have been screened, assessed and monitored by a range of services and so be resistant to interviews and assessments, and who can blame them.

As a result we have asked ourselves critical questions about what the data collection tools already described do, and give, to the young people. They could be critiqued as tools to allow us to mine information from the young people for our own organisational benefit, whilst detracting from the programme, causing stress to the young people, and having little benefit for them. Whilst this is, perhaps, an extreme critique, it was one that we considered at length, and one that led to our development of a creative methods toolkit.

We can think of creative methods in two ways. First, using the same quantitative and qualitative methods discussed so far in this chapter, but with a creative approach (for example, the smiley faces introduced earlier in this chapter). Second, we can consider creative methods as quite separate from quantitative and qualitative methods.

By creative methods we refer to techniques that allow activity, reflection, playfulness and focus on the evaluation questions. They include everything, from visual, symbolic and musical to physical creations. Through the development of creative evaluation methods we believe that we have aided the shift of power in evaluations, both by finding ways to engage young people in evaluation that are palatable to them, and in ensuring that the activities are part of the developmental process for the young people.

Our use of creative methods is embedded in an **action research** approach. Although we have used the 'research' word, action research is as evaluative as it is research. There are five key aspects of action research. For us, its most important principle is that it involves research 'with' rather than 'on' young people (Reason, 2003). This is a subtle repositioning of the power structures. Secondly, action research/evaluation is based in the lived experiences and socially constructed worlds of the young people (Reason and Bradbury, 2001; Ritchie and Lewis, 2003); we genuinely seek to understand what life is like for them. A third principle of action research/evaluation, is that there are benefits for the participants (Winter and Munn-Giddings, 2001) as well as the evaluator. Fourthly the approach shares power, young people are offered real choices about what they do, and each creative method engages the young people in 'power sensitive' conversations (Haraway, 1988). Finally, this approach is small scale, investigating deep stories and rich narratives from those young people that want to engage rather than seeking to quantify population-wide views. Action research/evaluation is also committed to bringing about positive changes, rather than documenting an event, and this is also a reason why we use it, as our evaluations are purposeful, leading to consolidation of good practice, and changes to poor practice.

You can probably tell that creative methods are far removed from quantitative methods, and for us, this is a deliberate move. Many of the data collection tools described so far have focused on the written and spoken word (Flewitt, 2005; Prosser, 2009). This is problematic when oral or written communication is not the preference or strength of young people, and can exclude participation (Booth, 1996). We believe that the views of all the young people who wish to participate are important if we are to understand the programme fully rather than generalising (Reinharz, 1992). In seeking these multiple voices we are aware that we are living our participatory values, and engaging in a political act, as voice is far from neutral (Alcott, 2009). Creative methods allow us to overcome these difficulties in a number of ways.

Creative methods are accessible and inclusive – anyone can be engaged in art, music, dance, modelling; anyone can express themselves in one medium or another no matter how restricted their language skills (Burke, 2008). The act of creation prioritises action over cognition, and this both engages young people, and provides them with more time to cognitively process the evaluation question than a simple verbal prompt would (Gauntlett, 2007). We believe that this provides more young people with the opportunity of engaging and provides better quality data. Because creative methods are visual, audible and physical they allow multimodal expression and are not reliant on language alone, encouraging participation and depth of expression (Jewitt, 2009). Youth culture is also increasingly multi-modal and so this form of evaluation is more in keeping with youth culture (Prosser, 2009). Because the act of creation forces participants to reflect, create, express and describe, the approach has been described as 'double reflection' in that there is reflection on what to represent, and on how to represent it, leading to a richer thought process (Bolton, 2010). This contrasts with the process of answering a question, which can result in a single thought retrieved from the short-term memory bank. Gauntlett and Holzworth (2006) describe the difference as 'working through' the evaluation question rather than responding to the question. For this reason, many argue that creative methods surface deeper data and more of the 'intricacies' of their lives (Alatt and Dixon, 2004: 80). One of the most comprehensive longitudinal evaluations of youth work projects in the UK reviewed 'Positive Futures' over three years. This national evaluation also chose creative tools above quantitative methods, stating:

> One of the points of departure of this research from other elements of the existing monitoring and evaluation is our contention that meaningful evaluation of initiatives such as Positive Futures requires a methodological strategy that goes beyond quantitative analysis. It is only when the real benefits rather than spurious assumptions of quantitative research are utilised to support a qualitative approach that we can achieve an evaluation which communicates the social structures, processes, 'feelings' and context in which the participants find themselves, and in turn how they respond to such pressures. (Crabbe, 2006: 19–20)

The Positive Futures evaluation (Crabbe, 2006: 51) collected multiple visual artefacts created by young people. These included maps in which they demarcated safe and dangerous areas, collages about themselves, and personal time lines. Analysis of young people's timelines revealed the complex and non-linear nature of young people's journeys, and the need for adaptability in working with them. The complexity of these journeys and the youth work process needed to accompany them would not have been captured with a simple statistical account of life-long activities, the visual nature of the data brought them to life.

As with the Positive Futures evaluation, a range of creative tools can create rich tapestries or 'bricolages' of meaning (Yardley, 2008) and are deemed highly appropriate for the social sciences by many (Dadds and Hart, 2001; Broussine, 2008; Plowright, 2011). This is not to say that they are widely accepted. Creative methods remain undervalued by evaluators that work in the positivistic paradigm (McIntosh and Sobiechowska, 2009). Creative methods are undervalued because they are not 'objective', 'valid' or 'reliable' according to positivistic assumptions. If the post-positivistic paradigm is adopted these methods are not problematic, as this paradigm does not seek objectivity or validity in the same way. Creative methods have also been derided by some as distorting data as they are non-naturalistic, they create data in a deliberately unnatural way (Pink, 2007), again, this is only an issue if you are working within a positivistic paradigm. To overcome this, many evaluators combine creative methods with quantitative methods in a mixed method approach (see the next chapter). When choosing to use these methods you may feel the tension between meeting the needs of the young people who would benefit from a creative approach, and the needs of the stakeholders who want a statistical approach (Walmsley and Johnson, 2003). For this reason the practical use (the method) and the data sought (the evaluation questions) should both point to the use of creative methods (McIntosh and Sobiechowska, 2009).

Setting the paradigmatic assumptions to one side, some problems remain with creative methods. Firstly, not everyone is creative, and for some young people the sight of paint and collage materials is equally as terrifying as a questionnaire. Young people may need assurance that it is the process, not the end product that is of value. Secondly, there are few ethical guidelines that refer specifically to creative methods (Prosser, 2000b), and we know from our experience that the depth of reflection in creative methods may lead young people to think about, and even disclose more personal information than they might when answering a direct question. This means that you need to carefully consider what you ask, how you ask it, and how you ensure the safety of participants in creative methods.

There is no limit to creative tools. There are hundreds of activities that you could do, and the creative approach can be used for both qualitative and quantitative data. Deciding what to do is a case of working out which activity the young people will most enjoy and benefit from, or allowing them to decide, and which activity will give you the best quality data for your questions.

Here are a few that we have used, and many more can be found on the Methodspace website.

Shields

Shields are essentially questionnaires, but written in a more creative way. The outline of a shield can be divided up so that each box represents an evaluation question. You can read out the questions and ask the young people to draw or write an answer in each corresponding box. Shields are obviously therefore appropriate for any evaluation question, qualitative or quantitative.

Line outs

Just as you have an ordinal scale on evaluation forms, so you can create such a scale on the floor. You can tape a line on the floor and then read out your evaluation questions. The young people can stand on the line to represent their self-score. The advantage of this approach is that they can then discuss why they are standing where they are with friends next to them, helping them to refine their answers. This is quick and simple but will require that you either draw what you see or take a photograph (as we did here) to record where people stood on the line. You can label the line with pre-prepared words or you can add numbers to it depending on what data you want to collect.

Journey maps

Figure 7.3   A journey map

A journey map is a visual representation of the life of a young person drawn either as a line on a graph showing ups and downs, or as a route map showing choices and crossroads. You will need to think about how much guidance you give when you set this activity up – you could describe it step by step or leave it open ended. You could give stickers with set words on, or leave the young people to do what they want. You will certainly need some questions to help them to create these maps. Overall they record key details of the young person's life and how the programme has fitted in. You can add photographs to illustrate your evaluation, and/or analyse them visually, and/or get the young people to explain them so that you have a narrative data set too. An example is shown in Figure 7.3.

Lego

Three-dimensional play is engaging. After a period of free play and re-familiarisation, you can ask the young people to make a model of something. In the example shown in Figure 7.4 we asked young people make a Lego model of who they are at school. Young people will need varying degrees of support to engage, and you will want to prepare some questions and prompts to help. As with the journey maps you can use photos of these illustratively; you can analyse them visually, or you can collect narrative data alongside them. Gauntlett (2007) famously used Lego to research identity in adults.

Creative canvases

As you have probably gathered, you can use art to any effect. Here we let young people have free play with a canvas and art resources, asking them to reflect on what they got out of a week-long programme. They divided the canvas up and each used a space to great effect.

Figure 7.4   A Lego model

This is a small selection of creative tools. Puppetry, dance, drama, music can all be used to great effect as data collection tools. Increasingly databases and analytical tools are becoming more sophisticated at storing multi-media data. Some (Views, Substance) even allow you to write multi-media case studies so that you can make full use of this rich data. For more ideas of how to evaluate creatively please see Sage's Methodspace where we have published a full toolkit.

Tools to Show Distance Travelled

One way to overcome the shortcomings of published assessment tools is to design your own measures of the distance travelled by the young people. The obvious advantage of this approach is that you can tailor it to the needs of the young people and your programme outcomes. This approach is increasingly common, as demonstrated by youth work organisations such as the Prince's Trust in the UK, who use their own design of distance travelled tool. The approach may convince most stakeholders and funders of the effectiveness of your interventions, but there will, no doubt, be some agencies or organisations that will insist on an externally validated assessment tool as described above. So it is always worth checking with your stakeholders before you invest time in designing your own distance travelled tool.

Essentially a distance travelled tool seeks to measure the young people's capabilities against the programme outcomes at the start of the programme and at the end (Siegel and Castellan, 1988). This means asking them the same set of questions in a classic pre-test, post-test measure. Most distance travelled tools collect quantitative data, so that you can quantify the change numerically. This doesn't mean you can't design qualitative tools to assess how far your young people have moved on, by, for example, asking young people to describe the changes that they have experienced.

How to show distance travelled

The first step is to decide on the outcomes that you need to measure – try to only include the ones that are really vital to your programme. We tend to ask practitioners to only have five or six outcomes, otherwise you get too many questions for young people to answer. The second step is to try to convert your outcomes into sentences or phrases that young people will understand and be able to relate to. Some young people, for example, may not understand the term 'self-efficacy', so that outcome might need changing into something like 'I believe that I can achieve what I want in life'. Having changed your outcomes into other words or sentences, you then need to decide on how you will measure them.

    You could use an ordinal scale going from one upwards. Deciding on the upper number is a case of deciding how much change you anticipate, how meaningful the scale will be to young people, and whether you want a middle 'fence sitting' number or not. One to five scales allow someone to sit on the fence by ticking a middle score, a one to six scale means that answers are over half way or below half way. A one to 10 scale is easy to convert into percentages, but could a young person really discriminate between ten different shades of being able to communicate?

My communication skills (one is low):   1 2 3 4 5 6 7 8 9 10

My communication skills (one is low):   1 2 3 4 5

My communication skills (one is low):   1 2 3 4 5 6

To overcome these difficulties, some people use Likert scales, so young people tick a box which has a verbal label like the examples shown below:

My communication skills are: Excellent / Good / Average / Okay / Rubbish

My communication skills are excellent: Strongly disagree / disagree / agree / strongly agree

---

Finally, you then need to decide how to present the questions. You could present them in a list in a questionnaire, or you could be more creative and present them as stars, ladders, snakes – anything linear really, such as the example in Figure 7.5.

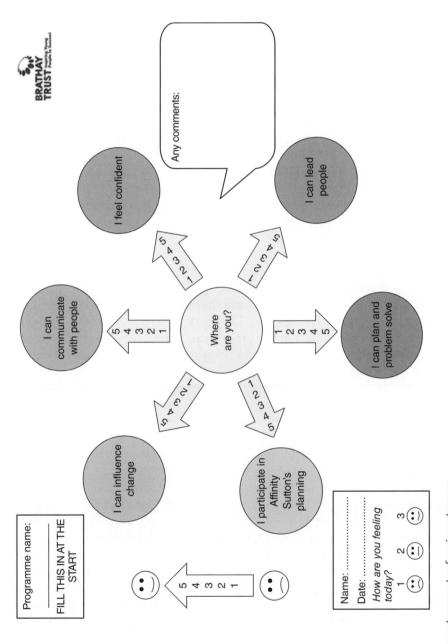

Figure 7.5   An outcome star for six outcomes

In deciding how to present the distance travelled tool you are always weighing up:

- Will the young people be able to fill this in easily?
- Will it give me the data that I need?
- Will I be able to analyse it?

When to use distance travelled

There is some debate about the timing of use of distance travelled tools with young people. Theoretically and classically they would complete these before the programme starts, or on the first day of the programme, and then again on the last day, or at the end of the programme. This would provide you with a clean data set of abilities before and after, allowing you to measure the gains made. There is a flaw in this design however. Our experience has shown that young people are very unlikely to provide accurate indications of their abilities at the programme for two fundamental reasons. Firstly, they may not feel confident enough to indicate that they have weak skills in the outcomes at the start of the programme as they may not want the practitioners that they have just met to think badly of them. They may therefore have a bias to overestimate their abilities in order to maintain face. Secondly, they may not fully understand what you are measuring. They may think that they are good at communicating, until they attend the programme, and only then do they realise how complex it is. They may therefore unknowingly overestimate their abilities at the start of the programme. This poses serious problems to the evaluation, and we have scratched our heads over the years as distance travelled forms such as those above were returned showing that young people had lost rather than gained skills! The same has happened to other organisations, as explored in the Fairbridge Vignette 7.8. There are two options available to you to overcome this issue. The first is to do the before and after assessments at the end of the programme, getting the young people to reflect back on their abilities at the start, and then think in the moment for the end measure. This works for the young people, but methodological sticklers may not think that this is a true pre-test–post-test measure and may dismiss your evaluation. The other route around the issue is to do a start measure, then at the end do a revised start measure and the end measure. This approach is used by the Prince's Trust. The Prince's Trust uses a self-designed distance travelled tool as part of their monitoring and evaluation process. The 'record sheet' is completed by young people at the start of the programme and at the end of the programme in a bar chart format. As you can see from Figure 7.6 there is also an opportunity for the young person to reflect on and revise their start score. The record sheet also asks young people how much the programme has helped them to develop each of the skills. This is an excellent way of establishing **attribution**, or the extent to which the youth project led to the improvement in skills. The Prince's Trust also tracks young people longitudinally using a telephone survey so that they can see the duration of these outcomes and the acquisition of hard outcomes, a truly robust evaluation process.

My Journey

on Get Started

Prince's Trust

Name: _____

Date: ____ / ____ / ____

Use the My Journey Scale to decide your rating for each skill, then colour in the squares to create your own skill journey.

Start: At the start of your programme rate your skills.
Reflect on start: During your programme you will learn more about the skills and yourself; rate your skill level for the start of the programme again.
End: At the end of your programme rate your skills.

	Start	Reflect on start	End
6			
5			
4			
3			
2			
1			

Example
1 = low score
6 = high score

	Start	Reflect on start	End
6			
5			
4			
3			
2			
1			

Communication
Speaking, listening, paying attention

	Start	Reflect on start	End
6			
5			
4			
3			
2			
1			

Working with others
Teamwork, getting on with people, respecting others

	Start	Reflect on start	End
6			
5			
4			
3			
2			
1			

Setting and achieving goals
Motivation, planning and organising, problem-solving, hard work

	Start	Reflect on start	End
6			
5			
4			
3			
2			
1			

Managing feelings
Dealing with issues, coping, managing problems

	Start	Reflect on start	End
6			
5			
4			
3			
2			
1			

Confidence
Self-esteem, self-belief, self-respect, self-awareness, dealing with nerves

	Start	Reflect on start	End
6			
5			
4			
3			
2			
1			

Reliability
Time-keeping, meeting deadlines, taking responsibility, attendance

Complete this page on the final day of your programme to help us improve the Get Started programme. Please answer the questions below:

Tell us how much the programme helped each skill:	Not at all	Very little	A little	Some	Quite a lot	A lot
Communication						
Working with others						
Setting and achieving goals						
Managing feelings						
Confidence						
Reliability						

	Not at all	A little	Quite a lot	A lot
Did you get what you wanted from Get Started, such as overcoming your challenges or achieving your goals?				
How much do you feel Get Started has increased the opportunities available to you for getting into or staying in education or training?				
How much do you feel Get Started has increased the opportunities available to you in your career or getting into self employment?				

Would you recommend Get Started to others?
- [ ] Yes
- [ ] No

How helpful was the guidance from staff on Get Started for deciding what you want to do next?
- [ ] Not at all
- [ ] A little
- [ ] Quite a lot
- [ ] A lot

How much has Get Started helped how satisfied you feel about your life?
- [ ] Not at all
- [ ] A little
- [ ] Quite a lot
- [ ] A lot

Have you been supported to get help with reading, writing, numbers or computer skills while on Get Started?
- [ ] Yes
- [ ] To some extent
- [ ] No
- [ ] Not needed

How much did the theme of your Get Started programme (e.g football, music) help to keep you interested in the course?
- [ ] Not at all
- [ ] A little
- [ ] Quite a lot
- [ ] A lot

What did you think of the Taster Day?
- [ ] Excellent
- [ ] Good
- [ ] Satisfactory
- [ ] Poor

What did you think of the venue where Get Started was held?
- [ ] Excellent
- [ ] Good
- [ ] Satisfactory
- [ ] Poor

What did you think of the support you received from Prince's Trust staff?
- [ ] Excellent
- [ ] Good
- [ ] Satisfactory
- [ ] Poor

What did you think of the support you received from Get Started trainer(s)?
- [ ] Excellent
- [ ] Good
- [ ] Satisfactory
- [ ] Poor

What part of Get Started did you enjoy the most and why?

What part of Get Started did you enjoy the least and why?

Do you have any suggestions on how Get Started could be improved or any other comments?

Complete at the end of your programme – Do we have your current mobile number?
→ The Prince's Trust will send you two simple surveys about how you are getting on by text message
→ One at three months and another at six months after you finish your Prince's Trust programme, it helps The Prince's Trust if you reply
→ If you do not have a mobile phone we will contact you another way
→ It is free to reply to the text message surveys and you do not need any credit to respond
→ If you do respond you'll be entered into a prize draw

Mobile number:

Second mobile number:

The information on this form and the text survey questionnaires will help The Prince's Trust and organisations working with us to run, fund and evaluate our work.

Please sign and date to say that you have read and understood this form.

Name:

Signature:

Date completed this page:

Returning the forms:
Please return forms to: The Prince's Trust National Administration Team, 1st Floor Paragon House, Seymour Grove, Old Trafford, Manchester M16 0LN.
The forms should be returned within two weeks of the programme ending.

Figure 7.6   The Prince's Trust record sheet

Vignette 7.8   Fairbridge's Problems with Distance Travelled (Knight, 2012)

The report used in this vignette brings together findings from three evaluation studies which Fairbridge conducted over the past decade that tested the theory that 'soft' outcomes in personal and social skills drive 'hard' outcomes in improvements in the life of the young person. Fairbridge developed their own distance travelled measure of young people's perceptions of their personal and social skills. This is called the 'Who are you? quiz'. In the quiz each young person completed a series of statements and was asked to rate 'how good am I at':

- Letting other people know what I mean
- Understanding what people are saying to me
- Getting on with people
- Making and keeping friends
- Keeping my feelings under control
- Understanding why I like some people and not others
- Understanding that different people have different ways of thinking
- Sorting problems out
- Understanding other people's point of view
- Give and take
- Thinking and planning ahead
- Learning from my successes and mistakes
- Accepting my share of the blame when things go wrong
- Thinking through what will happen to me and other people before I do something

In completing the quiz, the young person was asked to choose from one of the following categories:

1. Very good
2. Good
3. OK
4. Could be better
5. Need to work on this

After one week, the test results showed an across-the-board improvement of 13% in personal and social skills. However, this figure masked important variations between young people in Fairbridge. Further analysis revealed that 30% of young people had made 'significant gains' in personal and social skills, and 40% had made 'some gains', while 30% had made 'no gains' (and in a small number of cases gone backwards).

However, these good results did not last. When the young people completed the 'Who are you? quiz' at four months, mean personal and social skill levels

(Continued)

(Continued)

had regressed to where they had been at the beginning. Some of the young people were at a lower point than they had been when they joined Fairbridge. Scores gradually picked up again, however, so that after 10 months they exceed the score at the baseline and continued to rise.

It appears that progress through Fairbridge is not linear, but curvilinear. In the early stages, it appears to be a question of 'two steps forward and one step back'. The evaluator put forward three theories to explain this. One was that the group were experiencing group development (Tuckman, 1965) and were in a stage of 'storming' that led to their low self-perception. The second possible explanation comes from research on attitude change, and the role played by **'cognitive dissonance'** (Cooper, 2007). As people change, two opposing ideas may come into their mind at the same time, and the resulting conflict produces discomfort. As the new belief takes over, the conflict is resolved, and people are able to move on and make progress. The third is that, as with Maslow's learning theory (1943), there is a stage of unconscious incompetence that precedes competence, and operating out of this stage of development would mean that young people would self-score higher than their actual skill set.

Reflecting on this we note that such openness in evaluation is refreshing and compelling. Fairbridge found issues with their short-term distance travelled measures and theorised what these might be. Which of the three theories explain the dip in skills remains unclear, however, as Knight (2012: 14) says:

> what all three theories have in common is that there is a critical point in development in which disruption, and hence discomfort, is a necessary feature of progress. What Fairbridge perhaps does is to shake people out of their complacency to reveal to them that there is something important to address. Only when that disruption has taken place can a new identity take hold.

Distance travelled is a relatively new evaluation concept that seeks to understand more than just the attainment of X qualifications or Y end outcomes. Many evaluators seek to show uniform distance travelled (as suggested above) in order to allow them to report progress consistently. Some argue that this is a flawed concept, as the distance travelled should be distance towards the young people's own goals, which will never be uniform, and so neither will the ways in which it will be captured (Dewson et al., 2000; Lloyd and O'Sullivan, 2003). As such you may want to allow the young people flexibility in describing their own progress using a tool such as the journey maps, rather than something set like the tools above. This approach was adopted in one of the largest and most robust distance travelled evaluations ever completed, which was carried out in the UK on a programme called Positive Futures (Crabbe, 2006). The distance travelled evaluation was conducted using qualitative data over three years in a suite of three reports highlighted in the further reading which are well worth following up to see just how well a qualitative distance travelled report can be compiled.

Having discussed the nine data collection tools we now offer a summary (Table 7.7) so that you can more easily compare them.

Table 7.7   Summary of data collection tools

	Best used for...	Advantage	Disadvantage
Questionnaires	Large scale data	Easy to analyse	Surface rather than depth of information
Interviews	Small scale studies	Deep rich information	Time to transcribe and analyse
Focus groups	Group narratives	Collects multiple views and so time efficient	Hard to get everyone to speak
Diaries	Personal experiences	Completed in personal time	Ethical use
Documentary evidence	Contextual information	Easy to collect	May not answer your questions
Assessments	Quantitative studies	Valid and reliable	Impersonal and lengthy
Observations	Recording behaviours	Unobtrusive	Time to record
Creative methods	Engaging young people	Depth of information	Some may not accept them as valid techniques
Distance travelled	Showing a quantitative change even with qualitative data	Convincing comparative data	Issues such as cognitive dissonance

Summary

This chapter has described the key differences between qualitative and quantitative data collection tools. We have outlined eight different data collection tools and how they can be used to show distance travelled. The vignettes and case studies show some of the strengths and weaknesses of each of the tools. From this you can deduce that the strength of any tool is in its applicability to the context and questions that you seek to answer. Choosing the right tool(s) is important, and as such, we have summarised the main advantages and disadvantages of the tools to help you distinguish between them. In this chapter we have also positioned creative tools as a key approach to be explored and used by youth workers, as they address power imbalances, and are inclusive and multi-modal. Supporting your use of these tools is the Sage Methodspace where you can access our full creative toolkit.

Key Points

1. Data collection tools all have advantages and disadvantages; deciding which one to use is always a trade off.
2. Think about which tool will best suit the young people and your evaluation questions.

3. Put some time into designing and testing your data collection tools.
4. Mixed methods often help overcome the limitations of using a single data collection tool and so will be fully discussed in the next chapter.

Further Reading

Better Evaluation (2014) is an international collaborative website aimed at improving evaluation practice and theory by sharing information about methods, tools and approaches.

Crabbe, T. (2006) *'Going the Distance': Impact, Journeys and Distance Travelled* is the third interim national Positive Futures case study research report. It provides a good example of mixed data sets.

Gray, D. (2009) *Doing Research in the Real World* has a chapter providing more detail on most of the data collection tools described above (excluding creative methods).

Methodspace (2014) is the Sage online community for researchers. It is a great place to access discussions about research tools.

NECF and Horsley, K. (2009) *The Evaluator's Cookbook* is a well-known online resource providing excellent resources for participatory evaluation.

Stuart, K. and Maynard, L. (2011) *Brathay's Evaluation Toolkit* provides an online resource full of creative methods.

8

USING MIXED METHODS
IN EVALUATION

Chapter Overview

- Introduction
- What are mixed methods?
- Benefits of a mixed methods approach
- Challenges of a mixed methods approach.

Introduction

This chapter builds on the methodological debates introduced in Chapter 2 of positivistic and post-positivistic paradigms. As the title suggests, mixed methods draw from both paradigms, creating what some have referred to as a third paradigm. This third paradigm adopts an anti-purist approach, rejecting the idea of a qualitative versus quantitative debate in favour of combining the approaches. Mixed methods are presented as a potential bridge between positivism and post positivism as the mixed methods approach overrides the separate paradigmatic debates. The assumptions within this are that the weakness of either method will be compensated by the strengths of the other (Amaratunga et al., 2002). Compared to previous dominant paradigms, this third paradigm has seen a relatively recent surge of interest (Brannen, 2005), for example, Tashakkori and Teddlie's (2003) *Sage Handbook of Mixed Methods Research*. Situating creative methods within a mixed methods paradigm, further illuminates their participatory potential.

What are Mixed Methods?

At a simplistic level, we can think of evaluation methods being: (a) a mix of different quantitative methods (for example, two different surveys); (b) a mix of different qualitative methods (for example, focus groups and individual interviews); or (c) a mix of qualitative and quantitative methods (for example, a survey followed by an individual interview) (Brannen, 2005). Niglas (2000) defines these further (Table 8.1). Our discussion here focuses on the latest of these three and Niglas' third category of 'mixed design'. However, each of the areas can be thought of in terms of creating a multi-dimensional, rather than one-dimensional, understanding, through one method. Furthermore, mixing can also be thought of not just in terms of data collection tools, but also in terms of mixing participants, for example young people, youth workers, parents/carers.

Table 8.1   Niglas' (2000) classification of mixed methods

Pure Designs	Multi-method Designs	Mixed Designs
Purely quantitative or purely qualitative designs (may involve the use of several data sources and/or data gathering instruments from the same approach). Also known as mono-method studies.	Designs where both quantitative and qualitative approaches are used, but they remain relatively independent until the interpretation stage.	Designs where elements of quantitative and qualitative approaches are combined in various ways within different phases of the study.

Pause for Thought

Think of evaluations of projects you may have read:

- Do they fit into either Brannen's (2005) three categories, or Niglas' (2000) three categories?

This discussion is related to the concept of **triangulation**. Triangulation is when two or more methods are used to look at a particular phenomenon. Rothbauer (2008) states that the concept of triangulation is 'borrowed' from navigational and land surveying techniques that determine a single point in space with the convergence of measurements taken from two other distinct points. In the social sciences, data from multiple sources provide greater confidence and validity in findings.

Similarly the term crystallisation has grown from the concept of triangulation. Richardson (2000) states, from a post-modern perspective,

> We do not triangulate, we crystallize ... the central image for 'validity' for post-modern texts is not the triangle – a rigid, fixed, two-dimensional object. Rather, the central imaginary is the crystal, which combines symmetry and substance

with an infinite variety of shapes, substances, transmutations, multidimension-alities, and angles of approach. (2000: 934)

However, a mixed methods approach is not simply a matter of using a few different methods in our evaluations. This is a 'patchwork' of understanding using different techniques. Denzin and Lincoln (2000) calls this a **bricolage** and we can think of the evaluator as a 'bricoleur' piecing together and building understanding. The importance of gaining this multi-dimensional understanding allows us to look at the situation from multiple perspectives and gather a more holistic understanding. To appreciate this further, we can relate it to the discussion of methodology in Chapter 3 and the beliefs and assumptions that underpin the evaluation (ontological, epistemological and methodological).

Assumptions of mixed methods

At an ontological level (or the reality in which we understand the world), we see worldviews meeting in the middle of the positivist–post-positivist continuum. This is a position which values both objective and subjective views of reality. There is a belief from this position that we must see both depth and breadth. Therefore, a mixed methods paradigm is based on the assumption that reality is observable from multiple perspectives and is actually best viewed in this way, rather than biased to one end of the continuum or the other.

At an epistemological level (or where we define how knowledge is constructed), we see knowledge being constructed from different and complementary perspectives. This assumes knowledge can be, and should be, constructed in multiple ways. This values the knowledge of what has come before and is pre-defined as truth, as well as the knowledge people hold and know of as their truth. The meeting of these truths creates new and deeper understanding. Descriptions of knowledge add depth to previous generalisations and predictions of knowledge.

At a methodological level (or our approach to knowledge generation), we see evaluations being approached from multiple perspectives. That is, from objective and detached viewpoints, as well as from insider subjective viewpoints. This values approaching an area from a neutral perspective to observe or test pre-defined facts, as well as participating within the phenomena in order to get to know it and clarify its detail. This assumes that the two approaches will complement each other, with one leading from, or leading into, another.

These assumptions provide an underpinning justification for using a mix of both qualitative and quantitative methods. This unites the casual relationships identified between controlled variables (such as the impact of A on B), with detailed descriptions of the social situations (such as the meaning young people attach to an experience). This produces numerical data for statistical analysis, mixed with narratives and rich descriptions which are analysed for key themes.

Previously opposing positions unite as they aim to 'describe their data, construct explanatory arguments from their data, and speculate about why the outcomes they observed happened as they did' (Sechrest and Sidani, 1995: 78). Collectively, a mixed methods approach aims to provide empirical data to address questions (Johnson and Onwuegbuzie, 2004).

Vignette 8.1 introduces a mixed methods evaluation from the Netherlands.

Vignette 8.1   Effective Peer-to-Peer Support for Young People with End-stage Renal Disease: A Mixed Methods Evaluation of Camp COOL – Netherlands (Sattoe et al., 2013)

The Camp COOL programme aims to help young Dutch people with end-stage renal disease (ESRD) develop self-management skills. Fellow patients already treated in adult care ('buddies') organise the day-to-day programme, run the camp, counsel the attendees, and also participate in the activities. The attendees are young people who still have to transfer to adult care. This study aimed to explore the effects of this specific form of peer-to-peer support on the self-management of young people (16–25 years) with ESRD who participated in Camp COOL.

A mixed methods research design was employed. Semi-structured interviews (n = 19) with initiators/staff, participants, and healthcare professionals were conducted. These were combined with observations during two camp weeks and retrospective and pre and post surveys among participants (n = 62).

The self-reported effects of participants were: increased self-confidence, more disease-related knowledge, feeling capable of being more responsible and open towards others, and daring to stand up for themselves. According to participants, being a buddy or having one, positively affected them. Self-efficacy of attendees and independence of buddies increased, while attendees' sense of social inclusion decreased (measured as domains of health-related quality of life). The buddy role was a pro-active combination of being supervisor, advisor, and leader.

This shows how the mixed methods approach yielded a variety of data which was able to be summarised into key findings. This was then discussed and implications and recommendations made, such as the following:

Camp COOL allowed young people to support each other in adjusting to everyday life with ESRD. Participating in the camp positively influenced self-management in this group. Peer-to-peer support through buddies was much appreciated. Support from young adults was not only beneficial for adolescent attendees, but also for young adult buddies. Paediatric nephrologists are encouraged to refer patients to Camp COOL and to facilitate such initiatives. Together with nephrologists in adult care, they could take on a role in selecting buddies.

Reflecting on this we can see from this that there were multiple perspectives that needed to be represented in order to show a holistic understanding of the project within the evaluation. There was breadth of understanding from surveying a relatively large sample of people; depth of understanding from carrying out individual interviews, which can add detail; and context added by the evaluator observing the programme for themselves and getting to know its idiosyncrasies that might not be represented in either of the other data collection methods. This exemplifies the triangulation or crystallisation approach, as it looks at the project from multiple perspectives, using multiple data collection tools.

The patchwork of data which has been described above needs to be analysed and drawn together in its writing up. Mixed data sets obviously require mixed data analysis tools. This can be an extra challenge for evaluators. This relates to the discussion within Chapter 9 of coding and analysing data. What is important in the mixed methods approach is that this analysis is clear and transparent allowing the writing of this to smoothly blend the findings and robustly attribute their sources.

The findings generated from mixed methods evaluation can help speak to multiple audiences (this is discussed further in Chapter 10, which covers writing up for different audiences).

Benefits of a Mixed Methods Approach

The mixed methods approach shown in Vignette 8.1 provided a variety to the data allowing them to say more and explain themselves further. Interviews were carried out with a selection of people, observations made and participants measured before and after the intervention. Brannen's (2005) summary of the multiple benefits of adopting a mixed methods approach is adapted here to show the advantages of this evaluative approach:

- Qualitative evaluation facilitates quantitative evaluation.
- Quantitative evaluation facilitates qualitative evaluation.
- Qualitative evaluation facilitates the interpretation of relationships between variables.
- Quantitative evaluation captures the structure and qualitative evaluation the process.
- Combining qualitative and quantitative evaluation helps to bridge the gulf between 'macro' and 'micro' levels.
- Words, pictures, and narrative can be used to add meaning to numbers.
- Numbers can be used to add precision to words, pictures and narrative.
- Adds insights and understanding.
- Can provide stronger evidence for a conclusion.
- Increase the generalisability of the results.
- Qualitative and quantitative evaluation used together produce the more complete knowledge necessary to inform theory and practice.

For young people, a mixed methods approach can provide engagement options and further opportunities of involvement, or progression. For example, having taken part in a survey, a young person might wish to take part in a more detailed interview.

Pause for Thought

Think about a project you have been involved in:

- Would any of Brannen's (2005) list of benefits of mixed methods be useful?

So far, this discussion has not demonstrated the more creative methods that a mixed method approach lends itself to and what this book advocates. These are better exemplified by drawing from the mixed methods used in the Step Up case study. This case study has exemplified elsewhere in this book how the evaluator gathered qualitative and quantitative data. The creative methods used within this consisted of journey posters which were used as a stimulus for individual interviews. Practitioners also provided pen–portraits for each young person. In addition, all project materials were gathered as evidence (e.g. Asdan folders, creative projects, photos and video footage). This was then combined with quantitative attendance and attainment data, which was gathered from school databases. A comparison of data was made, pre-project, post–project, and six months on as well as comparing to year group data. The Step Up case study below details this further, focusing on the creative methods and showing the participatory benefits of a mixed methods approach.

    Step Up Case Study

A large piece of paper was rolled out in the middle of the circle of young people. On this roll of paper was the outline of a winding road which culminated in a T junction at the end of the road. The scene was introduced as a journey map, with the T junction representing a decision point, choosing one way or another. The group was then asked to create a mythical character in their group. The character was drawn on a separate flip chart and details regarding their name, gender, age, etc, were added. The group was then asked to describe the character's journey on the large map, the left-hand-side representing time before the programme and details of their upbringing and living situation. Detail was added as they moved along the journey map to the right, through time and through the programme. Details about thoughts, feelings, scenarios, and other people, were annotated on the journey map. This was semi-structured, in as much as there were initial questions such as 'What did they enjoy?', 'What did they learn about themselves?', or 'How will this help them in life?' This led to the decision point at the end, where the group chose two possible futures for the young person (one positive and one negative).

The group ran this process for several different characters. The aim of this was to allow young people to participate, but one step removed; not disclosing information about themselves, but being able to project their opinion onto the character. This provided a safe option for the young people to share their opinions about the course. Often they would start with a comment such as 'Sam felt like this' and then add comments such as 'I think Sam learnt that about himself' or 'Sam is just like me actually, and I felt like this when that happened'. This can be thought of as a creative way to run a focus group, as young people were in discussion about the detail, with ideas sparking off of one another.

The young people were then invited to create a journey map of their own. This allowed them to be able to detail ideas that might have come up during the previous discussion, which they did not feel comfortable sharing in the group, or to add more depth to what they had shared. They were asked to incorporate answering the same semi-structured questions as in the group activity, but apart from this they could create the journey map in whichever way they pleased. Creative materials were provided, or pre-drawn journey maps were offered. After creating their journey map, they were invited to explain it to the evaluator or project worker. The journey map was the stimulus of this interview conversation which was either recorded, or noted down.

The aim of this data collection process was to allow young people to build confidence in participating and sharing their opinions. They could do this in an abstract way and/or a personal way. They could engage at the level they wanted to and in a way they wanted to. Some people did not want to do a detailed creative map, but spoke in detail in their interview; others hardly said anything in the group mapping, yet spoke in detail in the individual interview; whilst for some young people, the creative part of the process gave them the opportunity to express their thoughts and feelings, enabling them to be better able to articulate these in the interviews. Others did not want to do an interview, but wrote in detail on their individual journey maps.

This case study better highlights the participatory benefits of adopting a mixed methods approach in the evaluation of projects with young people and how these benefits can be more inclusive of young people. Young people have more opportunities to choose methods that suit them and this can be in keeping with the patchwork that is being created. Young people are not restricted to one particular method and the evaluation could afford the same questions to be asked/answered through a variety of mediums, for example, visual and audio.

This allows young people to participate at the level they wish to. For example, collectively asking a group about an abstract character's experiences, allows them to give opinions. It should be noted, that this is valuable data in itself, even if the young person doesn't detail personal experiences.

The benefits of a mixed methods approach can also be further enhanced when a more participatory approach is employed. When young people have more involvement in the evaluation design, they may choose a mixture of qualitative and quantitative methods that will be more appropriate for themselves and other young people. They will further understand, for themselves, the benefits of mixed methods and the data they can yield. This, of course, is speaking the language of choice and power which is discussed in detail in Chapter 5.

Challenges of a Mixed Methods Approach

There is still a lack of comprehensive theoretical background for mixed method designs and therefore mixed method studies can seem to many practitioners, consumers and evaluators as 'mixed-up models' one cannot rely on (Datta, 1994: 59). A more recent argument suggests there is still a need to develop greater understanding and skills from the polar perspectives, as well as understanding the mixed method paradigm, which means greater training, time and resources (Brannen, 2005). This includes quality criteria for assessing mixed methods evaluation.

Further, some still argue from a purist perspective that quantitative notions such as being generalisable, valid, reliable and replicable ought not to be applied to qualitative evaluations (Spencer et al., 2003). Others argue that we should rather, draw upon the likes of Lincoln and Guba's (1985), broadly equivalent concepts that can apply to qualitative evaluation. For example, credibility/trustworthiness leading to internal validity; fittingness leading to external validity; auditability leading to reliability.

This still leaves the question, in doing mixed methods evaluation, how far do we work with these separate criteria or do we work to develop new specific or convergent criteria for mixed method evaluation? This uncertainty is perhaps resulting in complicated, unbalanced or failed evaluations. Vignette 8.2 below provides an example of such challenges.

Vignette 8.2   Youth Offending

This vignette is drawn from our early experience of being commissioned to provide research and evaluation services. An inner city youth offending team manager commissioned the IT solutions company which ran the city's youth offending data analysis software package to analyse offending data. The company had access to quantitative data for the last ten years. The company analysed this data in order to show various criteria, such as offending trends, gender, age, geography, etc. The company decided that they would like to provide some qualitative research to support their quantitative research. The hope was that this might qualify some of the results they were finding. The Brathay Research Hub was commissioned to carry out focus groups and interviews with a variety of young people who had been involved or at risk of being involved with youth offending. The qualitative research aimed to gather young people's experiences and opinions of offending, to be included within the mixed methods report. We used a variety of creative approaches to better engage this marginalised sector of young people. The company had data on some of the young people we spoke to and so a case study was written using mixed methods data. The case studies aimed to show trends in offending and then understand these better through the stories of the young people's journeys. This mixed methods approach provided richness to what would have been a more one-dimensional report.

For example, the offending trends of one young person's profile were able to be contextualised by their qualitative narrative. This showed crisis points in the young person's life that matched the dates of the offending within her profile. These included, her Dad being imprisoned, committing suicide and when she was later taken into care.

However, there were complexities within this. The company had 10 years' worth of quantitative data, compared to one month of time to gather 19 young people's opinions and experiences. This is not showing the balance of mixed methods values detailed in the assumptions described within this chapter.

It could be seen as a tokenistic gesture and is not in keeping with participatory practice with young people.

Reflecting on this, there is a challenge in combining approaches within a mixed methods study to ensure this is shared and authentic. Two opposing approaches coming together is not necessarily the same as coming from the same mixed methods paradigm.

Summary

In this chapter we have presented mixed methods as 'no stats without stories and no stories without stats'. This approach bridges values between external, objective, quantitative statistics and internal, subjective, stakeholder-led qualitative perspectives. The way these methods complement each other in the evaluation of a project is what matters most. Creative methods, for example, enable engagement and rich detail, whilst a questionnaire would allow you to quantify change, bridging the gap between funder and young person. Mixed methods allow you to present a holistic view of the project. Mixed methods also draw purists from their opposing positions to see the benefits of each other's work. Planning a mixed methods study will demand reflective practice as you identify which approach to use to answer which research questions and for what reasons.

Key Points

1. A mixed methods approach is where elements of quantitative and qualitative approaches are combined in various ways within different phases of the study.
2. This has been called a third paradigm, drawing from the previous two dominant paradigms of positivism and post-positivism. It has its own set of values and assumptions on which it is founded.
3. Qualitative and quantitative data collection tools used together produce more complete knowledge necessary to inform theory and practice.
4. Can provide stronger evidence for a conclusion and increase the generalisability of the results.
5. To be successful you need to ensure that all parties share the values of a mixed methods approach.

Further Reading

Brannen, J. (2005) *Mixed Methods Research: A Discussion Paper* provides an easy to read paper which gives a good overview discussion of the area of mixed methods.
Tashakkori, A. and Teddlie, C. (2003) *SAGE Handbook of Mixed Methods in Social and Behavioral Research* provides a pivotal text for those employing a mixed methods approach.

9

ANALYSING EVALUATION DATA

Chapter Overview

This chapter presents a guide to the collation, sorting, analysis and interpretation of data.

- A variety of data is considered alongside a number of different techniques to analyse it
- Participatory approaches to evaluation are discussed
- Reflection and reflexivity are highlighted as aiding data interpretation.

Introduction

Most people have had some experience of collecting and analysing data of one sort or another. However, it is often this part of the evaluation process that causes new evaluators the most anxiety and, unfortunately, can put people off doing evaluation altogether. In reality, data analysis is actually quite straightforward and, depending on the type of data you have and the depth you want your analysis to go into, you can start to make sense of your data by using some very simple techniques. At the heart of data analysis are the tasks of trying to sort through the data you have collected, working out what your data is 'saying' and choosing a method of presenting your findings in a meaningful and clear way. As we have already seen, there are different types of data (e.g. words, numbers and images) and for each of these there are a variety of techniques available to help you make sense of the data you have and present your findings. Throughout the book we have talked about different types of evaluation strategies. As you can probably imagine, these different forms of evaluation lend themselves to different techniques of analysis.

This chapter will introduce you to some very simple, straightforward, ways of making sense of your data. It will also guide you through a number of examples of data analysis and introduce you to a number of ways to take your data analysis further.

Approaches to Data Analysis: Deductive and Inductive Reasoning

One of the first things to be aware of when analysing data, is the very general way in which you are approaching your evaluation. For example, are you collecting data to give you some ideas of what might be going on in a project, what people are thinking or how they are responding? Or, are you collecting data to help you make a decision about whether something is working or not, to support or refute your hypotheses about a particular intervention? There are two main approaches to analysing data. One way starts with a hypothesis or theory. Data is collected to test the hypothesis. This is called **deductive** analysis, as you are trying to deduce or test whether your predictions or hypotheses are correct. For example, you might be asked to evaluate whether introducing a new activity leads to an increase in participation. Given the past record of the activity, we might predict that its introduction will increase participation. Our evaluation sets out to collect evidence that allows us to support (or reject) our hypothesis. This type of approach is often aligned with outcome evaluations. Data is collected and analysed to see if the intervention has had the intended effect.

The other approach to analysis starts with no preconceived ideas about what might be going on. The analyst turns to the data and uses it to develop ideas, theories or hypotheses. This is called inductive analysis. Inductive analysis suits process evaluations really well, particularly when you have no idea why something is working or not. You collect your data, and then let it speak to you.

As you will probably have guessed, these two approaches not only align with different types of evaluations and different types of data (e.g. quantitative or qualitative), but also reflect the two main paradigms of evaluation that we introduced in Chapter 1. Positivism tends to concern itself with testing ideas out and uses data to confirm and disprove those ideas, whereas interpretive methods start with the data and use that to develop ideas. **Inductive** reasoning involves observations from the data leading to hypotheses and wider generalisations. Deductive reasoning involves starting with a universal view or hypothesis and testing it out, working from the more general to the specific (Denzin and Lincoln, 2003; Gray, 2009). These different forms of reasoning are shown in Figure 9.1.

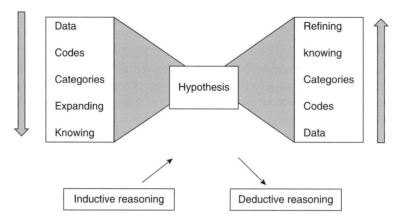

Figure 9.1   Inductive and deductive reasoning

Now that we have provided you with an introduction to deductive and inductive reasoning, we will guide you through a six-step process for each in turn.

Six steps for deductive analysis

1. Identify the theory or hypothesis that you are testing. There may be one or more, so state them as simply as possible.
2. Establish what types of data is needed to test your ideas. Identify what your data will need to look like (qualitative or quantitative) to enable you to confidently decide if your hypothesis is correct or not. This will be your analytical framework.
3. Collate your data sets. It is likely you will have a lot of raw data to work with. Try to organise it into some meaningful categories – chronologically, by young person, by type of data, by theme – whatever makes most sense to you. You will need to explain what you did to the reader when you write the report. At this point you might carry out some **descriptive analysis** of your data.

4. Search the data sets you have collated for indicators that your theory or hypothesis can be supported. This will mean your findings appear to be going in the way that you predicted.
5. Search the data for indicators that your hypothesis or theory cannot be supported. This might mean that the evidence you have collected appears to be refuting your hypothesis.
6. Weigh the evidence for and against your hypothesis and decide which carries most weight. This becomes you conclusion. It might be that you don't appear to have strong evidence either 'for' or 'against'. This is where **statistical analysis** might come in handy.

Now we will look at inductive analysis.

Six steps for inductive analysis

1. Collate your data. By now you might have a large set of data. The first step is to find a way to organise or collate your data that allows you to understand it. This could be done under your evaluation questions, under outcome headings, by type of project, by type of young person, etc. – whatever makes most sense to you and will be comprehensible by the reader and helps you to feel familiar with it. A common sorting tool for distance travelled evaluations is a 'before' and 'after' category.
2. Carry out some basic descriptive analysis or read and code your data. If you are working with narrative data, as you read the data different codes, ideas or messages will jump out at you. You might want to highlight them in the text or give them a number or a name. Write each one down with its colour or code as you go on another sheet of paper. This gives you your code list.
3. Re-read the data and check for all the codes all the way through the data, as the ones you wrote down at the beginning might have been missed at the end of the process.
4. Sort the codes into categories. Categories are like large drawers that might have lots of similar but smaller codes in them. Once you have a list of codes, you can then sift through them and decide whether they can be placed into larger themes or categories. Collating the codes into categories creates a clear theoretical framework, or findings.
5. Analyse your data to see what it is saying to you. Cross-check your data sets with the questions you set out with. What are the common or significant themes coming back? Check for significant themes that clearly jump out at you, as well as relationships or patterns. These become your findings.
6. Draw conclusions, generate theories and make predictions for future evaluation.

These frameworks have been developed from Boyatzis' (1998) thematic analysis, Friese's (2012: 92) analysis process, and Braun and Clarke's (2006: 16) analytical steps.

As you can see, there are different starting points for data analysis and it's useful if you clarify which approach you are using before starting your data analysis. To help you do this, start by asking yourself, what kinds of questions am I asking of my data?

Having introduced inductive and deductive reasoning, we will now introduce you to the basic techniques of data analysis. First we will cover quantitative techniques, then qualitative techniques, mixed method techniques and then participatory techniques.

Analysing Different Types of Data

As you can see, regardless of whether you are working inductively or deductively, a key part of data analysis is working with the data you have collected and trying to make sense of it. As we have already discussed, there are different types of data, the most typical being numbers and words. However, there are others too – for example, pictures and sound. It might be that you have collected one or more of these types of data. However, depending on what type of data you have, there are a variety of ways you can start to make sense of it.

Numerical Data

Perhaps the most common, and traditional, forms of data are numerical data. As we discussed in Chapter 7 numbers might be used in a variety of ways in the data analysis process (e.g. nominal, ordinal and interval scales) and, depending on what types of numbers you have, there are a variety of ways of analysing them. If you have used numbers in your evaluation a good place to start is with summary descriptive data analysis. Descriptive statistics are summaries of gathered data. The most common form includes measures of **central tendency** (mean, median or mode) and measures of **dispersion** (e.g. the range). Graphs and charts are also useful ways of displaying data.

Summarising data

Let's take a typical questionnaire that uses a variety of questions and types of measurement, and look at some of the different ways that the data can be summarised. This questionnaire was designed to investigate the profile of the current users of a youth centre, their view of the facilities available and their suggestions for improvement. In this section we will look at the numerical data collected and a variety of ways that are available to you to summarise this data and start your analysis.

Example Questionnaire: The Youth Zone

Many thanks for picking up this questionnaire. We would like to know your thoughts about the Youth Zone and how we might improve the services we provide for you. If you have five minutes to spare we would really like you to let us know your thoughts. If you want help filling in the questionnaire please contact Janice in the Youth Zone office. The questionnaire is anonymous so please feel free to let us know your thoughts. Thank you.

Q1:   Are you Male __ or Female __ ? (please tick)
Q2:   What is your age?
Q3:   What do you currently do?
Q4:   On a scale of 1–10, how highly do you rate the current facilities offered at the Youth Zone?

$$1 - 2 - 3 - 4 - 5 - 6 - 7 - 8 - 9 - 10$$

Not at all   Very highly

Q5:   What do you like about the Youth Zone?
Q6:   What don't you like about the Youth Zone?
Q7:   What suggestions do you have for how the facilities at the youth centre could be improved?

Pause for Thought

- What would you do with this data?

- How would you start to organise it and make sense of the participants' responses?

The first step of data analysis is to enter your data onto a data table. One simple way of starting your analysis is to record the responses of each participant to each question on a data table. For the example above this might look something like Table 9.1.

You can do some very simple analysis on this data.

The first thing you might want to know is how many people filled in questionnaires. By doing a quick **frequency count** of the number of completed questionnaires you received, you can work out that there were 10 participants. This can be entered into your data summary table (Table 9.2) as N (number of participants) is 10.

If you know how many questionnaires were picked (let's say 20), you can work out the return rate in the form of a **percentage**.

Question 1 asks participants to state whether they are 'male' or 'female'. Answers to this lead to the participant being placed into one of two categories – 'male' or 'female. These categories are separate groups as participants can't be both. They have to be one or the other. Again, a simple way of presenting categorical data is by way of a frequency count. In the below example, there are 4 males and 6 females.

Table 9.1   Example of collated data

	Sex	Age	Status	Rating	Positives	Negatives	Improvements
Participant 1	F	16	Student	5	Meeting people	Not enough to do	Coffee bar
Participant 2	F	18	Unemployed	9	Somewhere to go	Closed on Mondays	Computers
P3	F	17	Employed	2	Sports teams	Poor netball pitch	New sports facilities
P4	M	16	Student	5	Place to hang out	Poor equipment	New music equipment
P5	M	17	Student	6	Somewhere to hang out	Outdated equipment	New music facilities
P6	F	17	Student	8	Meeting people	No social space	Coffee bar
P7	M	16	Student	6	Place to hang out	Lack of seating	Comfy seating
P8	M	19	Unemployed	8	Somewhere to go	Poor equipment	New sports equipment
P9	F	18	Unemployed	9	Somewhere to spend time	Poor facilities	New social area
P10	F	19	Unemployed	8	The people	No music	New equipment

Table 9.2 Data summary

Total number of participants % response rate	Gender	Status	Age	Rating of facilities	What you like	What you don't like
N = 10	Male: 4 (40%) Female: 6 (60%)	Student: 5 Unemployed: 4 Employed: 1	Mean: 17.3 Median Mode	Rating of facilities		

Now we know the total number of participants and the number of males and females, we can take our data analysis one step further and work out the percentage of males and females we have. The box below shows you how to calculate percentages.

How to calculate percentages

$$\frac{\text{Number of cases collected} \times 100}{\text{Total number of cases}} = \% \qquad \frac{4 \text{ males} \times 100\%}{10} = 40\%$$

A really useful way of visually displaying percentages is with a **pie chart**, as shown in Figure 9.2.

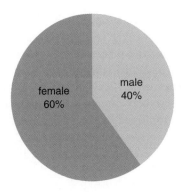

Figure 9.2   Pie chart showing the breakdown of males and females in the sample

You could do a similar frequency count for Question 3 (What do you do?). However, before working out frequencies you first need to sort the responses into **categories**. The simplest way of doing this with the data you have, is to work through the answers given and group together similar responses. From the questionnaires we have received back it is clear that our participants come from three separate groups:

Group 1: students
Group 2: employed
Group 3: unemployed.

Once we have identified groups or categories we can carry out a frequency count for each.

In analysing the responses to our questionnaire, a frequency count reveals that we have 5 students, 4 unemployed people and 1 employed person. Again, we can work out percentages and visually display our data in pie charts (see Figure 9.3).

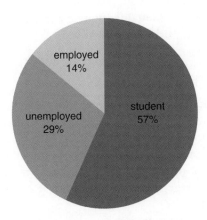

Figure 9.3   Pie chart showing the breakdown of the status of the sample

As you can see, through some very simple analysis you can start to draw out some interesting patterns in your data. Of course you can develop these themes even further and go on to work out the proportion of the males and females with each status (e.g. how many male students), and so on.

A bar chart is also another useful way of presenting category data and enables comparisons to be made between categories. Usually the **categorical variable** (e.g. student, unemployed, employed) is placed on the x-axis (horizontal) while the value for each category is place on the **y-axis** (vertical). A bar chart for the frequency of gender within each category is shown in Figure 9.4.

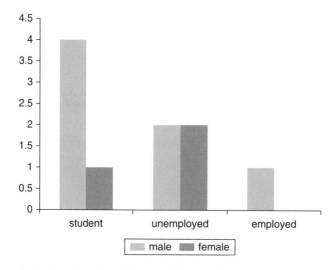

Figure 9.4.   Bar chart showing a breakdown of the sample by gender and status

When identifying categories, you can either label your categories with a 'name' (e.g. male or female) or a number (remember nominal scales) – e.g. Student: 1, Unemployed: 2, Employed: 3. If you decide to use numbers this will enable you to engage in an even more detailed quantitative analysis of your data such as working out the mode, including using statistical tests.

Measuring variables

Question numbers 2 and 4 use a different type of measurement to score the answers. Question number 2 asks participants to give their age, whereas question number 4 asks participants to respond by rating how much they liked the Youth Zone. These types of numbers represent forms of interval (age) and ordinal (rating) data. There is a variety of different ways such data can be analysed. Working out central tendency (e.g. average) and the dispersion (e.g. **range**) are common ways of dealing with such data.

Central tendency refers to working out the most central or typical value of a data set. There are three key measures of central tendency – the **mean**

(or average), **median or mode**. Depending on the type of data you have (i.e. nominal, ordinal or interval) one form of central tendency might be more appropriate than another.

Mean

This is most appropriately used with interval data. In our questionnaire this would be most appropriately used with the question asking for participants' ages, when we want to find our 'what is the average age of our participant?'

To find the mean of a data set, simply add each value together and then divide the total by the number of cases (N) in the data set. In our data this would give us an average age of 17.3.

$$16 + 18 + 17 + 16 + 17 + 17 + 16 + 19 + 18 + 19 = 173 \text{ (Total)}$$

$$173/10 \times 100 = 17.3$$

Means are a very useful statistic. However, they can be misleading, as a 'rogue' score (unusually high or low score) can distort the data. For this reason sometimes other measures of central tendency are used.

Median

This is the central value of a data set. You could use the median with ordinal or interval data. The median is easier to work out if you have an unequal data set. To work out the median, arrange all your scores in numerical order and the median is the middle score. If you have an equal data set, the median is worked out by taking the middle scores (which are the 4th and 5th scores in our data set) adding them together and dividing by 2:

$$16, 16, 16, 17, \textbf{17, 17}, 18, 18, 19, 19$$

$$\text{Median age} = 17$$

Mode

This is useful when we have nominal data (e.g. Q1 or 3) or ordinal data (e.g. Q4) and we want to find out which is the most frequent category (e.g. male (1) or female (2)) or rating given. In the case of the participants' sex, we can either count the number of males or females we have, or code the categories with a number (Male: 1 and Female: 2) and then work out which is the most common number. We can also use this method with ages. In our data set the most common age groups would be 16 and 17.

Table 9.3 shows three different measures of central tendency for our participants' ages.

Table 9.3   Central tendency for age

Measures of Central Tendency: Age	
Mean age	17.3
Median age	17
Mode	16 & 17

Using the measures of central tendency for the ordinal data on our participant's rating of the youth zone we get results shown in Table 9.4.

Table 9.4   Central tendency for Youth Zone ratings

Measures of Central Tendency: Youth Zone Ratings	
Mean rating	Not really appropriate 6.6
Median rating	6
Mode rating	8

Using the measures of central tendency for the nominal data on our participants' status' we get following results shown in Figure 9.5.

Table 9.5   Central tendency for status

Measures of Central Tendency: Status	
Mean	NA
Median	NA
Mode	Students/1

Measures of central tendency help us to start drawing out some key themes in our data. From the simple calculations we have carried out, it appears that the mean age of people using the Youth Zone is 17 years; they are more likely to be female and more likely to be students. Our participants are also moderately happy with the services that the Youth Zone provides.

As you can see, these basic techniques give you the foundations for identifying some key patterns in your data. Of course, there is nothing to stop you using these techniques more creatively. You might want to go even further and, for example, work out if there is a difference between the rating scores between males and females or employed and students by comparing the modes for the two groups.

Line charts

Line charts are useful for plotting the progress of groups over several measurement intervals and so are very appropriate when carrying out evaluations. Using our example of 'The Youth Zone', let's say after our first questionnaire has been analysed, we decide to make some changes to the Youth Zone and invest in some new equipment. In order to see if this raises the ratings of the Youth Centre, we may then ask our participants over the next few months to rate the facilities again. We can then plot 'ratings' over a 12-month period. In this example, the mean ratings have been taken for each of our status groups over a 12- month period, as shown in Figure 9.5.

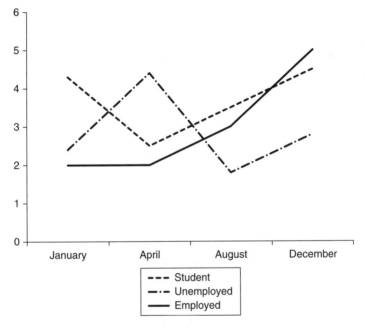

Figure 9.5 Line chart showing ratings for the Youth Zone over 12 months

Measures of dispersion

Dispersion is a measure of the extent to which all the values in a data set vary around the central or typical value. The simplest measure of dispersion is the 'range'– the distance between the top and the bottom value of a data set.

In our evaluation of the Youth Zone, it would be useful to know the range of ages participating in our evaluation and the range of rating scores given. We do this by working out the difference between the highest and lowest age or rating given, which give us these results shown in Table 9.6.

Table 9.6 Ranges

	Range
Age range	3 (16–19)
Rating range	7 (2–9)

As a 'one-off' the range of a set of scores might not be very useful, particularly as it does not take into account unusual or 'extreme' scores. However, if you are interested in taking a quick 'snapshot' of your data sets to check out how similar they are, for example, the range is a simple and quick way of doing this.

So, for example, in the Youth Zone example, your first set of data analysis showed that your sample's range of rating scores was 7. However, when you take the second rating four months later, the range has increased. This suggests that there is more variety in the ratings you are getting and some of your participants are rating the Youth Zone at the more extreme ends of your rating scale. In such cases it might be useful to look at why this is so. Why are some people really enjoying what you provide, and others not. What has caused these more varied responses.

If you want to achieve a more representative value of the dispersion of your data, the **mean deviation** is sometimes a better way of expressing the variety of the scores in your group.

The concept of deviation refers to the spread of values in a data set. A deviation score is simply the amount by which a particular value deviates from the mean. The mean deviation is therefore the mean of all the deviations in the data set.

In our data set we have already worked out the mean/average age of our participants is 17.3 years. We have also worked out the range of our ages is 3. To work out deviation scores we now work out the difference between each age (e.g. 16) and the mean age (17.3). In the first example, this would give us a deviation score of 1.3 years. To work out the mean deviation we would do this for every score. This would give us a score of 1.1. Again, on its own this score doesn't mean very much. However, both measures of central tendency and dispersion are useful measures to use when working out the key features of your group before you start your evaluation, your baseline data, or when you want to compare the key characteristics of a number of groups you might find yourself working with. They are useful checks to use if you want to find out how similar or different groups are. These values are also useful if you go on to implement an intervention. You can use measures to build up a before and after picture.

Correlation – the measure of relationship between two variables

Correlation is the measurement of the extent to which pairs of scores are related. For example, many people would agree that there is a relationship (or correlation) between height and weight, and that as people get taller they also get heavier. Correlation analysis allows us to work out whether variables are indeed related, and if so what the extent of that relationship is.

There are a number of different types of relationships that exist: **positive** and **negative correlations** are the key types.

Positive correlations occur when as one variable increases or decreases, the other increases or decreases too. For example:

- The longer you spend revising, the higher your grades
- As temperatures increase, the sales of ice cream increase.

Negative correlations occur when one variable increases as the other variable decreases. For example:

- As temperatures decrease, the sales of woolly jumpers increase
- The more you earn, the lower your credit card bills.

To get a basic idea of whether variables are related or not, you can plot a simple **scattergraph**. In Figure 9.6 we can see that as temperature increases, the sales of ice cream have done too.

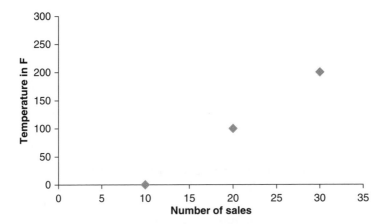

Figure 9.6   Scattergraph showing the correlation between ice cream sales and temperature

In the second example in Figure 9.7 we can see that as the temperature increases the sales of woolly jumpers decrease. Scattergraphs are therefore useful for showing trends or patterns in the data.

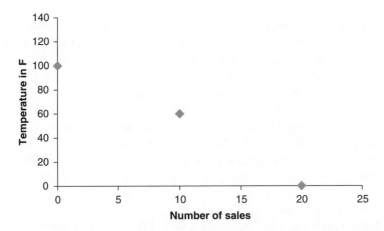

Figure 9.7   Scattergraph showing the correlation of sales of woolly jumpers and temperature

When there is no relationship between variables a scattergraph would look some-thing like Figure 9.8, which mapped the relationship between temperature and pen sales.

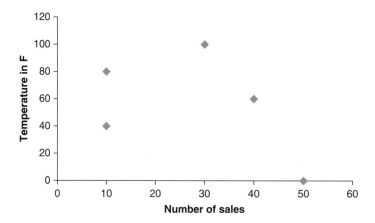

Figure 9.8   Scattergraph showing no correlation between temperature and pen sales

By plotting out the scores you have gained for each participant on two values (usually interval data) you can get an idea of whether any form of relationship exists. If you find a pattern does exist, there are statistical tests available which enable you to work out how strong the relationship is. This is technically known as a **correla-tion co-efficient**. The key tests for correlations are Spearman's rho or Pearson's test, both of which are outside the scope of this book.

By carrying out some very basic analysis, you can start to build a picture of the patterns in your evaluation findings. For example, from the data collected you might be able to work out who rates the services the most highly – male or females and whether their age correlates to status. You could also find out if there is a relationship between age and rating of the services (for example, as you get older, does your rating of the services go up or down?).

There are lots of techniques available to you to help you make sense of your raw numerical data. We have covered just a few of them. The reading list at the end of this chapter will direct you to a number of more specialist texts that will enable you to take your data analysis further.

Descriptive analysis enables you to draw out patterns from your data. For exam-ple from collecting data about the number of school truancies before and after an intervention it might appear that average truancy rates have fallen. Depending on the nature of your evaluation, descriptive analysis will enable you to make a quick assessment of how your programme is working and if it is having the desired effect. In other words, it will provide you with some evidence to base your evaluation on. However, descriptive analysis only enables you to glean and represent patterns in your data; they don't prove anything. It might be that you find a difference, or relationship, in your data, but how much of a difference does there need to be to enable you to say with confidence that something is really going on – that the intervention is having the effect you expected? This is where statistical analysis comes in. Statistics don't answer the questions for you, but they allow you say with more confidence that the patterns that you have found in your data are not accidental (or the result of chance) but are likely to be because of the treatment you have implemented.

There is a wide variety of different kinds of statistical tests that you can use to analyse your data. Some tests test the degree of difference between groups to enable you to assess how significant it is; others help you work out the degree of relationship. The kind of test you use depends on the kind of evaluation you have carried out and the kind of numerical data you have (e.g. nominal, ordinal or interval). It is beyond the scope of this book to work through the different tests that are available and how to use them. However, at the end of this chapter we have suggested a variety of books that you might find useful and which will give you guidance on the range of tests available, when to use them, how, and how to interpret them.

Vignette 9.1 Longitudinal Transition Outcomes of Youth with Emotional Disturbances (Wagner and Newman, 2012)

This study investigated transition outcomes of youth with emotional disturbances using data from the National Longitudinal Transition Studies. The study compares two cohorts of youth aged 18–21 and again when they were young adults aged 21–25, and who were out of high school up to 4 years in 1990 and 2005, on their rates of high school completion, post-secondary education enrolment, employment, independent living, and criminal justice system involvement. The study provided descriptive statistics for outcomes at each time point.

The study showed significant increases over time in rates of high school completion, post-secondary education and arrest, and there was a significant decline in employment. Analyses of young adults with emotional disturbances in 2009 show that 82.5% had completed high school, and 53% had had some post-secondary education. Although 91.2% had been employed at some time since high school, 49.6% were employed when interviewed; 63.1% had lived independently, 60.5% had been arrested, and 44.2% had been on probation or parole.

The conclusion of the study is that youth with emotional disturbances trail the general population in positive transition outcomes, and high rates of criminal justice system involvement suggest more effort is needed, including early intervening, with response to intervention strategies and self-determination training, to help these young adults succeed after high school.

Reflecting on this we can see the value of descriptive statistics to show change. The question remains, however, how these results were attained, and what meaning they have for the young people; to find this out we would need qualitative data.

Narrative and Visual Data

So far we have looked at making sense of numerical data. Now we turn to narrative data. Numbers are only part of the story, and, in fact, can be used to develop 'spurious assumptions' (Crabbe, 2006) about the efficacy of a programme. Qualitative data analysis looking at narrative and visual data allows more exploration and understanding of what happened, why, and with what impact. **Content analysis** is a key approach to analysing narrative data. There is a range of ways that narrative data might be collected – as responses to open ended questionnaires, interviews, diaries, poems, documentary evidence. Questions 5, 6 and 7 in our example, show you how narrative data might be generated by an open ended question. However, regardless of the manner in which you collected your data, the most common way of making sense of it is by using **coding** and **categorisation**. We already used a simple version of coding when we analysed Question 3 where we asked an open-ended question about participants' status. We then worked through the different answers given, coded them and allocated categories. This simple process of coding and categorising is fundamental to the analysis of all forms of narrative data.

Coding narrative data

In our questionnaire, we asked the question 'what do you like about the Youth Zone'. The answers given included:

- I really liked the staff, they make me feel really safe.
- I love the range of things to do. I think that they are brilliant.
- Going to the Youth Zone keeps me off the street and the staff and things we do are ace.

Coding means picking out relevant answers and working out if they fall into any common categories – from our analysis we worked out that some answers were to do with staff and some were to do with activities. These two areas then become our categories.

Once we have identified categories (as in our Youth Zone example), what we do with our data can go one of two ways – quantitative or qualitative analysis. Although both types of analysis start off at basically the same point, with coding words, sentences or phrases, and creating categories, how these are treated differs significantly. With a quantitative approach it is likely that you will engage in some form of frequency count of the number of examples that fall under different codes or categories, to support your claims (e.g. 'X% of our participants cited "social reasons" as the most important feature of The Youth Zone' or '7 out of our 10 participants claimed that ...'). The aim of such analysis is to reveal the **manifest content** of a text, the visible, obvious, surface messages that can be measured and quantified. However, if we chose to follow a more qualitative interpretation of the data we are more likely to look for the subtle, underlying messages reflected in the data, the **latent content**.

As we have already described how to analyse numeric data, we will now look at qualitative forms of data analysis, particularly content analysis.

Coding involves identifying and sorting data into units. It's useful to start the process by deciding whether you are going to create a code list before you look at the data or create it as you go along. The advantage of setting up a code list before analysis is that you are clear what you are looking for. This works well for simple data (e.g. gender, status) but risks imposing our ideas on the data and thus missing answers that you had not thought of. Coding as you go means that the analysis builds out of the data, ensuring that you don't miss anything. This approach is good where you have more complex data (e.g. interview data, life course analysis), however it can take longer as code lists need refining and you will need to check for all the codes in the whole data set once you have developed the code list from it.

The next stage of coding is to decide what types, units and size of language you need to code. Depending on what you want to find out you could look to code single words (e.g. favourite colour), sentences (what did you learn?), paragraphs (how the programme impacted on your life), or even whole narratives (case studies/life histories). You could also use a combination of these approaches. Coding sentences is the most common approach in social sciences. You also might be interested in more subtle messages in your text, such as evidence of 'fear of failure' or 'lack of confidence'. These could also be coded in your data. In all of these examples, the next step is to work through your data, often with a different colour highlighter pen for different codes, and pick out key words or phrases.

Once you have spent some time in the initial coding of your data, it is useful to spend some time reflecting on the codes that you have used and the units of data that fall under these and consider whether you can start to combine early simple codes into larger constructs that will eventually combine into categories. Final categories are a kind of hierarchical step above substantial codes.

With this qualitative analysis, on the other hand, the evaluator is more likely to be interested in the latent content of a text, the 'hidden or subtle messages' that could include cultural attitudes, prejudices or social norms that are encoded in message. Such messages might reveal themes or concepts that say something about the subject's place in society or how certain phenomena or people are perceived. This form of analysis depends much more on interpretation, and the evaluators need to be very aware that their interpretation of the data might be very much influenced by their particular position in the world and the lens they bring to their analysis. We will revisit this later in the chapter. When carrying out qualitative analysis, the evaluator is more likely to support their interpretation of the data by drawing on examples or quotes from their raw data.

Corbin and Strauss (2008: 159) describe the process of coding as: 'Extracting concepts from raw data and developing them in terms of their properties and dimensions' (Corbin and Strauss, 2008: 159). The purpose of the coding is not to reduce the data to 'chunks' or to 'count' and so quantify the data, but to generate a full analysis of the range of ideas within it and their inter-relationships.

Codes need to be revisited and revised many times ensuring that they are representative of the data, and that connections (of similarity and difference) are acknowledged. This resonates with steps three to five in the inductive process listed above.

There are ICT packages that allow you to code qualitative data online (e.g. Invivo or Atlas.ti) but these may be outside your budget or time scale to use. In this case, equip yourself with a set of highlighter pens or index cards or post-it notes, some sort of stationery that will allow you to mark and collect together words/sentences/paragraphs that say the same thing. Now you can report on each pattern, providing the number of people who said the same thing (n = 8) with some illustrative quotes to show the evidence, bring the report to life, and contextualise any statistics.

Vignette 9.2   A Canadian Study of Suicide and Prostitution Among Street Youth: A Qualitative Analysis (Kidd and Kral, 2002)

A research study conducted in Canada used only quantitative data, collected from 29 young people's narratives, to understand youth suicide and prostitution. A history of attempted suicide was reported by 76% of the participants and the analysis revealed themes of isolation, rejection/betrayal, lack of control, and most centrally, low self-worth, as forming the basis of their experiences concerning suicide. Additionally, it was found that trading sex, in which most participants had been or were currently involved, was linked with their suicidal experiences and may account for the high attempt rate. Finally, variables related to suicide were found that have not been examined previously in the literature on street youth, including loss of control, assault during prostituted sex, drug abuse as a 'slow suicide', and breakups in intimate relationships.

Reflecting on this and the previous vignette we can certainly see the difference between qualitative and quantitative data. Here we have the 'what and why' data, but not the 'how many'. You can see that you really need a clear question in your mind before you know which type of data to collect and which tools to use.

Analysing Creative Data

We have covered some basic principles of analysing narrative and numerical data sets. However, the same principles can be applied to the analysis of data generated by more creative methods.

I-poems

I-poems work in the same way as the qualitative data analysis described above but with a number of additional steps woven in to ensure the evaluator remains attentive to the different voices in the data. Additionally, data is arranged in a set manner and analysis takes place at the level of the narrative or poem. The data analysis described above can render the individual voices of young people invisible and this analytical technique directly tackles that by turning narratives into poems that are cited as wholes, each line starting with an 'I', and by forcing the evaluator to 'listen' to those voices in the analysis. The technique is called the 'listening guide' and is described below. As it works with narratives it is not useful for short excerpts of data.

1. Step one: read the data text and listen to the plot or storyline in the data – what is happening, or what is being described as happening? As you read note down your responses to the data explicitly bringing our subjective selves into the analysis rather than trying to exclude them.
2. Step two: re-read the data and highlight all the first person pronouns, i's and we's, and then extract these sentences and arrange them in a poem in the order you extracted them. This process is called the 'I-poem' (Debold, 1990). This focuses your attention on the voice of the participant and allows you to see how they view themselves. Sometimes this process captures something that was not originally seen in the whole text.
3. Step three: re-read the data listening for opposing voices, as people often have contradicting voices internally. These could be of compliance and rebellion, separate and connected selves, justice and care, resilience and distress, happiness and depression. Underline each voice in a different colour.
4. Step four: pull together what you have learnt about each question from the perspective of your own subjectiveness, what the participant said happened, what they say about themselves as an I and as other voices.

As you have probably guessed, this approach is best used when evaluation requires listening to different aspects of a person's expression of their experiences. The way in which it reveals different voices can be either a strength or a weakness, depending on what your evaluation question is.

Vignette 9.3   I-Poem Analysis (Balan, 2005)

There were no I-poem analyses for young people available. This study high-lighted looked at women's experiences of being involuntarily displaced from their corporate workplaces.
  An excerpt of Samantha's 'I-poem' is provided here:

I decided

I've been through

I think I'm still going through

I worked

I had

I had been with them for about a year

I was put into a role

I had had a friend and a mentor; I'll call him Sam

With the exception of myself

(Continued)

(Continued)

All of my colleagues left the company

I allowed, I was manipulated, I feel

I didn't want, I wasn't qualified for, I didn't perform well

I was earning about $30,000 less than any one of my peers

I think, relates to the fact that I'm a female

I think, easier to manipulate

I wanted to make up that gap

I was, I allowed, I guess, I found myself in a competitive state

I probably have a couple of more years of experience

A couple more years older than he is

Finding myself in a state of competition with Frank, with really no support from Mike

Feeling as if I was set up to fail, I realized I had pushed myself beyond

I thought, my limits, I knew that my health was being affected

I knew, stress level was beyond what I felt I could cope with

Through the creation of this i-poem, the researcher then identified a range of different voices that Samantha speaks in: a voice of silence, a voice of dissonance, and an awakened voice. Overall the researcher concludes that Samantha's experience is that of a war zone casualty:

Metaphor: War Zone Casualty

The metaphor that struck me [the researcher] to best describe Samantha's transitional period is that of war zone and Samantha as a casualty. Her repeated mention of competition, of pushing herself beyond her limits, of betrayal, of lack of choice, of manipulation paints a picture of constant upheaval and mistrust. Her longing for a collaborative environment is in contrast to the backdrop of the technology industry's bust that seems to be exacerbating the competitive, cutthroat corporate culture she finds herself in. The constant stress and her resultant health problems are not a surprise. (Balan, 2005: 13)

Reflecting on this we can see a powerful performative voice. The i-poem process has almost made the data more than it was originally. It has enhanced it by the way it has formatted it. Whilst this has allowed multi-voicedness to emerge, it begs the question as to whether these would have value to a range of stakeholders.

Visual images

Having discussed how to analyse metaphors in text, it is perhaps only a small step to analysing the metaphors in visual work. Visual data includes everything that you can see with your eyes; pictures, posters, photos, films, objects, dance, drama. Evaluators may typically use these as mere decoration in our evaluation reports, but they too are important data that you can analyse to add weight to your analysis. The process of analysing visual data is a form of content analysis. You look at the image/object and note what it contains – who, what, where, what happens, what emotions can be seen, what symbols or images. It is very likely that your analysis will tell a story through coding and categorising in the same way as the qualitative narrative analysis we have seen before. There are well recognised metaphors employed in some people's art work, for example, light and dark, smiley and unhappy faces, ups and downs. We can also use these as the units of analysis showing a distance travelled. Equally creative work sometimes contains words, and these give us direct qualitative data to work with.

Ideally you would also have a taped or written explanation of the art work or play or dance by the young person, but even if you do not have this, we suggest that you can interpret the clear use of metaphor in creative work.

The strengths of this approach are that the art work illustrates reports and perhaps shows more depth than statistical analysis; the drawback will be how much you can infer and how open your audience is to analysis of visual images.

Vignette 9.4   Visual Image Analysis (Literat, 2013)

This study used participatory drawing as a visual research method in qualitative research with children and youth. The author states that:

> Because of its co-constructed and playful nature, as well as its lack of dependence on linguistic proficiency, participatory drawing emerges as a highly efficient and ethically sound research strategy that is particularly suited for work with children and young people across a variety of cultural contexts. (Literat, 2013: 84)

The power of drawing as an evaluative tool is illustrated by this example taken directly from Literat's paper.

The two drawings demonstrate the efficiency of participatory drawing as an endline strategy of program assessment. In order to understand the perceived impact of the digital storytelling program, the students were asked, at the end of the school year, to draw a portrait of themselves before and after taking part in this project. Navya's pair of drawings [Figure 9.9] paints a rich picture of the way in which the program equipped her with novel skills and transformed her understanding of formal education.

(Continued)

(Continued)

Figure 9.9   Drawing in response to 'Draw a portrait of yourself before and after taking this digital storytelling course' (Literat, 2013: 92)

In addition to this the researcher also listed what the young person said about the pictures she had drawn:

> Navya's narrative: Before taking this course, I thought school was useful but not very interesting. Now I enjoy it much more, and I have computer skills and camera skills. My parents were very impressed with my skills, and they told everyone that their daughter is a filmmaker now. Other students don't have the opportunity to study these things in school, but I think it would be useful if all children could film our country and our life. (Literat, 2013: 93)

Reflecting on this we see compelling evidence that change has happened, and that pictures do indeed paint a thousand words. This data is equally as valid as a Likert scale in a questionnaire. Many evaluators steer away from visual analysis, but this beautifully demonstrates how simple and compelling visual methods can be.

We have shown you a variety of ways in which you can begin to analyse your data. However, there are lots of ways you can develop these ideas and suggest that once you feel confident using some of the methods we have introduced, that you look into more advanced qualitative and quantitative techniques.

Participatory Analysis

When analysing your data we would like to encourage you to think about **participatory analysis**. This is where you involve your participants as much as you can in the data analysis process. Working in this way helps you avoid just giving your 'version of events' and instead enables you to draw in the views and perspectives of your participants. This is particularly valuable when you are working with participants that differ from you in (for example) age, culture or background. Participatory analysis also conveys a sense of respect and value to your participants and can further reinforce their learning and develop their critical thinking skills.

Mixed Methods Analysis

When analysing mixed methods data sets you will need to decide on how you will use the two (or more) data sets. You may have collected all the data to analyse deductively or inductively, or you may use the quantitative data to prove your hypothesis (deductively) and the qualitative data to explore the reasons for it (inductively) or vice versa. You may use one data set as the prime data showing the findings and the other set to confirm them. Alternatively, you may have collected the different data sets to answer different questions.

Another way of mixing methods is to analyse the qualitative data in a quantitative way (e.g. counting the frequency of each quote). This is called quantitizing and has been criticised for losing depth of meaning. You could also apply a qualitative analysis to quantitative data (e.g. exploring the themes from a questionnaire). This is called qualitizing and has been criticised for being one-dimensional (Driscoll et al., 2007: 20). You can probably recognise that it may be better to analyse the numeric data quantitatively and the narrative and visual data qualitatively.

The timeline for your data collection will also affect how you analyse mixed data sets. For example, those that are collected concurrently will usually be used to corroborate one another, whereas those collected sequentially will usually be analysed sequentially, providing findings to guide the next round (and style) of data collection. A common example of this is a survey used to generate a range of interview questions.

Aside from these decisions as to how to treat each data set and when to analyse them, the actual analytical process for each is as described above. The trick in mixed methods is to use the findings in the best way so that the different data sets generate richer findings – whether they confirm or contradict one another.

Transparency, Reflection and Reflexivity

There are three features of analysis that we have not yet discussed, and which apply to all forms of data analysis. These are **transparency**, reflection and **reflexivity**.

Transparency is an important part of analysis. It means describing how you have carried out your analysis as simply and clearly as possible so that the reader can follow what you have done and see how robust it is. The more transparent, the more likely the reader is to follow your analysis and to agree with your findings. This does not mean a lengthy description in your reports, just a concise account of the steps that you took to develop the findings from the data.

Reflection is a second important analytical process. We stated in the introduction that reflective practice is a really important part of the evaluation, and this is particularly the case in the analysis. The reflective evaluative cycle (Figure I.1) encouraged you to continually:

(a) Think of the questions and criteria for success
(b) Gather data in an appropriate way
(c) Analyse the data to see what it says
(d) Apply the learning to the next project

Obviously in the analysis you are focusing on step (c) – analysing the data to see what it says. You need to reflect on the programme and its purpose, the way in which you gathered the data, and the way in which you analyse the data and comment, transparently, on your reflections as to how effective this evaluative process is. You will also be carrying out step (d) – applying the learning to the next project when you write the conclusions, and this will require you to reflect on existing practice, and the findings from your evaluation and what that might mean for future practice. We will explain the process of writing up more in the next chapter.

A final part of this reflective process is reflexivity – this is really the gold star of reflective practice. Reflexivity refers to your awareness of who you are, what experiences you have, what beliefs you hold, and how that shapes the way you have conducted the evaluation. You might, for example, find that your experiences of being female have been a barrier to you understanding male youth culture, or your preference for numbers has influenced your decisions about how you collect data. We always have to guard against using creative methods just because we like them! When you comment on the efficacy of your evaluation reflectively, you can take the opportunity to add any ways in which you might have been predisposed to assumptions because of who you are. It would be useful at this point to get a peer to check your interpretation – this is called a peer review or **inter-rater reliability** – to ensure that it is balanced.

The Step Up case study on the following page provides examples of how some of the data was analysed and put together in the evaluation report.

Step Up Case Study

The analysis of the data collected on Step Up commenced with descriptive statistics on the demographics of the young people to demonstrate that the project had recruited the target audience.

The project worked with 16 young people. The young people were all in year nine going into year ten (ages 14–16). Thirteen (81%) of young people defined themselves as 'White British'; one defined themselves as 'British Pakistani'; and two defined themselves as 'Asian – Other' (Figure 9.10). There was an equal split of eight young men and eight young women (Figure 9.11). Seven young people were in foster care; four had been fostered by family members; four were living in a residential unit; and one young person was fostered but then moved into a residential unit (Figure 9.12). Three young people declared they had dyslexia and had additional support at school.

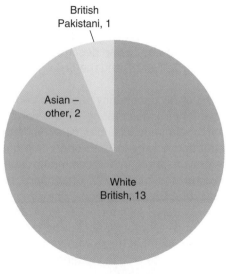

Figure 9.10   Pie chart showing Step Up ethnicity

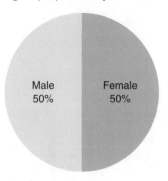

Figure 9.11   Pie Chart showing Step Up gender

(Continued)

(Continued)

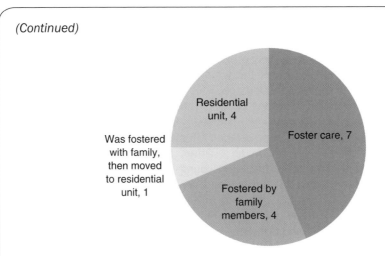

Figure 9.12   Pie chart showing Step Up care situation

The second analytical step was to use descriptive statistics to show the volume of work that had been delivered, and the percentage of sessions attended by the young people.

The project consisted of 26 community sessions and three residential sessions (each three days long), incorporating 27 sessions. Fifty-three sessions were delivered in total (community sessions plus residential sessions).

Young people's attendance ranged from one community session and one residential (10 sessions in total) to 26 community sessions and all three residentials (53 sessions and thus 100% attendance at all sessions). This equated to an average of 65% attendance. Nine of the 16 young people's attendance was above average. Figures 9.13, 9.14 and 9.15 illustrate how there was a core group of 6–11 young people who regularly attended the project. The Youth Worker reported that those who 'dropped out' of the course did so because of changes in 'personal circumstances'.

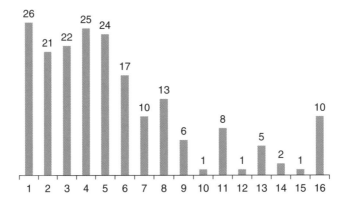

Figure 9.13   Bar chart showing Step Up community session attendance

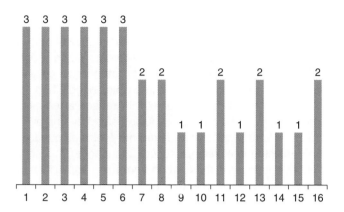

Figure 9.14   Bar chart showing Step Up residential attendance

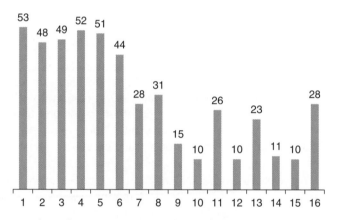

Figure 9.15   Bar chart showing Step Up total attendance

The third stage of the analysis was to measure impact against the programme outcomes. Here we provide you with some of the analysis against the three outcomes so that you can see how the data was used to substantiate claims that the programme was successful.

1. Decrease unauthorised school absence in participants

    The Step Up sessions were all voluntary and out of hours. It is significant in itself that the young people opted to attend sessions out of school time to help them achieve the accreditation.

    Overall, school attendance figures increased by 2%. Those who had average or above average attendance levels on the project (63%), had both high and improved attendance levels at school. This suggests the project had a positive impact on school attendance. This was further supported by evidence

(Continued)

(Continued)

showing that those who had low attendance on the project also had low and/ or reduced school attendance. However, there were some variations to this. For example, one young person had a high attendance on the project but decreased attendance at school; and three young people had below average attendance on the project but high and/or increased attendance at school. The second of these variations could be explained by improvements in life circumstances which meant that they did not feel they needed the project, and this was reflected in increased school attendance. This showed that the project could not been seen in isolation from the complexities of the rest of the young peoples' lives. One Foster Carer further showed this complexity:

At first the project had an effect on her school work, her attendance was good and she was trying hard. She has been having some problems lately but she has started to pick up again.

2. Support the transition from key stage 3 tto 4, and after GCSEs

The project's duration spanned the transition from key stage 3 to 4. The young people's school attendance (detailed above) is evidence in itself of the support the project provided through the transition from key stage 3 to 4. In addition, the project supported other transitions that the young people went through, such as moving school, home and area. The impact of these transitions was shown in one young person's comments:

Yeah it's a big year this has been for me. It's been an important year. A very big important year. Starting this [Step Up]; moving in with me foster home; school. I ain't moved school but that I just want to do well with my GCSEs.

3. Another young person's foster carer also illustrated this:

The project has helped [Name] with confidence. It helped her when we moved back into the area. It was a boost to her confidence because she didn't know many people. [Name] is better at talking to people.

For some, the project was something constant in times of change. One young man's Foster Carer identified how the project had supported him in times of transition:

Very pleased that [Name] has completed the programme. He did have a 'wobble' half way through, round about when he changed schools. Workers were very patient with him. Visited him at school to keep him involved. [Name] tends to start groups and not complete them. Boxing, cadets, local youth club ... [Step Up] has helped stop him getting into even more trouble. Workers have been there for him to talk to at the sessions. Just knowing someone is there has been good for him.

4. Improve academic attainment for participants

Schools were contacted to ascertain grades and predicted grades for the start and finish of the project. These grades were returned for seven young people (these were the seven who had most regularly attended the project). Figure 9.16 shows that these ranged from one young person dropping three grades, to another young person increasing nine grades across all subject areas. This is an average of 2.14 grade increase. For the one young person with the negative score, the project had helped in some areas of her life, but was unable to make a significant impact in all areas of her chaotic life. Her Social Worker commented:

Her confidence has massively improved. School attendance and attitude to school has worsened.

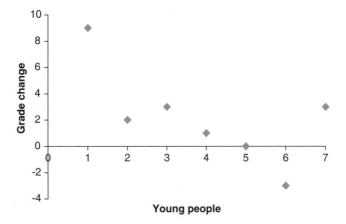

Figure 9.16   Bar chart showing Step Up changes in predicted grades

Nine young people (56%) sustained the commitment and a submission made for the ASDAN CoPE award.

Finally, four young people's stories or narratives were included in the report to illustrate in greater detail the diverse experiences of the young people and how the project had an impact on each of their lives. One is reproduced here (Figure 9.17) as an example.

Extract from the Step Up evaluation: Simon's story

Simon was referred to the Going Places project by his social worker who thought it might be a positive activity for him to get involved in. Simon has experienced a lot of upheaval in his life. He explained,

(Continued)

(Continued)

'When I were ten I had a crap upbringing. Used to have crap clothes. Mum didn't look after me much, but I had a good relationship with me dad, because he were funny and we always had a laugh with each other. I smelt quite bad, because me mum didn't used to get me bathed or owt. At 10 I got arrested for assault, that were me first warning. At 12 I got bullied a bit and I bullied, to try and forget about being bullied. I got in trouble at school and I didn't use to want to learn'.

Simon's Youth Worker described how one day, when Simon was at school, his real mum texted him saying she was going to kill herself. Simon went to every class to find a specific boy he was looking to beat up. After a very violent outburst Simon was excluded from school.

'When I were 13, I met an amazing group called Brathay. Got fostered. I live with me brother. My life got better. I moved schools to [name of school]. I stopped seeing me dad because he didn't get in touch with me Social Worker, but I kept seeing me mum. At 14, this were like three week ago, I got arrested for public order. I'm working with the YOT team, I'm on bail and I'm doing community service, at some time. I want to change my life and it is changing. I'm long-term fostered now … and I'm not gunna turn out like my mum and dad … What I wanna do is join the army and be a good mechanic. Everyone will supports me and I'll love my life … The thing that tempted me was me friends. But all people that mattered stops me from taking the bad route and the bad life'.

On the project Simon worked well with the larger group but he struggled with most forms of written work. He had a short attention span and got distracted very easily. He changed schools because of concerns for his academic achievement. During the project he became more confident in his academic abilities and was on track to achieve the equivalent of a grade B at GCSE through completing his ASDAN CoPE Level 2 portfolio.

His foster carers recently said,

> '[Simon] gets involved with lots of activities like cadets and boxing but never sticks to anything. Going Places is something that he has stuck to for nearly a year. That's a massive achievement for him. He particularly enjoys the weekend residentials, when he comes back from them he's buzzing for days afterwards'.

Simon attended all three residential weekends at Brathay Hall in the Lake District. At times Simon's behaviour was difficult to manage. He seemed to want to be popular and liked to act like the 'class clown' to get the attention that he wanted. This, at times, made the community sessions and residential weekends difficult. However, towards the end of the project the youth workers worked with Simon to use his popularity and influence to be a positive role model within the group.

Simon was involved with Brathay's 'Big Prom' event and attended planning sessions beforehand to make decisions with the group about colour schemes, raffle prizes, running order, etc. On the actual night of the event Simon's behaviour was impeccable. He was polite and courteous all night and did not have to be spoken to about his behaviour.

Simon was recently presented with an award by the Lord Mayor for Bradford for his achievements on the project, as well as a Looked after Children's educational award.

These examples of data led to the following findings:

The outcomes of the Step Up project seem to have both met as well as exceeded the original project aims and objectives. The evidence suggests that, on the whole, young people's attendance improved by 2% and attainment improved by 2.14 grades. Furthermore, the names of nine young people were submitted for the ASDAN Award (equivalent to GCSE grade B).

Of most significance was young people's development of confidence and self-worth. This was attributed to the supportive environment created throughout the project and the mixture of community and residential experiences. These provided the young people with both support and challenge to stretch and grow. The project employed an informal and experiential approach to learning which proved extremely valuable in raising the young people's emotional well-being, self-esteem and self-worth, as well as attitudes to learning.

The young people developed friendships with other young people in care. This was a novel experience which was based on empathy and a sense of collectiveness. These are fundamental principles of collective action, away from disempowerment and towards empowerment. This should not be underestimated and could perhaps be made more explicit within the project.

The role of the Youth Worker was also significant within this supportive environment. Consistency and longevity appeared to be important for these young people, where their lives may have previously been, and continued to be, chaotic. One Youth Worker in particular was widely referred to and praised for her support. It would be interesting to investigate further the specific characteristics that the young people valued, so as to model these in future projects.

Summary

There are many analytical techniques and you need to choose one that suits the overall design of the evaluation and that will provide you with the answer to your questions. You can always mix methods; you do not have to be confined to one alone, as described in the mixed methods chapter. Mixing analytical methods can build strength. Analysis needs to be a logical, reflective and transparent process. Explain what you did and how you arrived at your conclusions. If you can, experiment with different analytical approaches as they can often reveal findings that were not valuable before, and may allow you to use data that you would otherwise use for illustration rather than evidence. Do not be afraid of using creative methods; they can be equally as valid as other analytical approaches.

Key Points

The key points are the nine stages of analysis.

1. Gather data.
2. Inductive or deductive?
3. Process or outcome evaluation?

4. What kind of data have you got? Numbers, words or pictures?
5. Collate data.
6. Data tables.
7. Analyse key themes – central tendency, categories.
8. Display key findings.
9. Return to question – what does your data say?

Further Reading

Doucet, A. and Mauther, S. (2008) 'What can be known and how? Narrated subjects and the Listening Guide' gives a comprehensive guide on how to analyse I-poems.
McIntosh, P. (2010) *Action Research and Reflective Practice: Creative Visual Tools to Facilitate Reflection and Learning* provides good examples of the analysis of visual data.
Salkind, N. (2011) *Statistics for People Who (Think They) Hate Statistics* provides an excellent introductory guide to statistical analysis.

10

WRITING EVALUATION REPORTS AND PRESENTING TO DIFFERENT AUDIENCES

Chapter Overview

- Introduction
- Purpose
- Structure and content
- Accessibility

Introduction

This chapter will highlight some of the key aspects of writing up and presenting evaluation findings. We discuss how the way you write and present the evaluation findings is dictated by the audience who will receive the information. This relates to the discussion of purpose and who will gain, outlined in Chapter 3 on ethics. Knowing this will dictate the suitability of the content. This also relates to how to structure a report, as well as the type of data and findings included. This, in turn, leads the discussion of how the findings are made accessible to different audiences, including how they are made physically as well as intellectually accessible to all stakeholders. Evaluators should consider not only how their evaluations support learning for young people, practitioners, projects and organisations, but also how they can promote awareness of important youth issues and inform policy change. We discuss the different mediums that can be employed to make this accessible and where this can be carried out.

Purpose

The audience is usually, but not limited to, the project stakeholders. These will have been identified in designing the evaluation (discussed in Chapter 6 on planning evaluations). Interest may be extended beyond this to other interested parties, who, for example, may be creating or already working in a similar project area, or evaluators looking at a collection of evaluations in a particular field. These stakeholders are unknown and thus are an anomaly. However, they can be catered for as we make the final report or presentation clear, transparent and replicable. Some evaluators (particularly from the more traditional positivistic paradigm) maintain that the validity of an evaluation is held in its ability to be replicated by another evaluator (Golafshani, 2003; Lewis and Ritchie, 2003). Although post-positivist assumptions critique this perspective, we should be aware that the audience of our evaluations may hold such a viewpoint and thus we should consider this in our write up. The most straightforward way to address this issue is to provide a clear justification of approach, methods and analysis.

More commonly, however, we are presenting findings to the stakeholders we know. Be aware that it is very important that all stakeholders are considered in our presentation of findings. We can all too frequently write a report for a project's funder and tailor the report towards them. In doing so we frequently see young people being excluded from this phase of the evaluation process, as the report is inaccessible to them. This could either be because they simply aren't offered access to the report, or it is articulated in language that doesn't engage them or that they cannot comprehend.

This is directly related to the purpose of the evaluation. For example, this might be for more funding, proof of impact, to better understand what happened, to improve and develop, or to showcase the project. This discussion of purpose is directly related to each stakeholder. The two areas of purpose and stakeholder are therefore equally entwined and mutually reinforcing. This is represented in Table 10.1. The table is useful in establishing the motives for the evaluation. It can be used as a tick box, or as a grading system, where each category is ranked. For example, if we think of Table 10.1 as representing the Step Up case study, you will see that each stakeholder's motives have been ranked on a 1–3 scale (3 = high). From this it can be seen that more funding was of greatest importance in total, as no funding had been secured for the project on an on-going basis. From the manager/practitioner perspective, this was seeking

Table 10.1   Matrix of evaluation purpose

		Purpose				
		More funding	Proof	Understanding	Improve/Develop	Showcase
Stakeholder	Young people	1	1	1	1	3
	Practitioner	3	2	2	3	2
	Manager	3	3	1	2	2
	Funder	3	3	2	1	1

more funding and from the funder's perspective this was about awarding more funding; whereas the young people had little knowledge of the funding issues and prioritised showcasing their experience to their friends and families.

Pause for Thought

Think about a project that you have been involved in:

- Use Table 10.1 to consider who the different stakeholders were and what they were most interested in.

Knowing the interested stakeholders and their motives will help us to gauge how to go about writing up and presenting findings. In the Step Up example the evaluation was written primarily for funders, with a big focus on getting more funding for the project. This became the evaluation priority. With this knowledge we can then consider the detail of its content and how it will be presented.

Structure and Content

Burnard (2004) suggests that there are no absolutes in report writing, stating that different evaluations will call for different sorts of report. The following frame-work can be used as a guide of what you may want to consider including in an evaluation report:

1. Evaluation title (clear, concise but engaging – it's the first thing to be seen)
2. Introduction to the report (what the reader should expect from the report)
3. Context (set the scene of the project, including where the project fits in global and local contexts and the rationale for the project)
4. Literature and/or policy review (linking to the above, you may wish to provide more detail on other practice, policy, evaluations)
5. Project aim, intended outcomes and theory of change (the latter being the inputs and activities needed to achieve the outcomes and overall aim)
6. Evaluation approach/methodology (how you went about evaluating the project, with justification, detail of methods used and how this was analysed)
7. Findings (what the data collection methods found)
8. Discussion and implications (relating this back to the wider context what does this show and mean)
9. Recommendations (what you surmise, changes and further investigation)
10. Appendix (this should detail any relevant information that is too lengthy for the main body of the report. You should try and summarise anything that goes in here also, so it is not too long).

This framework can also be applied to other types of presentation of findings (for example, verbal). More details of these are found later in this chapter.

We need to consider exactly what goes in to the evaluation report and how much of what. Just as we have argued in Chapter 8 for mixed methods in evaluating young people's projects, we would also advocate mirroring this in the context of the evaluation report. Again this is to give a holistic, rounded picture of the findings, which engages all audiences. For example, a combination of numerical data or statistics and case studies or I-poems, can provide a holistic understanding, as well as being powerful and emotive. In relation to this, we should not assume that funders will only want statistics and young people will only want stories. This is far from true on both counts.

The balance of detail and content will need to be made with concise writing and headline statements which stand out for the ever busy audience. Again it should not be assumed that reports for funders will be longer, more technical and more detailed than those for practitioners (for example). Both of these audiences have limited time for reading and so need the important information.

This further highlights the need to make any type of data understandable to all audiences. This needs to be intellectually accessible to all audiences. Some reports often have a youth version and a professional version, so as to meet these needs. Attention needs to be paid to the type of language being used to ensure the right balance. For example, this may be with regard to technical, political or organisation-specific language and abbreviations.

There are further debates surrounding whether reports should be written in the first person ('I found') or the third person ('the evaluation found'). This will of course depend on your audience, but participative approaches lend themselves to the use of the first person. Further, this is more likely to be 'we found'.

The suitability of the content is best gauged from proof reading and feedback. 'Youth proofing' has become a common process in evaluation writing. Although usually employed by organisations wanting policies or documents youth proofed to help them become more accessible to young people, this can be applied to evaluation reports as well. This process can of course be made more participatory, by young people being involved more deeply in the writing process, rather than simply signing it off at the end. Participatory evaluation would consider young people's involvement throughout the whole process, including writing and presenting.

Accessibility

As we have discussed elsewhere in this book (for example, Chapter 3 on ethics) stakeholders can include young people, project workers, managers, family, friends, community members, or funders. Not all stakeholders will want to be the recipient of evaluation findings; however we need to meet all of their needs in case they do want to receive them. We need to consider how each of these stakeholders will physically access an evaluation report and how we make it attractive and engaging to them.

We need to decide how we will present the findings of the evaluation. This is by no means limited to a written report. It can include verbal, digital or creative presentations.

Written presentation of findings

This is the most common medium for presenting evaluation findings. Written reports are easily emailed and shared within organisations as well as circulated to wider stakeholders. These can also be made accessible to wider audiences through publishing in professional publications (e.g., in the UK, *Children & Young People Now*) and academic journals (e.g. *Youth and Policy*). Both mediums also afford access to online opportunities. This is not only through online versions of the aforementioned types of publications and journals, but also through organisational websites, online forums and social media.

Verbal presentation of findings

The presentation of findings is also commonly a verbal presentation. This may be to the youth group, internally within the organisation, to project stakeholders, to funders, or, more widely, to other professionals or academics at seminars and conferences.

There has been a relatively recent push from the participatory perspective of encouraging young people to present findings. This can be more authentic as well as being a great learning experience for the young person. This must be the priority and we should ensure that this process never becomes tokenistic or for our own gain, more than the young people's. Appropriate ethical and safeguarding procedures should be in place. More specifically, informed consent (discussed in Chapter 3 on ethics) needs to surround this process to ensure the young person is safeguarded. In these circumstances, young people can present their perspective, their experience, their story, or their I-poem, for example. They can present more generalised evaluation findings as well as answering questions, just as any practitioner or evaluator would. However, the advantage of the young person doing this is that the content and answers to any questions are not interpreted by a third party (the evaluator for example); they are authentic and genuine.

Visual presentation of findings

Visual presentation can make findings far more attractive, engaging and accessible. This may allow the audience to more personally relate to and understand a particular theme being discussed.

The basis of a visual presentations may be as simple as numerical data often being much easier to comprehend if presented as a graph. Or visual presentations could include other mediums such as digital images, video footage, or recordings. These also open up other online mediums, such as YouTube. Poster presentations are a common feature of academic conferences, but this concept extends to within the youth project setting; for example, posters targeting findings to young people, the public, staff or other professionals in the setting.

Word clouds, or wordles, create visual representations of data. Themes are represented by key words, and the more prominent or frequent the theme the larger the representation of the word. Figure 10.1 shows what was important about a youth group to members of a US Senior High (The First Religious Group Carlisle, 2014). Specific terms that were listed by multiple people are in larger type, and those mentioned rarely are in small type. Whilst this is visually accessible, it does not allow you to accurately quantify the amounts of each, which may or may not be important in your report. Similarly, infographics (Figure 10.2) are commonly used as a graphic visual representations of information, data or knowledge intended to present complex information quickly and clearly (Newsom and Haynes, 2011; Smiciklas, 2012). Again, these are excellent ways to represent your data and grab attention, but you probably cannot show as much nuance in this format as you would in text, and you need to consider what assumptions are available for the reader to make. Figure 10.2 shows the Centre for Information and Research on Civic Learning and Engagement (2014) infographic showing poll results on youth from the 2012 US Elections (Bufkin, 2012).

Creative presentation of findings

There are several other creative ways of presenting evaluation findings. Adopting creative presentation techniques goes hand in hand with the creative methods for which this book advocates. Photos, images, art work, or drama can all open up evaluation findings to become more accessible.

We have presented findings at a variety of conferences, both academic and practitioner based, through ethnodrama. An ethnodrama is the written transformation and adaptation of evaluation data (e.g. interview transcripts, participant observation field notes, journals, documents, statistics) into a dramatic play script staged as a live, public theatrical performance (Saldaña, 2008). An example of this is shown in Vignette 10.1. A trained theatre practitioner performed the ethnodrama, however, in our experience, this works equally well with youth work practitioners and young people acting it out.

Figure 10.1   Example of a wordle

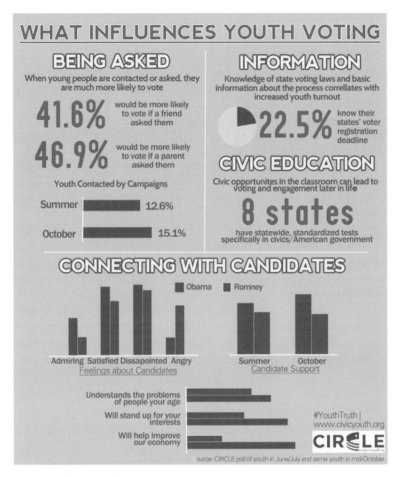

Figure 10.2   Example of an infographic

Vignette 10.1   An Ethnodrama (Maynard, 2008; Maynard and Smallman, 2009)

After a series of projects for young women at risk of sexual exploitation, we wanted to share the evaluation findings, not only with the funder (achieved through the required written report) but with wider audiences. We felt we had achieved significant learning within the project about working with young women in this particular situation and wanted to share this internally with colleagues, as well as externally with other professionals. The project had been a partnership between an inner city sexual exploitation service and Brathay Trust and had involved community and residential elements. This afforded a broad stakeholder and wider audience interest, incorporating police, social and care services, targeted services, youth workers and outdoor practitioners.

(Continued)

(Continued)

The young women's learning journeys through the programme had been particularly powerful and there had been some strong common themes amongst the young women and the way in which the programme had supported them. It was not an option for these particular young women to present their stories in person, because of their vulnerability and current context. However, with their permission we presented their stories through ethnodrama. This meant taking the stories of their experiences, compiled through direct quotations, and a colleague, who was a theatre practitioner, acting these out. The practitioner learnt the story word for word and, with the permission of the young women, listening to the transcripts to try and represent all the nuances of how their words were expressed.

The presentation used the ethnodrama to illuminate key themes from the experiences and implications for practice. This proved to be very emotive for audience members, bringing them closer to the project and the young women, and the ethnodrama was used to demonstrate the findings of the project, enabling the audience to conceptualise the young women's experiences.

Reflecting on this we can see the value of stepping out of the box and presenting findings in a different way. You could record the performance and use that as your evaluation report rather than writing one too, or some databases (e.g. Substance Views) allow you to embed multimedia into interactive evaluation reports.

Pause for Thought

- How have you been the recipient of evaluation findings in the past?

- Were these engaging?

- Did the way they were presented enhance the findings in any way?

- How could they have been presented better?

Summary

Reporting evaluation findings is a common requirement from funders, and general dissemination of your findings is important to support learning. This learning may be for the young people, practitioners, funders, other stakeholders, or wider interested parties. As youth work is pressurized in the UK, disseminating the results of evaluations is even more important to create a national acceptance of the value of the sector. We advocate the use of creative methods to present evaluation findings, for all the same reasons this book advocates creative methods of data collection.

Inclusivity, engagement and accessibility are just as important in the dissemination of findings, as well as in the approach to the evaluation itself. This may take more time and resources from evaluators or practitioners and so should be accounted for within budgeting and resourcing.

Key Points

1. It is important to understand who the audience is, as this guides the very design of the final report.
2. The report should include appropriate information, so it is justifiable and replicable.
3. The report needs to be well structured and uses language and content appropriate to the audience.
4. It is best practice to create two versions – a youth version, as well as a funder/practitioner version.
5. Powerful reports combine different mediums to ensure evaluation findings are attractive and engaging.

Further Reading

Burnard, P. (2004) *Writing a Qualitative Research Report* provides a useful structure to support and encourage the first-time researcher to write up their work in a systematic way (although within the discipline of nursing).

Saldaña, J. (2003) 'Dramatizing data: A primer' provides a 'how-to' piece for methods literature. Written by a theatre artist who later became an ethnographic researcher, it offers a personal primer in playwriting with qualitative data.

Saldaña, J. (2008) 'Ethnodrama' provides a good overview of ethnodrama.

CONCLUSION

We have positioned the work that we do with young people as 'non-formal'. In this type of project the staff facilitate learning, using flexible plans designed around the needs of the young people. Moreover, these projects feature active learning and learning takes place in a variety of settings. This approach stands in contrast to informal and formal learning. Although non-formal learning does not have a fixed curriculum, it does feature outcomes for sessions and is purposively developmental at heart. It is therefore equally as appropriate to evaluate it against these outcomes as it is to appraise formal education, and, indeed, we are missing a trick if we neglect to do so.

Evaluation is a core part of youth workers' practice. It may not be formalised, but youth workers' practice regularly involves them reviewing progress with the young people that they work with. This book has aimed to make the formalisation of evaluation processes as painless as possible, and, moreover, as engaging, meaningful and participatory as possible for the young people. They should benefit as much as we do. For this reason we have promoted participatory evaluation supported by a consideration of power which is often lacking in evaluations 'on' young people.

We have equally stressed the benefits of creative evaluation tools as important mechanisms that can support the engagement of young people in evaluation and that can transform evaluation into a meaning-making exercise for young people rather than a box-ticking exercise or interrogation. We have suggested ways in which you can collect and analyse this data that are as robust as, if not more so than, common 'standardised' forms of evaluation, such as happy sheets.

We do not subscribe to evaluating all work 'for the sake of it', rather the right degree of evaluation for the young people, stakeholders and project should be selected. Nor do we subscribe to the dominant form of evaluation promoted in the UK – evidence based practice. Rather we have argued for evaluation processes that are fit for purpose.

Evaluating projects with young people benefits them by revealing what they have learnt through their efforts on a programme. The end result is not some mystical gain, but a clear and tangible attitude, skill, knowledge, understanding or capability that they can use again. Evaluation also helps practitioners understand how and when they have contributed to these gains with their practice. This can help confirm and rein-force good practice, and challenge and point to the need to change poor practice. As such it is a learning process for young people, practitioners and organisations. Finally evaluation is also a vital tool to support the value of non-formal youth work – whether it needs demonstrating to project funders, local authorities, or the government.

To reap these evaluation rewards we need to be prepared to work our way through the whole of the evaluation cycle (Figure C.1).

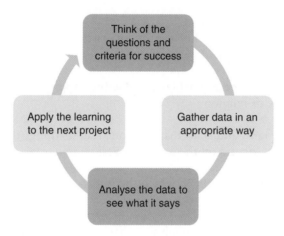

Figure C.1   The evaluation cycle

Thinking of questions is probably not problematic, and youth workers are used to thinking of criteria for success, or outcomes! Throughout the book we have encouraged you to gather data in an appropriate way, thinking through paradigms, methods, ethics, types of evaluation, and data collection tools. Analysis and com-munication of findings were described in Chapters 9 and 10. The final stage, applying learning to the next project is possibly one of the more difficult steps to achieve, depending on how challenging the findings of the evaluation are. We would also like to suggest that you do not confine your findings to your organisation, but that you also share them online, blog, tweet, use all the social media you can to share the findings of your work. This is so that you and your organisation gain a reputa-tion as people who take evaluation of youth work projects seriously. Sharing and disseminating will also provide blueprints and practice guides for other people to follow – both in terms of how to deliver youth work and how to go about evalua-tion. Finally, share and disseminate your work so that, together, we can build an evidence base of the efficacy of non-formal youth work projects.

The final task that we suggest for you is to reflect on your evaluation practice using the cycle above as a framework. This will mean that you continue to grow and develop as an evaluator, as well as a youth work practitioner. It is our sincere hope that this book and the accompanying toolkit will have aided you on that journey.

GLOSSARY

Action research is research initiated to solve an immediate problem or a reflective process of progressive problem solving led by individuals working with others in teams or as part of a 'community of practice' to improve the way they address issues and solve problems.

Anonymity aims to protect the identity of participants by ensuring personally identifying details are withheld or obscured.

Anti-oppressive practice is practice that does not oppress people on any grounds such as race, gender or religion.

Assets are the strengths and skills that someone has, or things that they can do. An asset based approach focuses on the attributes that people have.

Attribution refers to the extent to which the impact of a programme can be linked to that outcome rather than any other factors.

Bar chart – a bar chart or bar graph is a chart with rectangular bars with lengths proportional to the values that they represent. The bars can be plotted vertically or horizontally. A vertical bar chart is sometimes called a column bar chart.

Bricolage is a term that refers to a mixture of data sets brought together by a researcher or evaluator. It literally means 'do it yourself' in French.

Categorical variables are variables where cases are merely placed into independent, separate categories.

Category/categorisation refers to a class or division of people or things regarded as having particular shared characteristics.

Causal links describe the relationship between a cause and an outcome, for example that intervention A with young people B will always lead to outcome C.

Central tendency is a single value that attempts to describe a set of data by identifying the central position within that set of data. As such, measures of central tendency are sometimes called measures of central location. They are also classed as summary statistics. The mean (often called the average) is most likely the measure of central tendency that you are most familiar with, but there are others, such as the median and the mode.

Closed questions are questions that invite only a yes or no answer.

Coding refers to the process of giving similar observed instances (in text, behaviour) a symbol or category.

Cognitive dissonance refers to the discomfort that can arise when people change, and two opposing ideas come into their mind at the same time.

Confidentiality ensures access to participants' details or data is restricted.

Constructivism is a philosophical position that states that knowledge is constructed by human beings when new information comes into contact with their existing knowledge, and views all knowledge as developed through experience.

Content analysis is a search of qualitative materials (especially text) to find 'coding units' (usually words, phrases or themes); analysis often concentrates on quantitative treatment of frequencies but can be a purely qualitative approach.

Context, mechanism, outcome, pattern configurations (CMOCs) refer to the need to identify which contextual factors (e.g. class-size), lead to outcomes (e.g. increased learning).

Control group is the group used as the baseline measure against which the performance of the experimental group (or groups) is assessed.

Correlation is a (standardised) measure of the relationship between two variables.

Correlation coefficient is a number, between –1 and 1, which signifies the strength of the correlation (or relationship) between two variables.

Cost benefits refer to the identifiable benefits that the cost of an investment brings. The benefits should outweigh the costs for an investment to be worthwhile financially.

Creative methods involve collecting data through art, dance, drama, photography, poetry and other artistic, or creative forms of self-expression.

Critical consciousness focuses on achieving an in-depth understanding of the world, allowing for the perception and exposure of social and political contradictions. Critical consciousness also includes taking action against the oppressive elements in one's life that are illuminated by that understanding.

Critical pedagogy is a form of education in which students are encouraged to question dominant or common notions of meaning and form their own understanding of what they learn. This type of approach is especially popular in potentially subjective fields of study such as literature, art, and even history. One of the central ideas of this teaching method is that students are able to build their own meaning when learning, and teachers should facilitate that process rather than 'force' meaning upon the students. Critical pedagogy tends to accomplish this end by striving to help students 'unlearn' previous lessons that may enforce dominant thought and 'relearn' their own ideas.

Data set refers to a group of data points or values which can be summarised or analysed.

Deductive – a deductive approach would accept that the researcher has an idea of what is likely to be found and will more often than not take a theoretical stance at the start of the research. In this light data is analysed according to these preconceptions, and is used to support or refute the original research hypothesis.

Deficits are problems that someone has, or things that they are missing. A deficit approach focuses on the attributes that people do not have.

Dependent variables – a dependent variable is what is measured in an experiment as a result of the manipulation of the independent variable. It is called dependent because it 'depends' on the independent variable. In a scientific experiment you cannot have a dependent variable without an independent variable.

    Example: You are interested in how stress affects heart rate in humans. Your independent variable would be the stress and the dependent variable would be the heart rate. You can directly manipulate stress levels in your human subjects and measure how those stress levels change heart rate.

Descriptive analysis aims to summarise raw data and uses techniques such as percentages, central tendency, graphs and charts.

Developmental evaluation is an approach that can assist social innovators develop social change initiatives in complex or uncertain environments. It does not have any set methods or tools, is carried out in real time, and is very responsive to the situation.

Diaries require participants to record details of events, feelings and/or learning over a set period of time.

Disclosure is the act of sharing personal details or experiences with another.

Discourses are messages that are conveyed to us through spoken and written forms of communication as well as visual representations. They produce meaning about the nature of 'reality' in a way that is often out of our awareness. Young people, for example, are often presented in negative ways in the press, with few stories that balance that out by describing their positive attributes. This creates a discourse of 'youths' who are dangerous, lazy and worse than ever before.

Dispersion is a technical and general term and is used to describe any measure of the spread of scores in a data set. The range is a measure of dispersion. Measure of dispersion can denote how stretched or squeezed the distribution of data is.

Distal outcomes are outcomes that are a long way from the young person's current position and are dependent on other outcomes being achieved before they can be attained.

Distance travelled is a measure of the progress that a participant has made on a selected variable (e.g. confidence) from the start of the project to the end.

Distance travelled tools measure the difference between two points of achievement. This typically involves measuring young people's capabilities (or them self-assessing their capabilities) at the start of a programme and at the end, using the same tool, to demonstrate that there has been progression.

Ecological validity means that the methods, materials and setting of the study must approximate the real world that is being examined.

Emancipatory work seeks to increase people's sense of empowerment, of the power that they personally have over their lives.

Empirical method is a way of gaining knowledge by means of direct and indirect observation or experience.

Empiricism is a theory that knowledge comes only or primarily from sensory experience and emphasises evidence, particularly as discovered from experiments.

Empowerment is the process by which individuals or groups increase their power, control and ability to act.

Epistemology refers to our beliefs about how knowledge is constructed (e.g. we observe and build knowledge from facts, or we base our knowledge on previous experience).

Ethics is the branch of philosophy which involves discussing and deciding on the principles of moral conduct. In research and evaluation ethics informs the planning, implementation, analysis and dissemination of evaluation and findings.

Evaluation is a process that helps determine whether an initiative (like a programme or project) has been worthwhile in terms of delivering what was intended and expected.

Evidence based practice is a scientific approach to proving the efficacy of a project through the collection of quantitative data, random control trials, demonstrating causality, and proving the replicability of the project.

Experimental evaluations/experiments seek to test a hypothesis (for example that a programme leads to a positive impact for young people) and prove whether it is true or not by identifying the independent variable (programme), isolating this variable, controlling all other variables that might impact on outcomes and then observing the variable across conditions (e.g. programme vs programme) to see if the independent variable has the intended effect. This method proves a framework for positivistic approaches to evaluation.

Experiential learning is the process of making meaning from direct experience, i.e., 'learning from experience'.

Focus groups and **group interviews** refer to asking groups of people questions at the same time.

Formal learning is planned learning that takes place in schools, colleges and universities.

Formative evaluation is a method for judging the worth of a programme or project whilst it is forming (in progress). These evaluations track the progress towards outcomes, and the processes that are helping to achieve them.

Free market economy is where provision is based on supply and demand and there is competition between organisations for funding and clients.

Frequency data/count means counting the number of times an item occurs in a particular category.

Generalisable ideas or findings that emerge from evaluations can be generalised to wider society. For example, a programme that proved that intensive one-to-one work supported young people into employment might be generalised to all young people. The extent to which such generalisations are possible is contentious. Wide-scale scientific evaluations are sometimes believed to be more generalisable than small-scale interpretive evaluations. You may or may not aim to have generalisable findings when you start your evaluation.

Hard outcomes is a term used to refer to tangible outcomes that are easy to measure such as exam grades.

Hegemony refers to the hidden messages that exist in society about what is accepted and normal.

Hypothesis – a hypothesis is a theory that is being tested; for example, 'The world is round' or 'This programme led to change'.

Ideology is a set of conscious and unconscious ideas that constitute one's goals, expectations and actions. An ideology is a comprehensive vision, a way of looking at things, as in several philosophical tendencies, or it is a set of ideas proposed by the dominant class of a society to all members of this society (a 'received consciousness' or product of socialisation).

Impact is a marked effect, influence or change. In the context of evaluation of work with young people it refers to the effects, influences or changes that have occurred for the young people (and wider families and communities) as a result of engaging in a project or programme.

Impact evaluations seek to establish what changes have occurred for the participants in a programme or project as a result of the programme or project activities.

Independent variable – an independent variable is the variable you have control over, what you can choose and manipulate in an experiment. It is usually what you are interested in studying the effect of. In some cases, you may not be able to manipulate the independent variable. It may be something that is already there and is fixed, something you would like to evaluate with respect to how it affects something else.

Example: You are interested in how stress affects heart rate in humans. Your independent variable is the stress and the dependent variable is the heart rate. In your research you manipulate stress levels, for example by giving participants different tasks to do and then measuring how these impact on heart rate.

In-depth interviews aim to gather detailed, in-depth accounts from individuals about a particular issue.

Individuation has a range of meanings in the social sciences. In the context of youth work it is often used to refer to the process of placing blame on individuals. However, in the discipline of psychology it is used to express the process in which an individual's self develops and the person becomes an individual, distinguishable from other persons.

Inductive approaches – when a researcher takes an inductive approach they start their research with no preconceived ideas of what they might find. Instead they let the data speak to them.

Informal educators are educators that use informal education as their approach.

Informal learning is learning that is not organised or structured in terms of goals, time or instruction.

Informed consent is the practice of ensuring that participants understand exactly what is being required of them and that they voluntarily agree to participate and/or allow any data related to them to be used, shared and disseminated.

Interpretivism is a philosophy that believes that the social world is made up of meanings rather than facts. The subjective nature of the world can only be understood through the meanings that individuals assign to it and these can be observed by behaviour. Attending school, for example, implies that students think that school will help them get on in life. Because it is subjective, interpretivism seeks to understand the views and perspectives of research participants.

Inter-rater reliability is the degree of agreement among raters or evaluators. It gives a score of how much consensus there is in the ratings given by evaluators looking at the same data.

Interval data is a level of measurement at which each unit on a scale represents an equal change in the variable measured. An example of an interval scale is the measurement of length in cm.

Latent content is the underlying meaning of something, rather than the more obvious, objective appearance.

Likert scales are scales using a format where respondents select from an ordered range, for example 'strongly disagree' (10), 'disagree' (8), etc., and a ranked score is given to the responses as shown in the brackets.

Logic model is a pictorial map of a programme or intervention that shows your systematic thinking about the people who will come on the programme, what you will do and how that will lead to outcomes.

Managerialism is the management of people by inspection, indicators and paperwork.

Manifest content is the actual content of something, rather than the meaning that it holds.

Mean – this is measure of central tendency and relates to the 'average' score in a data set. The mean is calculated by adding up all the numbers in the data set and then dividing by the number of cases in the data set.

Mean deviation is a measure of dispersion and reflects the mean of all the deviations of each value from the mean.

Median – this is a measure of central tendency and refers to the middle value in a data set. To find the median, your numbers have to be listed in numerical order, so you may have to rewrite your list first.

Methods fit within and need to match the methodology. Methods refer to the specific ways in which we collect data, for example whether we will collect numeric data or narrative data (qualitative and quantitative).

Methodology is the approach to knowledge generation taken within an evaluation. It defines how you, the evaluator, will find out what you are trying to understand.

Mixed methods utilise the similarities and differences between qualitative and quantitative data, allowing the two to complement each other under the proviso that each fundamentally seeks the same goal – providing answers to evaluation questions.

Mode – this is a measure of central tendency. The 'mode' is the value that occurs most often.

Monitoring refers to the constant observation of changes over time within a given situation or context. In evaluations of work with young people attendance might be monitored so that (a) it can be managed and (b) it can be reported on as part of the end of project evaluation.

Narrative data is any account of connected events, presented to a reader or listener in a sequence of written or spoken words.

Naturalistic data collection tries to understand what is happening in as natural a setting as possible, rather than creating artificial data collection tools such as surveys.

Negative correlation is the relationship between two variables in which one variable increases as the other decreases, and vice versa.

Nominal data – a level of measurement at which numbers are only labels for categories. You can count but not order or measure nominal data. For example, in a data set males could be coded as 0, females as 1; marital status of an individual could be coded as Y if married, N if single.

Non-equivalent simply means that something does not match. When planning random control trials, it is important that the experimental groups and the control group are the same, or equivalent, on as many variables as possible (e.g. demographics, background, experience, motivation, etc.) so the 'independent variable' can account for any differences in the dependent variable. However, total matching is often not possible, in which case the control group is named 'non-equivalent' to note that other variables might be responsible for any differences observed between the groups.

Non-formal learning is learning outside the formal school, vocational training or university system.

Non-randomised studies do not use a random control trial.

Ontology refers to a person's view of the nature of reality (e.g. fixed and observable, or individual and subjective).

Open questions invite a longer answer than a yes or no; they invite dialogue.

Ordinal data – a set of data is said to be ordinal if the values/observations belonging to it can be ranked (put in order) or have a rating scale attached. You can count and order, but not measure, ordinal data.

Othering is the process of excluding or subjugating others by defining them as different and therefore inferior.

Outcome evaluations seek to establish what outcomes have been achieved by the participants in a programme or project as a result of the programme or project activities.

Outcomes are the end results – the observable consequence of any given action. The outcome of spending too much money could be debt, for example. In this context, programmes for young people often have outcomes that the group and individuals work towards.

Paradigm refers to a framework, pattern of thought or way of thinking. Positivism and post-positivism are the main two paradigms, or patterns of thinking, referred to in this book.

Participant observation refers to taking part in a programme whilst observing it.

Participatory analysis involves young people in the analysis and interpretation of the data.

Participatory/participative evaluation involves young people in the design and conduct of evaluations, and shares findings with them.

Participatory practice is a way of working that emphasises the rights of young people to have power, make choices and have their opinions heard.

Percentages – a percentage is a number or ratio expressed as a fraction of 100. It is often denoted using the percent sign, '%', or the abbreviation 'pct'.

Pie chart – a pie chart is a circular chart divided into sectors, illustrating numerical proportion. In a pie chart, the arc length of each sector (and consequently its central angle and area), is proportional to the quantity it represents. While it is named for its resemblance to a pie which has been sliced, there are variations on the way it can be presented.

Positive correlations show the relationship between two variables moves in tandem. A positive correlation exists when as one variable increases, the other variables also increase, and vice versa.

Positivistic/positivism is the paradigm of traditional science and is the oldest, most dominant, view of social science. It holds that there is an objective, observable and measureable reality.

Post-positivistic/post-positivism holds an alternative and anti-positivist viewpoint that believes one reality is not possible in a social world.

Power refers to the influence or control a person has or holds over a social situation, the self or other people.

Praxis is a process of bringing theory to practice and practice to theory, with the understanding that they are both essential components of knowledge development.

Pre-test–post-test designs are quasi-experimental methods that attempt to measure capabilities, skills, knowledge or outcomes before and after a programme. This is the technical name for a distance travelled tool.

Process refers to a way of working, the things that people did/do on a day-to-day basis. Process measures stand in contrast to outcome measures. Processes involve asking 'how' and outcomes involve asking 'what'.

Process evaluations seek to understand how well a programme is operating. They will assess the design and implementation of programmes and projects to provide feedback to stakeholders on how they are performing.

Proximal outcomes are those that are closest to the young person's current situation, and that will lead to more distal or further away outcomes.

Psychometric – a psychometric test is any standardized procedure for measuring sensitivity or memory or intelligence or aptitude or personality.

Qualitative data includes words, images and other non-numerical data.

Qualitative methods acquire a detailed description of the social situation being studied and focus on the meaning that people attach to their lives and experiences. The data is often language or image based.

Quantitative data refer to the numerical measurement of data.

Quantitative methods aim to collect and analyse numerical data, identifing the causal relationships between variables.

Quasi-experimental evaluations are studies used to estimate the impact of an intervention on its target population. Quasi-experimental research designs share many similarities with the traditional experimental design, but they specifically lack the element of random assignment to treatment or control groups.

Random control groups are a specific method used in scientific experiments, especially clinical trials. The process involves dividing evaluation participants 'randomly' into two groups – one that receives the project activities and one that does not – in order to prove that the activities alone led to the changes observed.

Randomisation/randomised control trials refers to the practice of assigning participants in a study to an intervention or a control group. This is a deliberate act that separates them in a random way in that they are not selected for entry to either group due to any characteristic.

Range is the difference between two numbers at the start and end of your data set. It shows the breadth, or dispersion of data.

Realism is the view that the world described by science is the real world, as it is independent of what we might take it to be.

Realistic evaluation is a post-positivist approach to evaluating social programmes. It assumes that knowledge is a social and historical product, and thus the social and political context as well as theoretical mechanisms, need consideration in analysis of programme or policy effectiveness.

Reflective practice is the process of thinking about practice as it happens, or after it has happened in order to understand issues, dilemmas, good practice and areas of weakness.

Reflexive practitioners are aware of who they are, what they believe, how they operate in the world, and how the world operates on them. They are vigilant to assumptions, discourses and hegemony.

Reflexivity refers to the evaluators' recognition that their personal perspective constructs the research interpretation. The position of the evaluator and its potential influence on the evaluation process is considered and discussed, along with possible alternative constructions or interpretations of the findings.

Relativist/relativism is the concept that points of view have no absolute truth or validity, having only relative, subjective value according to differences in perception and consideration, i.e. that truth is always relative to some particular frame of reference.

Reliability in an evaluation context means 'repeatability' or 'consistency'. A measure is considered reliable if it would give us the same result over and over again (assuming that what we are measuring isn't changing).

Replicable means that something can be done again. In an evaluation context, a programme is replicable if it can be delivered again in the same way and produce the same results.

Scattergraph/gram – a diagram showing the placement of paired values on a two-dimensional chart. It can be used to look for connections or a correlation between the two sets of data.

Selection bias or **selection effect** refers to the way that an error in the selection of participants may skew the evaluation results. This is particularly the case when a certain demographic dominates, or when young people have opted to participate.

Semantic differential scale – this is a type of a rating scale designed to measure the connotative meaning of objects, events and concepts. The connotations are used to derive the attitude to the given object, event or concept.

Semi-structured interviews are interviews with some of the questions predefined, but having flexibility to follow the line of conversation and pursue other themes that emerge.

Social construction refers to the way that society develops an understanding of the world and how it 'collectively' creates and defines categories, and attributes meaning, status and importance. For example, class, race and gender don't really mean anything. They have come to have meaning because society has given them a meaning. Social construction is also concerned with how the perspectives of certain groups (e.g. middle class, white, male) are privileged over others, and the impact this.

Social justice is the ability people have to realise their potential in the society where they live.

Soft outcomes is a term that is often used to refer to intangible and hard-to-measure personal development outcomes.

Stakeholder – a stakeholder is someone who has a 'stake' or an interest or claim in something that is happening.

Statistical analysis refers to the practice of analysing numerical data by employing a statistical test. Tests enable the user to process large amounts of data, identify and report overall trends, and assess the statistical significance of any findings.

Structured interviews/questionnaires have set questions that the interviewer sticks to no matter how the conversation develops.

Summative evaluation is a method of judging the worth of a programme or project at the end of its activities (summation). The focus is on the outcome.

Surveys are a method for collecting quantitative information, usually via questionnaires, from large samples.

Theory of change refers to a document or diagram that demonstrates the thinking that has underpinned a programme or project.

Transparent evaluations and **transparency** aim to make the process of research – including data collection, coding, and analysis – clearly visible to all readers.

Triangulation is the use of two or more different research methods.

Validity refers to the extent to which a conclusion or measurement is well-founded and corresponds accurately to the real world. The word 'valid' is derived from the Latin *validus*, meaning strong. The validity of a measurement tool (for example, the SDQ questionnaire) is considered to be the degree to which the tool measures what it claims to measure.

Variable is the factor (or value) that is being observed, manipulated or measured.

Visual analogue scales are where respondents mark their position on a line between two polar opposites and the distance of their mark from one extreme is measured as a score.

Voluntarism is where participants are given the choice whether or not to participate.

REFERENCES

Airthrey Ltd (2013) 'Making evaluation a priority' (http://www.airthrey.com/papers/airthreypaper_evaluationpriority.pdf).

Alatt, P. and Dixon, C. (2004) 'On using visual data across the research process: Sights and insights from a social geography of young people's independent living in times of educational change', in C. Pole (ed.), *Studies in Qualitative Methodology: Seeing is Believing? Approaches to Visual Research*. Oxford: Elsevier.

Alcott, L. (2009) 'The problem of speaking for others', in A. Jackson and L. Mazzei (eds), *Voice in Qualitative Enquiry*. Abingdon: Routledge.

Amaratunga, D., Baldry, D., Sarshar, M. and Newton, R. (2002) 'Quantitative and qualitative research in the built environment: Application of "mixed" research approach', *Work Study*, 51(1): 17–31.

Arnstein, S. (1969) 'A ladder of citizen participation', *Journal of the American Institute of Planners*, 35: 216–224.

Axford, N. and Morpeth, L. (2013) 'Evidence based programmes in children's services: A critical appraisal', *Children and Youth Services Review*, 35: 268–277.

Balan, N.B. (2005) 'Multiple voices and methods: Listening to women who are in workplace transition', *International Journal of Qualitative Methods*, 4(4): Article 5.

Baldwin, M. (2011) 'Resisting the EasyCare model: Building a more radical, community based, anti-authoritarian social work for the future', in M. Lavalette (ed.), *Radical Social Work Today: Social Work at the Crossroads*. Bristol: Polity Press. pp. 187–205.

Batsleer, J. (2008) *Informal Learning in Youth Work*. Sage: London.

Batsleer, J. (2010) 'Youth workers as researchers: Ethical issues in practitioner and participatory research', in S. Banks (ed.), *Ethical Issues in Youth Work*, 2nd edn. London: Routledge.

Beck, A.T., Ward, C.H., Mendelson, M., Mock, J. and Erbaugh, J. (1961) 'An inventory for measuring depression', *Archives of General Psychiatry*, 4: 561–571.

Beddoes, D., Hedges, A., Sloman, J., Smith, L. and Smith, T. (2010) *Engaging Children and Young People in Research and Consultation: A Review of Principals, Policy and Practice*. London: General Teaching Council for England.

Better Evaluation (2014) (http://betterevaluation.org/).

BIM Larsson Associates (2008) *The Aboriginal Youth Suicide Prevention Strategy: Summative Evaluation*. Alberta: AYSP.

Blueprints for Youth Development (2013) (http://www.blueprintsprograms.com/contact.php).

Bolton, G. (2010) *Reflective Practice: Writing and Professional Development*, 3rd edn. London: Sage.

Booth, T. (1996) 'Sounds of still voices: Issues in the use of narrative methods with young people who have learning difficulties', in L. Barton (ed.), *Disability and Society: Emerging Insights and Issues*. London: Longman.

Boyatzis, R. (1998) *Transforming Qualitative Information*. London: Sage.

Brannen, J. (2005) *Mixed Methods Research: A Discussion Paper. ESRC National Centre for Research Methods (NCRM) Methods Review Paper*. Southampton: NCRM.

Brathay Trust (2012) *Exit from Weapon Use Evaluation*. Ambleside: Brathay Trust.

Braun, V. and Clarke, V. (2006) 'Using thematic analysis in psychology', *Qualitative Research in Psychology*, 3(77): 1–10.

Broussine, M. (2008) *Creative Methods in Organisational Research*. London: Sage.

Buchroth, I. and Parkin, C. (eds) (2010) *Using Theory in Youth and Community Work Practice*. Exeter: Learning Matters.

Buck, A., Sobiechowska, P. and Winter, R. (2002) *Professional Experience and the Investigative Imagination: The Art of Reflective Writing*. London: Taylor and Francis.

Bufkin, S. (2012) 'Youth engagement rises ahead of election day, survey finds young voters still favor Obama' (http://www.huffingtonpost.com/2012/11/02/2012-youth-engagement_n_2065862.html?1351882717).

Burke, P. (2008) 'Play in focus: Children's visual voice in participative research', in P. Thompson (ed.), *Doing Visual Research with Children and Young People*. London: Routledge.

Burnard, P. (2004) 'Writing a qualitative research report', *Accident and Emergency Nursing*, 12: 176–181.

Butler, J. (1990) *Gender Trouble: Feminism and the Subversion of Identity*. New York: Routledge.

Cabinet Office (2012) *Social Justice: Transforming Lives*. London: HMSO.

Charities Evaluation Services (2014) 'About monitoring and evaluation' (http://www.ces-vol.org.uk/about-performance-improvement/about-monitoring-evaluation/).

Christian, C.G. (2005) 'Ethics and politics in qualitative research', in N. Denzin and Y.S. Lincoln (eds), *The SAGE Handbook of Qualitative Research*, 3rd edn. Thousand Oaks, CA: Sage. pp. 139–164.

Chouhan, J. (2009) 'Anti-oppressive practice', in J. Wood and J. Hine (eds), *Work with Young People*. Sage: London.

CIVICUS (2001) *Monitoring and Evaluation Toolkit*. Johannesburg: CIVICUS.

Clark, A. (1999) *Evaluation Research*. London: Sage.

Clough, P., Earle, K. and Sewell, D. (2002) 'Mental toughness: The concept and its measurement', in I. Cockerill (ed.), *Solutions in Sport Psychology*. London: Thomson Learning. pp. 32–46.

Community Sustainability Engagement (2014) *The Evaluation Toolbox* (http://www.evaluationtoolbox.net.au/index.php?option=com_content&view=article&id=11&Itemid=17).

Cooper, J. (2007) *Cognitive Dissonance: 50 Years of a Classic Theory*. London: Sage.

Copenhagen Youth Association (CYA) (2013) 'Impact' (http://www.cyproject.org/impact).

Corbin, J. and Strauss, A. (2008) *Basics of Qualitative Research*, 3rd edn. London: Sage.

Cousins, B. (2013) *Participatory Evaluation Up Close*. Ottowa: University of Ottowa.

Crabbe, T. (2006) *'Going the Distance': Impact, Journeys and Distance Travelled. Third Interim National Positive Futures Case Study Research Report*. Leeds: Substance.

Creswell, J.W. (1997) *Qualitative Inquiry and Research Design: Choosing Among Five Traditions*, 2nd edn. London: Sage.

Dadds, M. and Hart, S. (2001) *Doing Practitioner Research Differently*. Routledge: London.

Datta, L. (1994) 'Paradigm wars: A basis for peaceful coexistence and beyond', in C.S. Reichardt and S.F. Rallis (eds), *The Qualitative-Quantitative Debate: New Perspectives*. San Francisco, CA: Jossey-Bass. pp. 53–70.

Davies, B. (2005) 'Youth work: A manifesto for our times', *Youth and Policy*, 88: 5–27.

Davies, S. (2012) 'Embracing reflective practice', *Education for Primary Care*, 23: 9–12.

Davis, J. (2011) *Integrated Children's Services*. London: Sage.

Debold, E. (1990) 'Learning in the first person: A passion to know', paper presented at the Laurel-Harvard Conference on the Psychology of Women and the Development of Girls, Cleveland, Ohio.

Denscombe, M. (2010) *The Good Research Guide: For Small-Scale Social Research Projects*, 4th edn. Maidenhead: Open University Press.

Denzin, N. and Lincoln, Y.S. (2000) *Handbook of Qualitative Research*, 2nd edn. Thousand Oaks, CA: Sage.

Denzin, N.K. and Lincoln, Y.S. (2003) 'Introduction: The discipline and practice of qualitative research', in N. Denzin, and Y.S. Lincoln (eds), *The Landscape of Qualitative Research: Theories and Issues*, 2nd edn. London: Sage. pp. 1–46.

Department for Children, Schools and Families (DCSF) (2005) *Education Act*. London: HMSO.

Department for Children, Schools and Families (DCSF) (2007) *The Children's Plan: Building Brighter Futures*. London: HMSO.

Department for Education (1989) *The Children Act*. London: HMSO.

Department for Education and Environment (DfEE) (2001) *Transforming Youth Work*. London: Department for Education and Employment/Connexions.

Dewson, S., Eccles, J., Tackey, N.D. and Jackson, A. (2000) *A Guide to Measuring Soft Outcomes and Distance Travelled*. London: Institute for Employment Studies for the DfEE.

Doucet, A. and Mauther, S. (2008) 'What can be known and how? Narrated subjects and the Listening Guide', *Qualitative Research*, 8: 399–408.

Dozois, E., Langlois, M. and Blanchet-Cohen, N. (2010) *A Practitioner's Guide to Developmental Evaluation*. University of Victoria (BC): J.W. McConnell Family Foundation.

Driscoll, D.L., Appiab-Yeboah, A., Salib, P. and Rupert, D. (2007) 'Merging quantitative and qualitative data in mixed methods research: How to and why not', *Ecological and Environmental Anthropology*, 3(1): 18–28.

Economic Social Research Council (2013) *Research Ethics Guide Book for Social Scientists* (http://www.ethicsguidebook.ac.uk/).

Ellis, J. and Gregory, T. (2008) *Developing Monitoring and Evaluation in the Third Sector*. London: CES.

Ellis, J., Parkinson, D. and Wadia, A. (2011) *Making Connections: Using a Theory of Change to Develop Planning and Evaluation*. London: Charity Evaluation Services.

Emanuel, E., Wendler, D. and Grady, C. (2000) 'What makes clinical research ethical?', *Journal of the American Medical Association*, 283: 2701–2711.

Festeu, D. and Humberstone, B. (eds) (2006) *Non-formal Education through Outdoor Activities Guide*. Buckinghamshire: European Institute for Outdoor Adventure Education and Experiential Learning.

Flewitt, R. (2005) 'Is every child's voice heard? *Early Years*, 24(3): 207–222.

Flick, U. (2009) *An Introduction to Qualitative Research*, 4th edn. London: Sage.

Foucault, M. (1979) *Discipline and Punishment: The Birth of the Prison*. Paris: Gaillimard.

Foucault, M. (1982) 'The subject and power', in J. Faubion (ed.), *'Power': Essential Works of Foucault 1954–1984, Volume 3*. London: Penguin. pp. 326–348.

Fourtner, A.W., Fourtner, C.R. and Freeman Herreid, C. (2007) 'Bad blood: A case study of the Tuskegee Syphilis Project', in C. Freeman Herreid (ed.), *Start with a Story: The Case Study Method of Teaching College Science*. Dancers: National Science Teachers Association.

Fox, J. and Cater, M. (2011) 'Participatory evaluation: Factors to consider when involving youth', *The Journal of Extension*, 49(2): 1–4.

Franklin, A. and Franklin, B. (1990) 'Age and power: A political economy of ageism', in T. Jeffs and M. Smith (eds), *Youth Work in a Divided Society*. London: Macmillan. pp. 1–28.

Freire, P. (1970) *Pedagogy of the Oppressed*. London: Penguin.

Freire, P. (1972) *Cultural Action for Freedom*. London: Penguin.

Freire, P. (1974) *Education for Critical Consciousness*. London: Continuum.

Friese, S. (2012) *Qualitative Data Analysis with ATLAS.ti*. London: Sage.

Gaskell, G. and Bauer, M. (2000) 'Towards public accountability: Beyond sapling, reliability and validity', in M. Bauer and G. Gaskell (eds), *Qualitative Researching with Text, Image and Sound*. London: Sage.

Gauntlett, D. (2007) *Creative Explorations: New Approaches to Identities and Audiences*. London: Routledge.

Gauntlett, D. and Holzwarth, P. (2006) 'Creative and visual methods for exploring identities', *Visual Studies*, 21(1): 82–91.

Gawler, M. (2005) *Useful Tools for Engaging Young People in Participatory Evaluation*. UNICEF.

Gerber, M., Kalak, N., Lemola, S., Clough, P., Pühse, U., Holsboer-Trachsler, E. and Brand, S. (2013) 'Mental toughness and stress resilience', *Stress Health*, 29(2): 164–171.

Giroux, H.A. (2001) *Theory and Resistance in Education (Revised Edition)*. Westport, CN: Bergin and Garvey.

Gladstone, C. (2010) 'What happens when I leave school? Transition project', paper presented at the 33rd Collaborative Action Research Network Conference, Cambridge.

Goddard, C. (2012) 'Outcome measurement', *Children & Young People Now*, December: 25–30.

Golafshani, N. (2003) 'Understanding reliability and validity in qualitative research', *The Qualitative Report*, 8: 597–607.

Gramsci, A. (1971) *Selections from the Prison Notebooks of Antonio Gramsci*. New York: International Publishers.

Gray, D. (2009) *Doing Research in the Real World*. London: Sage.

Guba, E.G. and Lincoln, Y.S. (1994) 'Competing paradigms in qualitative research', in N.K. Denzin and Y.S. Lincoln (eds), *Handbook of Qualitative Research*. Thousand Oaks, CA: Sage. pp. 105–117.

Haralambos, M. (1985) *Sociology: New Directions*. Ormskirk: Causeway Press Ltd.

Haraway, D. (1988) 'Situated knowledges: The science question in feminism and the privilege of practical perspective', *Feminist Studies*, 14: 575–599.

Harris, V. (2009) *Community Skills Manual*. Sheffield: Federation for Community Development Learning.

Hart, R.A. (1992) *Children's Participation: From Tokenism to Citizenship*. Florence: UNICEF (Innocenti Research Centre).

Hart, R. (1997) *Children's Participation: The Theory and Practice of Involving Young Citizens in Community Development and Environmental Care*. Florence: UNICEF.

Heartland Alliance Social Impact Research Center (2014) *Challenges Facing Chicago Youth* (www.heartlandalliance.org/research/projects-publications/an-evaluation-of-youth-media-chicago.html#.U38zo8vjhdg).

Heath, S., Brooks, R., Cleaver, E. and Ireland, E. (2009) *Researching Young People's Lives*. Thousand Oaks, CA: Sage.

HM Treasury (2011) *The Magenta Handbook Guidance for Evaluation*. London: HMSO.

hooks, bell (1994) *Teaching to Transgress: Education as the Practice of Freedom*. London: Routledge.

House of Lords (1985) *Gillick v West Norfolk and Wisbech Area Health Authority and Another*. London: House of Lords.

In Defence of Youth Work (2013) 'About us' (www.indefenceofyouthwork.com).

Institute of Development Studies (1998) 'Participatory monitoring and evaluation', *IDS Policy Briefing*, 12.

International Program for Evaluation Development Training (2013) *Evaluation Ethics, Politics, Standards and Guiding Principles* (www.betterevaluation.org/resource/guide/IPDET_ethicsguide_mod14).

International Youth Foundation (2010) *Youth Empowerment Program: Executive Version*. Baltimore: IYA.

Jefferies, L. (2011) *Understanding Agency: Social Welfare and Change*. Bristol: Polity Press.

Jeffs, T. and Smith, M. (2002) 'Individuation and youth work', *Youth and Policy*, (76): 39–65.

Jewitt, C. (ed.) (2009) *The Routledge Handbook of Multimodal Analysis*. London: Routledge.

Jewitt, C. and Van Leeuwen, T. (2004) *The Handbook of Visual Analysis*. London: Sage.

Johnson, R.B. and Onwuegbuzie, A.J. (2004) 'Mixed methods research: A research paradigm whose time has come', *Educational Researcher*, 33(7): 14–26.

Kamran, S. (2010) 'Mobile phone: Calling and texting patterns of college students in Pakistan', *International Journal of Business and Management*, 5(4): 13–26.

Kellett, M. (2010). *Rethinking Children and Research*. London: Continuum.

Kellett, M. (2011) *Children's Perspectives on Integrated Services: Every Child Matters in Policy and Practice. Interagency Working in Health and Social Care*. Basingstoke: Palgrave Macmillan.

Kellogg Foundation (2004) *Logic Model Development Guide*. Michigan: W.K. Kellogg Foundation.

Kemmis, S. (2009) 'Action research as a practice based practice', *Educational Action Research*, 17(3): 463–474.

Kidd, S.A. and Kral, M.J. (2002) *Suicide and Prostitution Among Street Youth: A Qualitative Analysis*. Windsor: The Homeless Hub.

Kirkby, S., Cornish, H. and Smith, K. (2008) 'Cumulative cultural evolution in the laboratory: An experimental approach to the origins of structure in human language', *The Proceedings of the National Academy of Sciences*, 105(31): 10681–10686.

Kirkpatrick, D. and Kirkpatrick, L. (2006) *Evaluating Programmes: The Four Levels*, 3rd edn. New York: Berrett-Koehler.

Knight, B. (2012) *Back from the Brink: How Fairbridge Transforms the Lives of Disadvantaged Young People*. Newcastle Upon Tyne: CENTRIS.

Kolb, D. (1984) *Experiential Learning, Experience as the Source of Learning and Development*. Englewood Cliffs, NJ: Prentice Hall.

Kumar, R. (2014) *Research Methodology: A Step-by-Step Guide for Beginners*, 4th edn. London: Sage.

Lansdown, G. (2013) 'Protection through participation: An international perspective', paper presented at the Child Studies Conference 2013: Participation into Practice, Kings College, London.

Lazarus, R.S. and Folkman, S. (1984) *Stress, Appraisal, and Coping*. New York: Springer.

Ledwith, M. (2011) *Community Development: A Critical Approach*. London: Polity Press.

Le Grand, J. (2003) *Motivation, Agency and Public Policy*. Oxford: Oxford University Press.

Lenhart, A. (2009) *Teens and Sexting: How and Why Minor Teens are Sending Sexually Suggestive Nude or Nearly Nude Images via Text Messaging*. Washington: Pew International.

Lewin, K. (1946) 'Action research and minority problems', in G.W. Lewin (ed.), *Resolving Social Conflicts*. New York: Harper and Row. pp. 201–216.

Lewis, J. and Ritchie, J. (2003) 'Generalising from qualitative research', in J. Ritchie and J. Lewis (eds), *Qualitative Research Practice: A Guide for Social Science Students and Researchers*. London: Sage.

Liamputtong, P. (2006) *Researching the Vulnerable: A Guide to Sensitive Research Methods.* London: Sage.

Lincoln, Y.S. and Guba, E.G. (1985) *Naturalistic Inquiry.* London: Sage.

Lipsky, M. (1980) *Street-level Bureaucracy: Dilemmas of the Individual in Public Services.* New York: Russell Sage Foundation.

Literat, I. (2013) 'A pencil for your thoughts: Participatory drawing as a visual research method with children and youth', *International Journal of Qualitative Methods*, 12: 84.

Lloyd, R. and O'Sullivan, F. (2003) *Measuring Soft Outcomes and Distance Travelled: A Methodology for Developing a Guidance Document.* London: Department of Work and Pensions.

Lofgren, G. (2009) *How Are You Getting On? Charities and Funders on Communicating Results.* London: New Philanthropy Capital.

Loflin, K. (2003) 'Improving bradenton's after school programs through utilization-focused evaluation', *Evaluation Exchange* (1): 9.

McIntosh, P. (2010) *Action Research and Reflective Practice: Creative Visual Tools to Facilitate Reflection and Learning.* London: Routledge.

McIntosh, P. and Sobiechowska, P. (2009) 'Creative methods: Problematics for inquiry and pedagogy in health and social care'. *Power and Education*, 1(3): 296–306.

McLaren, P., Macrine, S. and Hill, D. (eds) (2010) *Revolutionizing Pedagogy: Educating for Social Justice Within and Beyond Global Neo-liberalism.* London: Palgrave Macmillan.

Madriz, I. (1998) 'Using focus groups with lower socioeconomic status Latina women', *Qualitative Inquiry*, 4: 114–128.

Mansoor, D., Kazi, A. and Hall, T. (2010) *Realist Evaluation of Aberlour Housing Support Service: What Works and in Which Circumstances.* Aberlour: Aberlour Child Care Trust.

Manzo, L. and Brightbill, N. (2007) 'Towards a participatory ethics', in S. Kindon, R. Pain and M. Kesby (eds), *Connecting People, Participation and Place: Participatory Action Research Approaches and Methods.* London: Routledge. pp. 33–40.

Maslow, A. (1943) 'A theory of human motivation', *Psychological Review*, 50(4): 370–396.

Mauthner, M., Birch, M., Jessop, J. and Miller, T. (eds) (2002) *Ethics in Qualitative Research.* London: Sage.

Maynard, L. (2008) 'Young women and sexual exploitation', paper presented at North West Regional Youth Work Unit Seminar, Manchester.

Maynard, L. (2011) *Step Up Evaluation.* Ambleside: Brathay Trust.

Maynard, L. and Smallman, E. (2009) 'The three E's of ethnodrama', paper presented at University of Cumbria Research and Scholarship Fest, Lancaster.

Mayne, J. (2008) 'Contribution analysis', ILAC, Briefing 16.

Mayor of London (2012) *Time for Action.* London: Greater London Authority.

Merton, B., Payne, M. and Smith, D. (2004) *An Evaluation of the Impact of Youth Work in England*, DfES Research Report, 606, DfES.

Methodspace (2014) (http://www.methodspace.com/).

Mindtools (2014) 'Stakeholder analysis' (http://www.mindtools.com/pages/article/newPPM_07.htm).

Moon, J. (2004) *A Handbook of Reflective and Experiential Learning.* London: Routledge Falmer.

Mullender, A., Ward, D. and Fleming, J. (2013) *Empowerment for Action: Self-directed Groupwork.* London: Palgrave Macmillan.

Munhall, P.L. (1991) 'Institutional review of qualitative research proposals: A task of no small consequence', in J.M. Morse (ed.), *Qualitative Nursing Research: A Contemporary Dialogue.* Newbury Park, CA: Sage. pp. 258–271.

NatCen (2011) *National Citizenship Service Evaluation.* London: NatCen.

National Youth Agency (NYA) (2004) *Ethical Conduct in Youth Work*. Leicester: The NYA.
National Youth Agency (NYA) (2014a) *Commissioning Toolkit* (www.nya.org.uk/dynamic_ files/finalcommissioning/Part%205.pdf). Accessed 21 May 2013.
National Youth Agency (NYA) (2014b) 'What is youth work?' (http://www.nya.org.uk/careers-youth-work/).
National Youth Development Agency (2012) *Study on Youth Volunteering Perceptions and Motivations in South Africa*. South Africa: NYDA.
NECF and Horsley, K. (2009) *The Evaluator's Cookbook* (http://cms.nottinghamshire.gov.uk/theevaluatorscookbook.pdf).
Neuman, W. (1997) *Social Research Methods: Qualitative and Quantitative Approaches*, 3rd edn. Boston: Allyn and Bacon.
Newsom D. and Haynes, J. (2011) *Public Relations Writing: Form and Style*. London: Wadsworth, Cengage Learning.
Niglas, K. (2000) 'Combining quantitative and qualitative approaches', paper presented at ECER 2000.
NSPCC (2012) *Gillick Competency and Fraser Guidelines. NSPCC Factsheet* (http://www.nspcc.org.uk/Inform/research/briefings/gillick_wda101615.html).
Organisational Research Services (2004) *Theory of Change as a Practical Tool for Action, Results and Learning*. New York: Annie E. Casey Foundation.
Oxford Dictionary (2013) *The Oxford Dictionary*. Oxford: Oxford University Press.
Pain, R. (2008) 'Ethical possibilities: Towards participatory ethics', *Children's Geographies*, 6(1): 10–13.
Participation Works (2014) (http://www.participationworks.org.uk/).
Patton, M.Q. (1986) *Utilization-Focused Evaluation*. Newbury Park, CA: Sage.
Patton, M.Q. (1996) 'A world larger than formative and summative', *Evaluation Practice*, 17(2): 131–144.
Patton, M.Q. (2008) *Utilization-Focused Evaluation*, 4th edn. Thousand Oaks, CA: Sage.
Patton, M.Q. (2010) *Developmental Evaluation: Applying Complexity Concepts to Enhance Innovation and Use*. New York: Guilford Press.
Pawson, R. and Tilley, N. (1997) *Realistic Evaluation*. London: Sage Publications.
Pawson, R. and Tilley, N. (1998) 'Cook-book methods and disastrous recipes', *Evaluation*, 4: 211–213.
Payne, M. (2009) 'Modern youth work: "Purity" or common cause?', in J. Wood and J. Hine (eds), *Work with Young People*. London: Sage.
Pearlman, D., Camberg, L., Wallace, J., Symons, P. and Finison, L. (2002) 'Tapping youth as agents for change: Evaluation of a peer leadership HIV/AIDS intervention', *Journal of Adolescent Health*, 31: 31–39.
Pink, S. (2007) *Doing Visual Ethnography: Images, Media and Representation in Research*. Sage: London.
Plowright, D. (2011) *Using Mixed Methods*. London: Sage.
Podd, W. (2010) 'Participation', in J. Batsleer and B. Davies (eds), *What is Youth Work?* Exeter: Learning Matters.
Price, A. (2004) 'Encouraging reflection and critical thinking in practice', *Nursing Standard*, 18(47): 46–52.
Prosser, J. (2000a) *Image Based Research*. London: Routledge Falmer.
Prosser, J. (2000b) 'The moral maze of visual ethics', in H. Simons and R. Usher (eds), *Situated Ethics in Education Research*. London: Routledge Falmer.
Prosser, J. (2009) 'Chapter one. Introducing visual methods: A road map', in ESRC, *Research Development Initiative*. London: ESRC.

Puma, J., Bennett, L., Cutforth, N., Tombari, C. and Stein, P. (2009) 'A case study of a community-based participatory evaluation research (CBPER) project: Reflections on promising practices and shortcomings', *Michigan Journal of Community Service Learning*, Spring: 34–47.

Puttick, G. and Mulgan, R. (2010) *Making Evidence Useful: The Case for New Institutions*. London: NESTA.

Reason, P. (2003) 'Doing co-operative inquiry', in J. Smith (ed.), *Qualitative Psychology: A Practical Guide to Methods*. London: Sage.

Reason, P. (2013) *The SAGE Handbook of Action Research: Participative Inquiry and Practice*. London: Sage.

Reason, P. and Bradbury, H. (2001) 'Introduction', in P. Reason and H. Bradbury (eds), *The SAGE Handbook of Action Research*. London: Sage.

Reinharz, S. (1992) *Feminist Methods in Social Research*. Oxford: Oxford University Press.

Richardson, L. (2000) 'New writing practices in qualitative research', *Sociology of Sports Journal*, 17: 5–20.

Ringrose, J., Gill, R., Livingstone, S. and Harvey, L. (2012) *A Qualitative Study of Children, Young People and 'Sexting'*. London: NSPCC.

Ritchie, J. and Lewis, J. (2003) *Qualitative Research Practice*. London: Sage.

Roberts, H. (2008) 'Listening to children: and hearing them', in P. Christensen and A. James (eds), *Research with Children: Perspectives and Practices*. Abingdon: Routledge.

Robson, C. (2002) *Real World Research: A Resource for Social Scientists and Practitioner-Researchers*. 2nd edn. Oxford: Blackwell.

Rosenberg, M. (1965) *Society and the Adolescent Self-Image*. Princeton, NJ: Princeton University Press.

Rosseter, B. (1987) 'Youth workers as educators', in T. Jeffs and M. Smith (eds), *Youth Work*. London: Macmillan Education Ltd.

Rothbauer, P. (2008) 'Triangulation', in L. Given (ed.), *The SAGE Encyclopaedia of Qualitative Research Methods*. London: Sage. pp. 892–894.

Saldaña, J. (2003) 'Dramatizing data: A primer', *Qualitative Inquiry*, 9(2): 218–236.

Saldaña, J. (2008) 'Ethnodrama', in L.M. Given (ed.), *The SAGE Encyclopedia of Qualitative Research Methods*. London: Sage.

Salkind, N. (2011) *Statistics for People Who (Think They) Hate Statistics*, 4th edn. London: Sage.

Sani, F. and Todman, J. (2005) *Experimental Design and Statistics for Psychology: A First Course*. Oxford: Blackwell.

Sapin, K. (2013) *Essential Skills for Youth Work Practice*. London: Sage.

Sarantakos, S. (1998) *Social Research Method*. London: Palgrave Macmillan.

Sattoe, J.N.T., Jedeloo, S. and van Staa, A. (2013) 'Effective peer-to-peer support for young people with end-stage renal disease: A mixed methods evaluation of Camp COOL', *BMC Nephrology*, 14: 279.

Saunders, M. (2000) 'Beginning a valuation via RUFDATA: Theorising a practical approach to evaluation planning', *Evaluation*, 1(6): 7–21.

Schön, D. (1983) *The Reflective Practitioner: How Professionals Think in Action*. New York: Basic Books.

Schwandt, T.A. (2003) 'Three epistemological stances for qualitative inquiry: Interpretivism, hermaneutics and social constructivism', in N.K. Denzin and Y.S. Lincoln (eds), *The Landscape of Qualitative Research: Theories and Issues*. London: Sage. pp. 292–231.

Scriven, M. (1991) 'Beyond formative and summative evaluation', in M.W. McLaughlin and D. Phillips (eds), *Evaluation and Education*. Chicago: University of Chicago Press.

Sechrest, L. and Sidani, S. (1995) 'Quantitative and qualitative methods: Is there an alternative?', *Evaluation and Program Planning*, 18: 77–87.

Select Committee (2011) *Services for Young People*. London: House of Commons Education Committee.

Sercombe, H. (2010) *Youth Work Ethics*. London: Sage Publications.

Shek, D.T.L., Lee T.Y., Siu, A.M.H. and Lam, C.M. (2006) 'Qualitative evaluation of the project P.A.T.H.S. based on the perceptions of the program participants', *The Scientific World Journal*, 6: 2254–2263.

Shephard, R. (2002) 'Ethics in exercise science research', *Sports Medicine*, 32(3): 169–183.

Shufflebeam, A. and Shinkfield, D. (1985) *Evaluation Theory, Models, and Applications*. London: Wiley.

Siegel S. and Castellan Jr, N.J. (1988) *Nonparametric Statistics for the Behavioral Sciences*, 2nd edn. New York: McGraw Hill.

Silverman, D. (2013) *A Very Short Fairly Interesting and Reasonably Cheap Book About Qualitative Research*. London: Sage.

Simons, H. (2009) *Case Study Research in Practice*. London: Sage.

Smart, S. (2007) 'Informal education, in (in)formal control? What is voluntary youth work to make of self-assessment', *Youth and Policy*, 95: 73–82.

Smiciklas, M. (2012) *The Power of Infographics: Using Pictures to Communicate and Connect with Your Audience*. Indianapolis: Que Pub.

Spence, J. (2004) 'Targeting, accountability and youth work practice', *Youth Work Practice*, 16(4): 261–272.

Spencer L., Ritchie J., Lewis J. and Dillon L. (2003) *Quality in Qualitative Evaluation: A Framework for Assessing Research Evidence*. London: Government Chief Social Researcher's Office, Occasional Papers Series 2.

Squirrell, G. (2012) *Evaluation in Action: Theory and Practice for Effective Evaluation*. Lyme Regis: Russell House Publishing.

Stern, J. (2011) 'From negative ethics to positive virtues in research', paper presented at Value and Virtues in Practice-Based Research Conference, York.

Stuart, K. and Maynard, L. (2011) *Brathay's Evaluation Toolkit* (http://www.brathay.org. uk/wp-content/uploads/2013/06/All-Evaluation-Tools-v2.pdf).

Stuart, K. and Maynard, L. (2012) *Brathay's Model of Youth Development*. Ambleside: Brathay Trust.

Suchman, E. (1967) *Evaluation Research*. New York: Russell Sage Foundation.

Tashakkori, A. and Teddlie, C. (2003) *SAGE Handbook of Mixed Methods in Social and Behavioral Research*. Thousand Oaks, CA: Sage.

Teder, M., Mörelius, E., Nordwall, M., Bolme, P., Ekberg, J., Wilhelm, E. and Timpka, T. (2013) 'Family-based behavioural intervention program for obese children: An observational study of child and parent lifestyle interpretations', *PLOS ONE*, 8(8).

The Centre for Information and Research on Civic Learning and Engagement (2014) *What Influences Young People to Vote*. (www.civicyouth.org).

The Commonwealth (2013) *Youth Development Index Results Report* (www.youth developmentindex.org/cms/cms-youth/_images/197918019952385f3219c75.pdf).

The First Religious Society in Carlisle (2014) *High School Youth Group – What's Important to Us*. (http://uucarlisle.org/index.php?page=high-school-youth-group).

The OMG Centre (2014) *Amplifying Learning in Systems Change Investments: An Experience of Developmental Evaluation*. Philadelphia: The OMG Centre for Collaborative Learning.

Thompson, S. and Thompson, N. (2008) *The Critically Reflective Practitioner*. London: Palgrave Macmillan.

Tilley, N. (2000) 'Doing realistic evaluation of criminal justice', in V. Jupp (ed.), *Criminology in the Field: The Practice of Criminological Research*. London: Sage. pp. 97–113.

Treseder, P. (1997) *Empowering Children and Young People: Training Manual*. London: Save the Children.

Tuckman, B.W. (1965) 'Interpersonal probing and revealing and systems of integrative complexity', *Journal of Personal and Social Psychology*, 3: 655–664.

UNESCO (2012) *Guidelines for the Recognition, Validation and Accreditation of the Outcomes of Non-formal and Informal Learning* (www.unesco.org/new/en/education/themes/strengthening-education-systems/quality-framework/technical-notes/recognition-validation-and-accreditation-of-outcomes/).

United Nations High Commissioner for Human Rights (1989) *Convention on the Rights of the Child*. Geneva: Office of the United Nations High Commissioner for Human Rights.

Wagner, M. and Newman, L. (2012) 'Longitudinal transition outcomes of youth with emotional disturbances', *Psychiatric Rehabilitation Journal*, 35(3): 199–208.

Walmsley, J. and Johnson, K. (2003) *Inclusive Research with People with Learning Difficulties*. London: Jessica Kingsley.

Weiss, C.H. (1998) *Evaluation: Methods for Studying Programs and Policies*, 2nd edn. Upper Saddle River, NJ: Prentice Hall.

Werquin, P. (2010) *Recognising Non-formal and Informal Learning: Outcomes, Policies and Practices*. Paris: OECD Publishing.

Winokur Early, K., Chapman, S. and Hand, G. (2013) 'Family-focused juvenile re-entry services: A quasi-experimental design evaluation of recidivism outcomes', *Journal of Juvenile Justice*, 2: 2.

Winter, R. and Munn-Giddings, C. (2001) *A Handbook for Action Research in Health and Social Care*. Routledge: London.

Woollaston, V. (2013) 'An adult at 18? Not any more: Adolescence now ends at 25 to prevent young people getting an inferiority complex' (www.dailymail.co.uk/health/article-2430573/An-adult-18-Not-Adolescence-ends-25-prevent-young-people-getting-inferiority-complex.html).

Yardley, A. (2008) 'Piecing together – a methodological bricolage', *Forum: Qualitative Social Research*, 9(2): 31.

Young, K. (1999) *The Art of Youth Work*. Lyme Regis: Russell House Publishing.

Young Foundation (2013) *The Catalyst Outcomes Framework*. London: Young Foundation.

Zimmerman, J.F. (1997). 'The Belmont report: An ethical framework for protecting research subjects', *The Monitor*, Summer.

INDEX

developmental evaluations (DE), *67*, 73–75, 204
developmental outcomes (soft outcomes), 11, 19–20, 213
diaries, 112, 126–127, **147**, 204
disclosure, 204
discourses, 16, 204
dispersion, 162, 169–170, 204
distal outcomes, 23–24, *24*, 61, 204
distance travelled, 20, **147**, 204
distance travelled tools, 61, 139–146, *141*, *143–144*, 205
documentary evidence, 127–129, *128*, **147**

ecological validity, 131, 205
Education Act (2005), 85
Ellis, J., 101–102
emancipatory work, 18, 205
Emanuel, E., 49
empirical method, 205
empiricism, 32–33, 205
empowerment, 205
epistemology
  definition of, 205
  mixed methods and, 151
  overview, 29–30, 32–33, **39**
  in Step Up Case Study, **42**, 94–95
ethics
  anonymity and, 49, 50–51
  confidentiality and, 49, 51
  definition of, 46–47, 205
  ethics panels and committees and, 53
  evaluation planning and, 95, 98, 105, 108
  evaluation's purpose and gain and, 47–48
  evaluation's sharing and dissemination and, 52–53
  informed consent and, 49–50, 54–55, 56, 195
  limitations of traditional notions of, 53–57, **57**
  participant validation and, 52
  risk of harm and, 48–49
  in Step Up Case Study, 51–52, 95
  youth work and, 3, 9–10, 18–19, **19**, 45–46
ethics panels and committees, 53
ethnodrama, 196–198
evaluation
  Catalyst outcomes framework and, 21–23, *22*
  challenges of, 9–26
  definition of, 2, 205
  difficulties of measuring youth work and, 19–21
  importance of, 200–201, *201*
  non-formal learning and, 10–12
  professional context of, 13–18, *17*
  purpose and focus of, 59–67, 192–193, **192**
  types of, 67–76, 95, 97–98, 105–106, 108
  value base of youth work and, 9–10, 18–19
evaluation planning
  contextual influences in, 94, 95–96, 106–107, 108
  design choices and, 99–101, *101*
  ethics and, 95, 98, 105, 108
  methodology and, 94–95, 96–97, 106, 108
  power and, 99

evaluation planning *cont.*
  reflective practice and, 107–109
  in Step Up Case Study, 94–95
  theory of change and, 101–107, *103–105*
  types of evaluation and, 95, 97–98, 105–106, 108
evidence based practice, 1, 14–15, 205
experiential learning, 20, 205
experimental evaluations, 67–71, *67*, **68**, **69**, 205
experiments, 112

Fairbridge, 145–146
family-based behavioural intervention programmes (FBIPs), 133–134
focus groups, 112, 124–126, **147**, 206
formal learning, 11–12, **12**, 206
formative evaluations, 64, *66*, 206
Foucault, M., 83–84
Franklin, A., 15
Franklin, B., 15
Fraser guidelines, 54–55
free market economy, 13, 206
Freire, P., 84
frequency counts, 114, 163, 206
frequency distributions, 114

Gauntlett, D., 40, 136, 138
generalisability, 33, 206
Gillick competency, 54–55
Gladstone, C., 90–91
Gramsci, A., 83
group interviews, 112, 206
Guba, E.G., 52, 156

hard outcomes, 11, 206
Hart, R., 85–86, *85*
Heartland Alliance, 128–129, *128*
hegemony, 83, 206
Holzwarth, P., 136
hypothesis, 118, 206
hypothesis testing, 32–33

I-poems, 176–178
ideology, 206
impact, 61, 64, 206
impact evaluations, 61–62, *66*, 206
in-depth interviews, 112, 207
incentives, 50
independent variables, 68, 206–207
individuation, 15–17, 207
inductive reasoning, 159–160, *160*, 161–162, 207
informal educators, 207
informal learning, 10, 11–12, **12**, 207
informed consent, 49–50, 54–55, 56, 195, 207
Institute of Development Studies, 87
inter-rater reliability, 182, 207
interpretivism, 31, 207
interval data, 207